Chindia Rising

How China and India will Benefit Your Business

Chindia Rising

How China and India will Benefit Your Business

Jagdish N Sheth

Kellstadt Professor of Marketing
Goizueta Business School
Emory University, Atlanta, USA

Tata McGraw-Hill Publishing Company Limited
NEW DELHI

McGraw-Hill Offices

New Delhi New York St Louis San Francisco Auckland Bogotá Caracas
Kuala Lumpur Lisbon London Madrid Mexico City Milan Montreal
San Juan Santiago Singapore Sydney Tokyo Toronto

Tata McGraw-Hill

Published by Tata McGraw-Hill Publishing Company Limited,
7 West Patel Nagar, New Delhi 110 008.

For sale in India, the Indian Subcontinent and Asia

This edition can be exported from India only by the publishers,
Tata McGraw-Hill Publishing Company Limited.

ISBN 13: 978-0-07-065708-3
ISBN 10: 0-07-065708-4

Managing Director: *Ajay Shukla*
Head—Professional and Healthcare: *Roystan La'Porte*
Publishing Manager: *R Chandra Sekhar*
Asst. Manager—Production: *Sohan Gaur*
Manager—Sales & Marketing: *S Girish*
Controller—Production: *Rajender P Ghansela*
Asst. General Manager—Production: *B L Dogra*

Published by Tata McGraw-Hill Publishing Company Limited, 7 West Patel Nagar,
New Delhi 110 008, typeset at Bukprint India, B-180A, Guru Nanak Pura, Laxmi Nagar,
Delhi 110 092 and printed at Gopsons Papers Ltd., A-2 & 3, Sector 64, NOIDA 201 301

Cover Designer: Kapil Gupta

Cover Printer: Gopsons Papers Ltd.

RAZYCDLYRQDCA

To

Jairam Ramesh, who coined Chindia
Minister of State for Commerce (Government of India) and
Economic Advisor to Congress (I) Party

Advance Praise

Eye opener! Shifted my thinking about China and India's global impact.

Philip Kotler, Ph D
S. C. Johnson Distinguished Professor of International Marketing
Marketing Department
Kellogg School of Management
Northwestern University

Prof. Jagdish Sheth does it again. He distills the implications of the growth of China and India through a wide ranging and thoughtful interpretation in *Chindia Rising* and its implications to global growth, prosperity, security and culture. A must read for all managers, politicians and security experts.

C.K. Prahalad
Paul and Ruth McCracken Distinguished University Professor,
Ross School of Business
The University of Michigan

Business leaders in East and West will surely read with interest Jagdish Sheth's thought provoking assessment of how the rise of China and India (Chindia) will prove to be an enormous boon to the worldwide economy. With his profound insight into global business trends, Prof. Sheth shows how Chindia's rise will not only stimulate the mature economies of the West but will also help birth economies in Asia, Africa, and Latin America.

Azim Premji
Chairman and Managing Director
Wipro, Ltd.

The rise of China and India will have a profound effect on businesses in the developed as well as the developing world. Any businessman who wants to be ready to benefit from these dramatic changes should read Dr Sheth's insightful book.

Patrick J. McGovern
Founder and Chairman
International Data Group

With detailed analyses of companies, economic trends, and historical patterns, the noted business management scholar, Prof. Sheth convincingly suggests that the rise of China and India as 21st century global powers can be as beneficial to the world as was the rise of the US in the early 20th century. This is a useful source for not only business leaders but anyone interested in this tectonic shift that is underway in the world today.

Dr Vishakha N. Desai
President
Asia Society

Jag Sheth has produced a thought provoking treatise on contemporary events involving China and India, which will have a major impact in the foreseeable future. India and China are the key players in globalization, that is changing the face of Asia, while transforming trade and commerce in the rest of the world. Sheth propounds an extremely well reasoned point of view of these developments, which will appeal to a wide cross section of readers around the world.

Ashok Ganguly
Chairman
Firstsource Solutions & ABP Group

While there have been many paens sung to the phenomenal rise of Chindia (and BRIC's), by relating this rise contextually to US and European Economic and Commercial history, Jagdish Sheth has done us all a favor. This book not only makes it easier for us contextually, but also gives us insights into the huge challenges and exciting opportunities for the world. Finally, how Chindia affects the world will depend upon the qualities of the institutions they build. These will reflect their society, culture, aspirations and impact they wish to have on the world. This book gives us the first insights into some of the thinking in that direction.

Gautam Thapar
Chairman and CEO
Avantha Group

Many articles and books have been written in the recent past on China and India, and their economic models and future. I find Prof. Jagdish Sheth's book *Chindia Rising* as a brilliant analysis of not only how China and India will occupy the prime position as two great economies in the future, but how they are different from economies that became success stories. Indeed in the 19th and 20th Century, Europe and U.S. were the main players, and later Japan and Korea, each followed a model based on their culture, resources, and markets. Both India and China are operating in a new environment, where capital is not scarce, entrepreneurship is a winner, globalization and communications is a reality for future growth, and we have abundance of bright human resources and huge domestic markets. These observations, and particularly the analysis of the differences between Western economies and Chindia, with enumerable examples, reads like a well researched case study; and certainly makes Prof. Sheth's book a 'Must Read' for all professional managers, entrepreneurs, economists, policy makers, and public at large. I thoroughly enjoyed reading the manuscript, and am grateful to Prof. Sheth for honoring me by sending me the manuscript before publication of this future best seller.

Suman Sinha
Chairman
Bata India Ltd.

Chindia Rising is a visionary work encompassing multiplicity of dimensions of the unprecedented impact and influence of the two great nations, India and China, on the world's industrial, business and also political future of few hundred years. The book is destined to become a milestone and extensively studied by scholars, influencers of the international industrial scene and general public. Dr Sheth reminds the global business community of the fundamental significance of the economic rise of China and India. With his typical acuity, he sees beyond the temporary dislocations caused by outsourcing or trade imbalances and discovers a future of worldwide economic growth, job creation, and expanding opportunity. I strongly recommend this book to scholars, students, international business leaders and general readers.

Dr KRS Murthy
CEO and Vice Chairman of the Board
SUNrgi—Power of 1000 Suns

The Chindia phenomena is at its nascent stage. The world hasn't seen anything like it. The book comes at an appropriate time and evaluates the subject holistically. The large domestic market, the huge, young and growing population, the realization of the future imperatives by the respective governments, the compulsions of multinationals and the rise of private enterprise all are working in favor of China and India. The book will enable both governments and enterprises to think about the challenges of becoming a dominant global force, employability of the youth, issues preventing the rural-urban divide, sustainability, collaborative energy, security, patents and IPR issues. Every citizen of the world must read it.

Rajeev Karwal
Founder Director
MILAGROW

What indeed jumps out is the new first generation companies emerging from China and India who are now global players. The sheer scale of Brownian movement of entrepreneurs in both the countries is moving the two global economies to operate globally; reading *Chindia Rising* is like reading a business thriller.

Sudhir Sethi
Founding Chairman & Managing Director
IDG Ventures India
Bangalore, India

So appropriate is the name of this book, *Chindia Rising*. I have focused and worked within the Indian and Chinese business communities for three decades, and I have personally seen the growth and the positioning of *"Chindia"* to accelerate far beyond the expectations of the global community. Dr Sheth continues to identify trends in the global economic landscape and so astutely explains how those trends impact our daily lives. I predict that this book will become a best seller and will continue the significant success that Dr Sheth has had within the global economic spectrum. Dr Sheth so clearly explains this trend of *Chindia Rising* that a reader can grasp the enormity of this trend while reading his book.

Kenneth A. Cutshaw
Honorary Consul of India
Business Executive and Global Attorney

Foreword

I am delighted to write this foreword to an important book on a subject that has long interested me. It was in May 2005 that I first put forth the idea of *Chindia* to capture pithily the re-emergence of the two Himalayan demographic neighbors as economic powers in the world. My idea of using the term *Chindia* was also to convey the idea of China *and* India, not China *or* India, since I have always believed that engagement, not confrontation is the destiny of the two ancient civilizations and modern nation-states.

The rise of China and India (Chindia) is not only inevitable but will be beneficial to the world. Advanced economies of United States, European Union, Japan, South Korea, as well as Canada, Australia and Singapore, will benefit through actively participating in the growth of consumer markets in China and India through organized retailing and services including mobile phones, hotels, consumer finance, as well as healthcare and education. Advanced countries will also benefit by investing in their manufacturing, especially automobiles and appliances, and in infrastructure industries including airports, seaports, roads, electricity and other utilities.

At the same time, both China and India are becoming globally integrated economies through economic reforms and government incentives. Although China's economic integration with the world has been through trade, similar to that of Japan and South Korea, India's global integration is more likely to be through large acquisitions of many mature industries of advanced economies. Examples include the recent large scale acquisitions of Corus Steel and Tetley Tea by the Tata Group in the U.K., as well as acquisition of Novelis by Hindalco (an Aditya Birla Group company) in the United States; and of course, this extends to worldwide acquisitions by Ranbaxy and Dr. Reddy's in the pharmaceutical industry, and by Wipro, Infosys and TCS in the engineering, IT and consulting services industries.

These acquisitions are primarily for future growth of Indian enterprises and, therefore, they will revitalize mature companies and industries of advanced countries. Also, they will transform Indian companies from export oriented ethnocentric corporations to large transnational corporations whose capital and talent will be of global origin and not just Indian origin.

I believe even bigger beneficiaries of the Rise of Chindia will be other emerging economies in Africa, Caribbean, Latin America, Southeast Asia, Central Asia, Eastern Europe and virtually the rest of the world. Both nations will, through trade and investments, speed up rapid development of emerging nations more through economic partnership and less on geopolitical ideologies. Chindia needs their industrial and agricultural resources and they need Chindia's technical and professional talent.

It is also inevitable that as China and India march toward becoming global economic powers through trade and investments, their cultural and political influence will also rise. In other words, just as we have experienced the Westernization of heritage-rich China and India, we will also experience the Easternization of the world in fine arts, literature, foods, fashion and more importantly, in the rich spiritual and philosophical traditions of China and India that have drawn from each other

I felt privileged when Prof. Jagdish Sheth asked me to write this foreword. I had, of course, heard and read about him for long but we became good friends beginning October 2002 when I was invited by Emory University in Atlanta, GA, as a Claus Halle Fellow. I am also pleased to see that the concept of Chindia has now become mainstream both on Wall Street and on Main Street and that, for the most part, the intellectual property rights for the term are respected!!

My best wishes!

Jairam Ramesh
Minister of State for Commerce
Government of India
Author of *Making Sense of Chindia: Reflections on China and India*
(India Research Press, New Delhi; May 2005)

Preface

Why the Rise of Chindia is Inevitable

The genesis of this book goes back to the late 1980s, when I became advisor to several governments for branding, positioning and marketing of nations. It became obvious to me that while the 20th Century was driven by economic and political ideology of advanced countries, the 21st Century will be driven by markets of emerging nations. In other words, the 70 plus percent concentration of trade and GDP among the 15 advanced countries of the world which included 12 European common market nations, United States, Canada and Japan was not sustainable in the future. Nor was it going to benefit the emerging economies of the world despite their post-war decolonization and political freedom.

In other words, no matter what ideology one followed to uplift growth of emerging economies, whether Communism, foreign aid, or access to markets, it was not sustainable due to several reasons. First, all advanced countries were aging and aging fast! They had low to no domestic growth as exemplified by Japan, Germany and France. United States was the exception because it was aging less rapidly mostly due to second wave of immigration from all around the world and especially from non-white countries such as Mexico, Latin America, Asia and the Caribbean. Thus market access for political or economic reasons was not sustainable and any outsourcing of work such as manufacturing or services would result in domestic political turmoil.

Second, political leaders of all advanced nations realized soon after the first energy crisis of the 1970s, and more recently after the collapse of Communism, that what matters most to people in elections across national and cultural boundaries, is hard core realities of economic growth as manifested in jobs and wealth creation for the masses. In other words, getting elected or re-elected was more due to economic boom or bust rather than party loyalty, personal charisma or future promises.

This was clearly evidenced when George Bush Sr., who was the most popular US President both domestically and internationally (soon after and as a consequence of the first Gulf War in 1990), lost the bid for re-election in 1992 because there was economic recession; and Bill Clinton was elected on the now famous platform: It is the economy, stupid!

Similarly, Helmut Kohl, the longest surviving Chancellor of Germany, made the fatal mistake of integrating East German economy with West Germany on an equal footing, which resulted in unprecedented unemployment in Germany since the Marshall Plan. Finally, Japanese government's leadership became an annual event all through the late 1980s and the early 1990s because Japanese economy remained deflationary despite very low, giveaway interest rates.

And this was not limited to advanced and politically mature economies. It happened in India with the defeat of the incumbent BJP Party whose "India Shining" campaign failed to deliver jobs and economic growth to non-urban masses. So was true in Brazil, Bolivia, and Argentina and so on. Consequently, economic pragmatism replaced ideology and rhetoric forever in politics.

A third factor for the rise of market forces was the dramatic and sudden collapse of Communism as an ideological counterbalance to market forces of capitalism. And this was a worldwide phenomenon not limited to the Soviet Union. Economic bankruptcy of Communist nations forced them to embrace capitalism. And they have embraced it with fervor and zeal comparable to what a convert manifests in religious conversion. Indeed, the best capitalist nations of today are mostly ex-Communist nations including China, Vietnam, Eastern Europe, Russia and to some extent India which had embraced a socialistic pattern of society and implemented Fabian economics through what is referred to as the "License Raj".

I have always been puzzled about why ex-Communist nations would or should do well with a capitalist mindset. And the answer again seems to be resource based advantages of ex-Communist countries. Despite all the ills of Communism, it created two key resource based advantages for the nation, mostly related to human capital. First, they made primary and secondary education mandatory and further invested in post secondary technical and vocational education to produce skilled workers for the factories and the military. Second, they made gender a non-issue. It did not matter whether you were a man or a woman; both had to go to school or work for the state. This resulted in an enormously large pool of talented and skilled people, both men and women, even in small countries.

If, in addition, the nation was also blessed with natural resources especially industrial raw materials such as coal, oil, gas, copper, iron ore, and bauxite, it provided additional resource advantages to these ex-Communist or ex-socialist countries such as China, Russia, Central Asia and India.

A final and more recent reason for the growth of emerging economies is access to global capital and technology. Most of the emerging economies, and notably China and India, are attracting enormous capital, whether it is Foreign Direct Investment (FDI), private equity or debt capital.

Access to capital became easier through liberalization of trade, contract manufacturing and re-emergence of their own stock market exchanges. The world became flat not just in terms of information technology (especially the mobile phones) and entrepreneurship, but also with respect to global access to capital, and global agricultural or industrial resources.

Chindia's Global Impact

Among the large emerging economies such as Brazil, Russia, Nigeria and Indonesia, it is the rise of China and India (Chindia) which will have (and already has) enormous business implications during the first half of this Century mostly beneficial to the world.

First, both nations will require enormous natural resources because not only are they manufacturing and service centers of the world, but because of their own rapidly expanding domestic consumer markets. And this demand for natural and industrial resources such as oil, gas, coal, copper, bauxite, aluminum, iron and steel will be for many years.

While China today is roughly nine times as big as India, it is expected that China will very soon become an aged and affluent nation, similar to what happened to Japan, Singapore, Taiwan and others and will begin to plateau its economic growth. Also, it will outsource manufacturing to other nations, especially in Africa and other resource rich nations. The rapid aging of Chinese population attributed to its one child policy implemented over two generations will impact its domestic economic growth. On the other hand, while India is at present one tenth in size of China, it will experience accelerated growth in less than ten years with better infrastructure, political reforms and financial transparency.

Also, India will refocus on manufacturing both for global supply as well as for its domestic demand. Unlike China, however, India's manufacturing will be selective and largely concentrated on high-end aerospace, military, space and consumer durables including automobiles and appliances. It will begin to catch up with China and some experts even believe that its growth rate will surpass that of China. In any case, both nations with more than a billion people each, will have enormous need for industrial, agricultural and other natural resources and raw materials. Since a vast majority of these untapped resources are in other dormant or emerging economies in Africa, Caribbean, Latin America, Central Asia and Russia, the rise of Chindia will create economic boom for them which otherwise did not happen for nearly 200 years of colonial rule.

Second, the global integration of China and India will be radically different. India's economy and enterprises will be globally integrated especially with other advanced countries (Europe, US, Canada, UK, Australia, Singapore, Japan, South Korea) through large scale acquisitions of well established and well respected foreign companies with technology, branding and manufacturing assets. The journey has already begun with Mittal Steel's acquisition of Arcelor, Tata Steel's acquisition of Corus Steel, and Hindalo's acquisition of Novelis (largest North American sheet aluminum company). And it will not be limited to industrial raw materials and to private enterprises of India. For example, several large public sector units (PSUs) of India such as ONGC (Oil and Natural Gas Corporation), Indian oil and SBI (State Bank of India), who have the domestic scale and capital reserve, are starting to flex their acquisition muscles. Similarly, Wipro, an information technology (IT), engineering services, as well as consumer products company, has recently made several worldwide acquisitions (including Infocrossing, a data center company in the US, and Unza, a personal care consumer products company in Singapore).

Finally, Ranbaxy and Dr. Reddy's have become significant players in the global pharma industry largely through acquisitions. So have Mafatlal and Raymonds in fashion and garments. In other words, India will contribute to global growth as much, if not more, through revitalizing and investing in Western assets as it would through growth of its domestic consumer markets.

On the other hand, China's growth will be proportionately more domestic and only on a selective basis through global acquisitions. This is due to several reasons. First, China has begun to focus on domestic demand especially in consumer markets such as consumer electronics, appliances, automobiles and financial services. It has the physical infrastructure as well as large scale domestic state-owned enterprises such as Haier, Lenovo, China Mobil, Petro China and China Development Bank to capitalize on domestic demand.

Second, the advanced world seems less willing to sell their assets to China (especially technology assets) due to what I believe are myopic misperceptions about the peaceful rise of China (in contrast to rise of India). For example, Chinese oil company, CNOOC's attempt to buy Unocal as well as Haier's (the largest Chinese appliance company) attempt to buy Maytag Company in the US, met with political resistance. The obvious exception is IBM's sale of its personal computer (PC) business to Lenovo. But it is more an exception.

Consequently, Chinese enterprises that have the scale and incumbency advantage to dominate the domestic Chinese markets will end up expanding globally by first going to other emerging economies such as countries in Africa, Caribbean, Latin American and the ASEAN as well as in Central Asia and India, both through trade as well as foreign direct investment (FDI). In addition, despite history and current uneasiness of rise of China, it is inevitable that both Japan and South Korea will quickly integrate their economies with China, just as what Taiwan has already done. This will result in rapid growth in bilateral trade as well as reciprocal foreign direct investment between China and Japan and China and South Korea. Consequently, the largest trading bloc will be Asia especially with free trade with India. This will require formation of a new currency comparable to the Euro; and it will become the dominant currency of the world similar to the rise of the dollar as a global currency after World War I.

While the global integration paths taken by China and India will be different, their impact on businesses worldwide either as suppliers, customers, partners or competitors will be beneficial and enormous. In fact, it is no exaggeration to state that the future survival of most admired enterprises from all advanced economies including the United States, Canada, Europe, Australia, Japan, and South Korea will depend on how quickly they participate in ensuing rise of China and India even if they have to distance from their own government's politics and public opinion. This includes companies such as General Electric, HSBC, Mercedes Benz, Siemens, Alcatel and many others.

Chindia's Geopolitical and Cultural Hegemony

Finally, it is inevitable that as China and India become the largest economy of the world, its geopolitical and cultural hegemony will expand. I firmly believe that the G-8 Forum will invite and integrate China and India to become the G-10 Forum—for its own relevance and survival. Similarly, most world forums (from Davos to climate change) and world agencies, must encourage significant involvement of bureaucrats and professionals from China and India. This includes the World Bank, IMF and various UN agencies such as WHO, ILO, UNIDO and UNESCO. Again, Indian professionals are more likely to be invited and encouraged to become leaders and advisors of the world bodies due to language, culture and political compatibility as compared to Chinese professionals and bureaucrats.

Rudyard Kipling who proclaimed that "East is East and West is West and never the twain shall meet" is already proven wrong with respect to Westernization of heritage-rich and tradition-based China and India. He will be proven wrong again as we witness what I refer to as the Easternization of the world. Indeed, the Western culture will more readily accept and adopt the arts, culture, fashion and *traditions* of China and India because of their prochange cultures. The Western world will also embrace spiritual and meditation practices of the East. For example, Emory University (where I am a Professor) recently formally inaugurated the Emory–Tibet Partnership with His Holiness, the Dalai Lama as the Presidential Distinguished Professor! The Emory–Tibet Partnership will attempt to blend the Tibetan Buddhist meditation practices with modern science, using brain imaging techniques to study how mind and body work together. Similarly, Emory University has invested in archiving Salman Rushdie's writings for scholars to research on contemporary authors. In exchange, Rushdie has also agreed to be a Professor at Emory University.

In short, it will be less a clash of cultures and more a fusion of cultures across arts, architecture, science, law, engineering, medicine and management traditions and perspectives.

The Real Show Stopper: The Environment

In my view, the only show stopper to the economic rise of China and India will be the environment and not geopolitics. Both nations, and the rest of the world, will realize that to carry out their economic journey will require understanding the impact of their economic growth on environment and proactively protecting it. In other words, sustainability is in their self interest and survival. Nature, like the human body and other living organisms, has a way of resisting its depletion and destruction.

Unlike the first Industrial Revolution which garnered the industrial age at the expense of the environment, this second industrial age anchored to emerging economies will be wiser and more experienced to manage economic growth conservation *through* breakthrough innovation and cloning of natural and biological resources.

Cloning of sheep, chicken, pigs and other living organisms is now a routine science. And just as in the last Century substituted plant, vegetation and animal based medicine with modern pharma and biotech and bioengineering technology, we will innovate to preserve and duplicate nature's resources. At least this is my hope in addition to my forecast.

The rise of Chindia is not only inevitable, but it will be beneficial to the world economy. It will be, of course, beneficial to businesses and entrepreneurs, but also to the masses at the bottom of the pyramid (people who earn less than two dollars a day). It will generate unprecedented innovation, probably more dramatic and breathtaking than the first Industrial Revolution, by making existing technologies more affordable and accessible and by inventing or discovering ways to replicate natural resources. Finally, *both* the advanced countries and the emerging economies will rapidly learn to innovate for conservation, sustainability and cloning of nature's resources.

JAGDISH N SHETH

Acknowledgements

First and foremost, I want to thank Mr. John Yow, who did research and writing of this book with me for six months. His ability to research, synthesize and express in writing is extraordinary. It was a joy to work with him again!

I want to thank Abhijit Agrawal, my research assistant and MBA student at the Goizueta Business School, Emory University, for carefully reading the manuscript, questioning my logic and language, as well as editing the manuscript and working closely with the publisher.

I also want to thank Roxanne Russell and Dr. Yuan Yuan Chen, Fellows at the India, China and America (ICA) Institute, for reviewing the manuscript and checking for accuracy. Additional thanks goes to Suresh Sharma, a great colleague, for his very helpful suggestions on cover design and the subtitle for this book. Also, I want to thank Robert Cady, ICA Institute Director of Development, for his suggestions about publicity of this book.

I am grateful to R. Chandra Sekhar, Publishing Manager, and Roystan La'Porte, Head of Professional and Healthcare McGraw-Hill Education, India, who persisted in signing me up, speeding up the editorial and production schedule, and agreeing to publish the book both in English and Mandarin Chinese. The editorial staff at McGraw-Hill was extraordinary both with respect to updating and checking the accuracy of research sources used in preparing this manuscript.

I am also extremely grateful to Isha Edwards who provided exceptional editorial assistance toward the publication of this book.

As always, my executive assistant, Elizabeth Robinson and my department's administrative assistant at Emory University, Sonya Owens, who both provided support and put up with my demands for more than three years since I started this project. Both have provided incomparable administrative support to me for more than 12 years!

JAGDISH N SHETH

Contents

Introduction

THE RISING TIDE

"The argument made in this book is that the rise of China in the early part of the twenty-first century is distinctive and has more in common with the rise of the United States in the twentieth century than with the advance of its Asian Neighbors; the repercussions of its climb are equally monumental."

— Oded Shenkar, *The Chinese Century*

"Never before in recorded history have so many people been in a position to rise so quickly."

— Gurcharan Das, *India Unbound*

By now we've become accustomed to statistics reflecting the spectacular growth of the world's two emerging economic superpowers China and India. But let's look again at two statistics that puts the story in a nutshell: By 2025, India's share of the world GDP, will have risen from 6 to 13 percent, making it the third largest economy in the world.[1] China by that time will have become the largest economy, and together China and India will account for a 39 percent share of the global output—about equal to the present share of the United States and Europe combined.

What are some of the signs of the Chindia's rising tide which laps at the shores of the world's economy? Here are a few of the most visible.

Multinationals on the Move

In 2005, China's Lenovo bought IBM's personal computer unit for $1.75 billion, immediately making the Chinese company the world's third largest computer manufacturer. In 2006, India's Mittal Steel bought Arcelor, Europe's largest steel manufacturer, for $34 billion and thus created the world's first 100-million-ton steel producer; Arcelor Mittal (as the new company is now called) is three times bigger than its closest rival Nippon Steel. These blockbuster deals are significant beyond the dollar signs they reveal the strategy by which China's and India's corporations are rapidly transforming themselves into serious competitors on the global stage. Discarding the old Japanese and Korean model of entering at the lower end of the market and depending on an export-driven economy, these new multinationals are building worldwide businesses through mergers and acquisitions, targeting both high-end as well as low-end markets. The speed with which these Indian and Chinese companies are moving into the world's markets make previous strategies adopted by Japanese and Korean companies seem slow.

Low-price Leaders

China and India can develop the strength of their multinationals while still enjoying their inherent low-cost advantage in a bid to establish themselves as world centers for global sourcing. Manufacturer to the world, China is the global leader in the production of toys, shoes, wooden furniture and clothing. Wal-Mart alone does so much business with China ($15 billion worth in 2003 alone) that if the American retail giant were a nation, it would be China's fifth-largest export market, ahead of Germany and Great Britain. In India meanwhile, 250,000 IT workers are answering phone calls from all over the world, or dialing out to solicit people for credit cards or other bargains. But these "call centers" mark where the game began. India now has at least 40 Internet service providers, and via the Internet "remote services" are exploding: under the rubric of "remote infrastructure management," Indian engineers in Bangalore and New Delhi are controlling the temperature inside U.S. factories, and even monitoring who enters and exits the premises. China's manufacturing and India's IT industry have created a powerful launching pad for global initiatives: China has stashed away $1 trillion in foreign reserves. India, which had approximately $1 billion at the outset of the economic reforms in 1991, now has $250 billion.

Geopolitical Giants

In Beijing in October 2006, an unprecedented meeting took place between China's top officials and leaders from 48 African nations—a summit that clearly signaled a new level of economic and political cooperation between China and Africa. It's the kind of partnership that will define the 21st century: China avails itself of Africa's resources to fuel its continued industrial growth, and Africa, in turn, avails itself of China's technical and engineering know-how to help meet its vast infrastructure needs. About the same time China was meeting with the Africans, India's Prime Minister Manmohan Singh and Trade Minister Kamal Nath were attending a trade summit in Helsinki with the top leadership of the European Union. The purpose: to start negotiations for a free-trade agreement between the EU and India. With business and trade ties rapidly strengthening between India and the United States, the EU was anxious to play catch-up.

With economic power comes political clout. Where the world's nations assemble—at the UN, at the WTO—China and India are now players. The eight geopolitical giants (G-8) could soon be the G-10.

Dollars for Resources

In 2005 China stunned the United States when CNOOC, one of China's largest government-owned oil concerns, bid nearly $20 billion to buy out the American oil giant Unocal. When that deal was scotched by the U.S. Congress, who saw the sale as a possible threat to U.S. energy security, China turned its sight towards Canada and bought up PetroKazakhstan for $4.2 billion. India, having been the losing bidder for PetroKazakhstan, has now successfully built up its own energy stakes in Venezuela, and is in talks with Iran and Myanmar about building gas pipelines into India. Of course, given that China and India together have roughly one third of the world's population, both are rapidly industrializing, and both are in the process of trying to raise millions of people out of poverty and into a consumption-oriented middle class. It's no wonder the two are scouring the globe in search of oil, gas, coal, and iron ore. As an important, and hopeful—sign of the times, however, let's note that instead of competing, China and India are partnering up. Under a series of agreements signed in late 2006 and early 2007, the two nations have agreed to work together in energy exploration, production, storage and stockpiling, research and development, and conservation.

Insatiable Appetites

China has already become, by far, the world's largest market for cell phones, with close to half a billion subscribers. India, now posting the world's largest month-by-month increase in subscribers, is gaining in on China. In 2007, China will pass America to become the largest beer consumer in the world; India already produces and consumes more milk than any other nation. China is No. 1 in cigarette smoking; India is No. 2. China and India also lead the world in the consumption of cement and steel as their infrastructures rapidly expand. In 15 years, the Chinese will be buying more cars than any other people in the world.

Mukesh Ambani's Reliance Industries Limited opened their first three supermarkets in late 2006. He confidently predicted that in the next three years there would be four thousand of his Reliance Fresh stores across the country. The point is that China and India won't just need more oil; as their domestic markets grow into the world's largest and also most voracious, they will need more of everything—from food to computers to cars to life insurance. This is of course good news for manufacturers and service providers everywhere.

Cultural Fusion

In the second half of the 20th century, the process of Westernization— export of the Western culture to the East—reached its zenith. The 21st century will see the pendulum swing back with the West increasingly absorbing a wide range of Asian cultural influences. The difference will be that while the modern, fast-paced, consumerist Western culture often imposed itself upon reluctant traditional societies in the East—i.e. culture clash, the culture of the East will be embraced by and assimilated into the West in a more or less tension-free process of "culture fusion."

In day-to-day consumer needs like food and clothing, in arts and entertainment fields like movies, music, painting and literature, and perhaps most profoundly—at the transcendental level of values, philosophy, and spirituality, the culture of the East will move westward piggybacking on the surging economies of China and India.

* * *

The question is no longer whether the Chindia tide is rising, rather what impact its waves will make along the shorelines of the global economy. In trying to view this rising tide from a historical perspective, analysts and commentators in China and India—as well as in the West—are all reaching a uniform conclusion: that the kind of rapid rise to economic supremacy now being witnessed in these two nations has happened but once before—in the United States, from roughly 70 years after the end of the Civil War, to the end of World War I. It therefore follows that the bursting of China and India into full economic bloom will have global repercussions—political, social, cultural, as well as economic. These repercussions are expected to be in the same order of magnitude as that at of America's hegemony throughout the 20th century. This book will argue that the transformations, which occur as a result of Chindia's rise, will be fascinating, far-reaching and, ultimately, positive.

First though, let's take a look at the premise. England, in the 1800s, also grew into a world-transforming power—indeed, a world-girdling empire. True enough, but even British historian Bernard Porter, a specialist on the English Empire, who painstakingly compares Britain's "imperial" stature with America's, comes to the unquestionable conclusion that "Britain once had an empire. America now has a super-empire. . . . She exceeds any previous empires the world has ever seen: for example in the spread of her cultural and economic influence . . .; in her military dominance; and in the extent of her ambition . . . to remodel the world in her own image."[2] I do not expect that Chindia will entertain "imperial ambitions," but it is likely to remodel the world in its image. The rise of Chindia might well compare to that of America's in its global ramifications; it will certainly pose an unprecedented opportunity, as well as challenge, for the West. How the West must respond to Chindia's rising tide is a question we will examine in our penultimate chapter.

Now, to lay the groundwork for analyzing Chindia's dominance, let's look at some of the interesting parallels between the rise of America in the late 19th and early 20th centuries, and that of China and India today; that is, let's establish a rationale for arguing that the rise of "Chindia" will be as far-reaching and transformational as has been that of the United States.

Vast Natural Resources: The Historical Advantage

Like the United States, China and India are huge land masses blessed with abundant natural resources. India, particularly like North America in this regard, is endowed with a rich and diverse topography. Especially important is that almost 60 percent of its land is arable, including the fertile Ganges plain. Instead of the "basket case" that India ended up becoming in the 1960s, when it had to import countless tons of grain from the United States, it now has the potential of itself being one of the world's "bread baskets," with food grains one of its most important exports. No less important is the nation's vast coastline, and the wealth of resources supplied by the surrounding oceans.

As for its "buried treasures," India is plentifully supplied with iron and manganese, which accounts for the fact that its critical steel industry is currently booming. It has the world's largest store of titanium, used these days in everything from weaponry to golf clubs. It has massive reserves of bauxite, or aluminum ore; aluminum manufacturing is another industry poised for take-off. Beryllium, an important alloy in copper, and monazite, a radioactive element used, among other things, for nuclear energy, are also abundant.

Though much of its terrain is forbidding and only 10 percent of its land is arable, China is also rich in natural resources. It claims more coal than any other nation in the world, with reserves estimated at 11 trillion metric tons. Because of the exploding urban growth and the burgeoning industrial sector, China in the last few years has become a net importer of oil, but its petroleum reserves are nonetheless vast. With an estimated 20 billion metric tons, the bulk of which has been discovered offshore, China can now lay claim to being second only to Saudi Arabia.

Like India, China is also plentifully supplied with mineral ores, including an estimated 40 billion metric tons of iron ore and 1 billion metric tons of aluminum ore. Its tin reserves are so abundant in fact, that the nation is responsible for more than 10 percent of the world's output. China also boasts the world's largest reserves of both antimony and tungsten. In addition, major uranium deposits have been discovered in Manchuria and elsewhere. Of course, these supplies represent only what the Chinese have already tapped into. There's no telling what might yet be discovered high on the Tibetan Plateau.

America too has enjoyed a wealth of natural resources, the exploitation of which formed the entire basis of its early economy. Virginia owed its survival to tobacco; South Carolina depended on rice and indigo, the Deep South on cotton. In the North it was cod, timber, and fur. But America began to develop into an economic power only when the basis of its economy shifted from agriculture and the export of raw materials, to manufacturing and the export of finished goods. This transformation began in the first half of the 19th century with a revolution in transportation and communications. Suddenly, steamboat power appeared on the nation's network of rivers and canals, followed quickly by thousands of miles of railroad track and, at the same time, a rapidly growing network of telegraph lines. "Almost overnight," Robert Hormats writes in the Harvard Business Review, "large numbers of what had been generally self-sufficient local economies found themselves, ready or not, part of a relentlessly changing and expanding national economy."[3]

Hormats, whose essay is aptly titled "Abraham Lincoln and the Global Economy," offers a telling anecdote to illustrate the parallels between Lincoln's time and ours. On a night in 1856, the steamboat Effie Afton crashed into a railroad bridge spanning the Mississippi between Davenport, Iowa and Rock Island, Illinois. Claiming the bridge was hazardous to navigation, the boat's owners sued the Rock Island Bridge Company for damages. The larger issue, however, was the competition between an established means of transporting goods (the steamship) and the newcomer that threatened to cut into this business (the railroad). To defend itself in the suit, the bridge company hired Illinois lawyer Abraham Lincoln, who saw perfectly that the real conflict was "between entrenched interests rooted in the past and the imperatives of the coming new economic order."

A few years later, as President during the Civil War, Lincoln was in a position to realize his vision for America's economic growth. He understood that manufacturing had to establish itself locally, that the colonial powers could not be allowed to continue buying up raw material and do all the value-adding in their own factories. Of course, Britain at first resisted the development of a competing industrial sector in America. For example, export of textile machinery, the technology that jump-started the Industrial Revolution, was strictly forbidden. Inevitably, it was stolen, and America had its first cotton spinning mill as early as 1790 because of people like Samuel Slater and Francis Cabot Lowell. But the American industry was still in its infancy in the middle of the 19th century, and Lincoln knew that it would have to be protected. He was perfectly willing to use protectionist tariffs to get the job done. It was his belief, writes Hormats, that "a nation must tailor its policies to its own political, economic, and social circumstances."

China's current leaders would obviously agree, based on their intransigence on the issue of devaluing their currency. As for India, consider these words from former President A. P. J. Abdul Kalam: "We need to play the multilateral game, attract foreign investments, have joint ventures and be an active international player. Still, we have to remember that those who aim high, have to learn to walk alone, too, when required."[4]

Given America's vast store of raw material and a growing industrial sector that could only get larger, the British and other Europeans understood how the game would have to be played. In effect, they outsourced their manufacturing to the United States, where labor was plentiful and costs were low. Moreover, to build factories in Britain required infrastructure—transportation, power generation, and the like—and smart money that Europe had for some time been investing in America's industrial infrastructure. The Baring Brothers of London, for example, had bought more than $300,000 worth of Erie Canal bonds. That was in 1821. By 1847, European investment in American securities was up to $193 million. A decade later, on the eve of Lincoln's election, that amount had doubled.[5] In this regard, the parallels between America's experience and the current situation in China and India could not be clearer.

Huge Domestic Markets: The Obvious Advantage

It might be argued that there is one important difference between the America of the past and the Chindia of today: while much of today's outsourcing in China and India is the work of American and European multinationals who have cast a covetous eye on the huge consumer markets in those countries, there was no domestic consumer market to speak of in America. That was more or less true at the beginning of the 19th century, and America's first manufactured goods were primarily produced for export. But the analogy holds. The first outsourced manufactures in China were also intended for export, considering the masses, China's population were too impoverished to constitute a viable market. But immigration from Europe into the United States throughout the 19th century—an astounding thirty million people between 1820 and 1914—created a vast consumer market where there had been none, just as today the economic boom in China and India is creating a consumerist middle class, the likes of which the world has never seen before. So it's quite reasonable to say that in both China and India today and in the United States of two hundred years ago, outsourced manufacturing was at first export driven but soon directed itself inward to a rapidly expanding domestic market.

A cornerstone of Lincoln's policy for building America's economy was his belief in upward mobility, so well illustrated in his own life. As

Hormats puts it, "just as Lincoln argued that America could not sustain itself as a nation half slave and half free, so he also believed that it could not sustain itself 5 percent rich and 95 percent poor." One crucial key to upward mobility, he believed, was property ownership, and to that end his Republican congress passed the Homestead Act, which granted settlers of the West 160-acre parcels. In Lincoln's words, "it is best for all to leave each man free to acquire property as fast as he can." In both China and India today, the top national priority is the elimination of poverty, and the expansion of a middle class which has a vested interest in economic growth and prosperity. In 1978, when Deng Xiaoping became convinced that private ownership was the one great incentive for production, China's economy at last began to free itself from state control. Gurcharan Das says of India, "to focus on the middle class is to focus on prosperity, unlike in the past, when our focus has been on redistributing poverty. The whole purpose of the enterprise is to lift the poor—and lift them into the middle class."[6]

It follows from Lincoln's belief in upward mobility that his policies emphasized the importance of the consumer sector of the economy. (By contrast, Europe had historically viewed the industrial sector, often subsidized by the government, as the great driver of the economy.) As America's population swelled and expanded westward, Lincoln foresaw the economic power of a growing domestic consumer market, and many of his reforms, particularly in the banking industry (including the creation of the first "greenbacks"), were intended to unify that market nationally. The Federal Home Loan Bank would follow, spurring the rise of savings and loan institutions across the country—and the commensurate surge in home ownership. Home-building, of course, is one of those "multipliers" in the economy; i.e., it supports players up and down the supply chain.

America too became the land of consumer-driven innovation. "Get the prices down to the buying power," Henry Ford famously advised, and his automobile assembly line did just that. As historian John Steele Gordon writes, "If the automobile was invented in Europe, the mass-produced automobile, sold at a price the middle class could afford, was a purely American idea, an idea that transformed the American and world economies."[7] With the introduction of his assembly line at the Highland Park, Michigan plant in 1913, a Model T could be fully assembled in 93 minutes. As production time dropped, so did price, down to $360 by 1916. In the early 1920s, despite the inflation that resulted from World War I, the price was still dropping; it eventually settled at $265. And talk about a great multiplier. In the 1920s, the auto industry was consuming 20 percent of the steel produced in the country, 80 percent of the rubber, and

75 percent of the plate glass. To reiterate the generalization, the nations of Europe, whose greatness tended to be achieved through conquest and empire, saw the military-industrial complex as the economy's great multiplier. America's power, meanwhile, has come through wealth rather than conquest, with its huge consumerist middle class largely driving its economic growth.

In the same way, China and India have come to recognize that their own domestic consumer markets are a source of virtually limitless economic power. Japan and Korea, relatively small nations with relatively small populations, grew their economies through export, but the situation in China and India reflects the changing face of Asia. Yes, both nations have huge workforces and low wage structures that together constitute a recipe for export, but the difference is that as more and more Chinese and Indians become money-makers and money-spenders, those nations' industries will not have to depend on export; they will not be at the mercy of trade agreements and currency fluctuations. Both nations will have the capacity for the kind of economic engine—a prodigious production-and-consumption machine—that can propel growth for years to come. (And as we know, American, European and more recently Japanese and Korean multinationals have been salivating over the size and hunger of the consumer markets in China and India.)

Entrepreneurship: The Real Advantage

Yet another factor in America's rise as an economic superpower was its spirit of entrepreneurship. Unlike Europe of the old, with its aristocratic disdain for "business" and the vulgarity of money-making, the United States had always revered entrepreneurship, always venerated the "self-made man." Benjamin Franklin himself epitomized America's central economic ethos—the possibility, and desirability, of rising in the world. Son of a Philadelphia tallow maker, Franklin became a newspaper publisher, inventor, merchant, and, in the process, a very wealthy man. His story is currently recapitulated in the astounding success of today's Silicon Valley billionaires; the high-achieving entrepreneur has always been a prominent actor on America's stage. The extent to which the "rags to riches" archetype reverberated in the American psyche is exemplified by the wild popularity of Horatio Alger's novels, the first of which appeared in 1867. And indeed, it was during the second half of the 19th century, building on Lincoln's foundation, that America's entrepreneurial giants—or "second founders," as historian Richard Parker calls them— "transformed America into the world's largest and fastest-growing economy." Their story is best represented by Andrew Carnegie (whose father, in one of capitalism's great ironies, was laid off from his work as a hand weaver by the Industrial Revolution). Carnegie began as a telegraph messenger boy on the Pennsylvania Railroad and by 1900 was manufacturing half the nation's structural steel. When he sold his empire to J. P. Morgan, he may well have been the world's richest man.[8]

China and India too have entrepreneurial DNA, but until recently their mercantile spirit had been driven overseas, stifled at home by politics, policies, and prejudice. In China, when the creation of the People's Republic in 1949 tolled the death knell for private enterprise, it also propelled a vast diaspora of Chinese traders and merchants to business-friendly cities far and near—from Hong Kong and Singapore, to San Francisco and London. For a quick measure of how much Chinese expatriates have contributed to other Asian economies, consider Indonesia, where ethnic Chinese account for 2 percent of the population but hold 70 percent of private capital. True, this imbalance has created internal tensions between the majority and the minority, but the problem is likely to be resolved positively as the Indonesian economy gets integrated with China and India through the ASEAN.

Ironically, India's independence and the establishment of its democracy in 1947 had much the same effect as did Communism in China. When Nehru chose to model his nation's economy on the Soviet state-controlled system, he effectively quashed entrepreneurial enterprise. Gurcharan Das offers this memorable statistic from the business-chilling environment of the "License Raj": Between 1960 and 1989, the Tatas made 119 proposals to start new businesses or expand old ones, "and all of them ended in the wastebaskets of the bureaucrats."[9] Nor were the aspirations of the Indian businessman abetted by the traditional caste system, in which the merchant class was afforded third place in the four-level hierarchy, just a notch above the laboring class. Not surprisingly, India's industrialists chose to expand their empires overseas. Notable examples include the Aditya Birla Group in Southeast Asia and the Patels in the U.S. hospitality industry. Also, more recently, graduates of the prestigious IITs and IIMs have become entrepreneurs in Silicon Valley, creating billions of dollars of new wealth.

After reforms in both countries unleashed the economic juggernaut, Chinese and Indian entrepreneurship is again trying to take root in native soil. Even under China's still-Communist system, in the booming cities of the southeast—Shanghai and Pudong and Shenzhen, where Deng created his first Special Economic Zones—the vibrant business environment is luring Chinese entrepreneurs back home. In India, no fewer than 27 businessmen have made room for themselves in Forbes' billionaires' club. The Brahmin prejudice against business may at last be dissipating. Two generations ago, young Indians worshipped Nehru and Gandhi. Now the objects of veneration and respect are the Birlas, the Tatas, the Mittals, Azim Premji and Dhirubhai Ambani, some of the titans of Indian business. As a perfect counterpoint to his story about the Tatas' frustration under the License Raj, Das recounts meeting a 14-year-old boy hustling tables in a roadside village café. It's his summer job, he tells Das. He's going to use the money he makes for computer lessons, so that he can grow up to run a computer company—like "this man Bilgay [Bill Gates] . . . the richest man in the world."[10] Again, the huge populations of China and India serve as a comparative advantage. With entrepreneurial success increasingly enshrined as a respectable and rewarding goal, vast resources of brains and talent will be redirected.

Research and Development: The Future Advantage

Another interesting parallel between the rise of America and the rise of China and India is related to investment in research and development. America's economic expansion began with technology imported—or stolen—from Europe, but the United States quickly moved beyond that dependence. Even before the end of the 19th century, the nation had begun to create land-grant universities that developed into centers for agricultural and technological research. In the 19th century, the great parade of American inventors was led by Thomas Edison, but Edison's greatest invention may well have been the industrial research laboratory he established in Menlo Park, New Jersey in 1876. As John Steele Gordon points out, "It was, in essence, an invention factory where engineers, chemists, and mechanics turned new technological possibilities into practical—and, most important, commercially viable—products."[11]

Moving into the 20th century, the U.S. government has generously underwritten the nation's technological hegemony, investing heavily in projects like the National Science Foundation, the National Institutes of Health, and the U.S. Department of Agriculture, to name just a few, while at the same time India's elite universities have continued to emphasize their research capabilities. As a result, India has attracted the world's brightest minds to the nation, where R&D investment has been a high priority. However, the United States continues to lead all other nations in intellectual property and patent values, as well as in the number of Nobel Prize winners in science categories. I now see China and India expanding beyond export manufacture and infrastructure improvement to R&D and knowledge creation—the ultimate realm of value addition. An interesting difference is that while America, at least initially, had to depend on brain-power imported from Europe, China and India are simply calling their own native sons and daughters back home. Particularly after World War II, Indians and Chinese flocked to U.S. colleges and universities, especially for advanced degrees in the sciences, but now a lot of these bright minds are headed back home, where bigger and better opportunities await. China is rapidly becoming a world leader in number of patents filed per month. In India, nobody is pressing harder for R&D investment than former President Dr. Kalam, who is well aware that economic security depends on technology development. "Whenever developing countries have to import technology and know-how from the developed countries," he writes, they find themselves in a "catch-22" situation: they "pay a very high price for old technological inputs and in return have to sell much more goods and services to balance the high price of technology imports." The only way out of this trap, says Dr. Kalam, is for the developing nation to "arm itself" with its own technological prowess.[12]

Of course, both these nations, more so China, have availed themselves of western technology as well as intellectual property. This has been by means of technology-sharing joint ventures with foreign corporations eager, sometimes too much so, to penetrate the enormous Chindian market. This is an issue we'll return to in a later chapter. For now it is enough to emphasize that China and India have got the message: like America did in the 19th and 20th centuries, they will have to invest in their own R&D centers and develop their own high-tech expertise in order for their economies to become true global powerhouses.

Capitalism Redefined: One More Time

The United States also set itself apart from previous and contemporaneous superpowers, including Britain, by giving capitalism freer reign. For example, the rulers of Britain's colonies, recruited from her governing class, had a patrician disdain for capitalism, and often strove to keep in check the profiteering impulses of British "settlers" in colonial territories. To offer a controversial illustration from Bernard Porter: it can be argued that one of the motives for anti-British resentment among the American colonists (along with the better known tea tax) "was their desire to continue their expropriation and elimination (even genocide) of the native peoples to the west of the original thirteen colonies, against the wishes of the imperial government."[13] More generally, as the industrial economies of Europe have evolved during the 19th and 20th centuries, they have been largely characterized by a balancing act between free-market forces and state supervision.

From the outset, however, the United States did not buy into the idea that key industries like telephone, railroad, utilities and defense were too "critical" to be left in the hands of the capitalists. Quite the opposite, in fact: there was considerable sentiment in the late 19th century that business could not be entrusted to the government, and for good reason. As John Steele Gordon points out, many of America's late-19th century business titans—Morgan, Rockefeller, Carnegie, etc. "came of age in the era of unprecedented government corruption and would never be able to conceive of government as a suitable instrument for reforming and regulating the economy."[14] What's more, in a number of instances the private sector stepped up to regulate itself. To formalize accounting practices, the Institute of Accountants and Bookkeepers was established in New York in 1882, followed five years later by the American Association of Public Accountants. More dramatically, when the Pennsylvania Railroad and the New York Central became entangled in their ruinous competition, it was J. P. Morgan who successfully mediated the dispute (at the famous meeting on his yacht Corsair). And it was the railroads themselves, frustrated by paralysis in the United States Congress, which finally established the nation's four time zones and put interstate transportation on a universal schedule. The U.S. government's first attempt to regulate a portion of the economy came in 1887 with the establishment of the Interstate Commerce Commission; there have been many attempts since. But the continued dominance of capitalism in this country was powerfully illustrated by the government's inability to break up Microsoft in 1998.

Just what kind of capitalism China and India will embrace remains to be seen. It now looks like budding capitalists in those two nations have chafed long enough under the restraints of state control (Communism in China, the remnants of the License Raj in India) and would like nothing better than to soar unfettered into the inviting air of the free market. In fact, not only in China and India, but wherever the capitalist spirit had been previously choked (like Vietnam or the former Soviet states), business is joyfully booming. But my prediction is that the no-holds-barred, full-steam-ahead model will not be suitable for Chindia in the 21st century. Chindian capitalism will have to relearn the fundamental lesson that the wealth capitalism creates must be returned to society; it will have to redefine capitalism to embody not just wealth creation but wealth distribution.

Indeed, already many of America's capitalists are trying to give the lie to Herbert Hoover's famous pronouncement: "The only thing wrong with capitalism is capitalists. They're too damn greedy." In these early days of the 21st century, private money by the billions is pouring in to solve some of the world's most intractable problems, in some of the world's most impoverished places. In many cases, private money seems to be working wonders where government aid—inefficient and agenda-driven—hasn't been able to; and in doing such work, capitalism is wearing its new face. As we will suggest in our final chapter, China and India, where social and environmental problems are staggering, must become exemplars of this new "enlightened capitalism."

Déjà Vu All Over Again?

These, then are some of the parallels between the rise of America in the 19th and 20th centuries and the economic explosion that China and India appear headed toward in the 21st. Will this explosion indeed have the global impact that America has exerted? Time will tell, but the signs are promising.

On the most general level, there seems abroad in the world today a far-reaching "economic pragmatism"—witness the withdrawal of governments worldwide from the "commanding heights" of the economy.[15] America has led the way toward an ideology-free, market-driven *zeitgeist* as never seen before. Will this "spirit of the times" prevail? Will Chindia's rise be a force for world peace and prosperity? The chapters that follow, I hope, will convincingly answer that question in the affirmative.

Notes

1. Das, Gurcharan, "Afterword," *India Unbound: From Independence to the Global Information Age* (New Delhi: Penguin Books India, 2002), p. 360.
2. Porter, Bernard, *Empire and Superempire: Britain, America and the World* (New Haven: Yale Univ. Press, 2006), p. 162.
3. Hormats, Robert, "Abraham Lincoln and the Global Economy," *Harvard Business Review*, August 2003.
4. Kalam, Abdul A. P. J., *India 2020: A Vision for the New Millennium* (New Delhi: Penguin Books India, 1998, 2002), pp. 24-25.

5. Gordon, Steele John, *An Empire of Wealth: The Epic History of American Economic Power* (New York: Harper Perennial, 2005), p. 185.

6. Das, Gurcharan, *India Unbound: From Independence to the Global Information Age* (New Delhi: Penguin Books India, revised ed. 2002), p. 352.

7. Gordon, p. 297.

8. Parker, Richard, "Pittsburgh Pirates," *New York Times Book Review*, Nov 5, 2006, p. 10.

9. Das, 93.

10. Das, xiv.

11. Gordon, p. 302.

12. Kalam, p. 189.

13. Porter, p. 46.

14. Gordon, p. 222.

15. Yergin, Daniel, *The Commanding Heights: The Battle for the World Economy* (New York: Simon & Schuster/Touchstone, 2002).

1

Chindia Multinationals Making Waves

When we think of China, we think of shoes, textiles and toys—the deluge of products that have earned China the sobriquet "workshop of the world." When we think of India, we think of IT, of call centers, of talking to technicians in Bangalore when something goes wrong with our PCs. Right now, however, those burgeoning economies are driven by something much bigger and much more globally significant than the outsourcing phenomenon that began to catch the world's attention a decade ago. Before analyzing the new reality of Chindia's global business, let's look at two examples.

Lenovo

Lots of casual electronics watchers were caught off guard when venerable IBM, pioneer of the personal computer, sold its PC unit to China's Lenovo for $1.75 billion in early 2005. Insiders weren't surprised that IBM was looking to sell; after all, thanks to cut-throat competition and collapsing margins, IBM's PC business had lost close to a billion dollars in the three years prior to the sale. The tougher question was why Lenovo wanted to buy.

Founded in 1984 as a retail enterprise selling everything from TVs to roller skates, the Legend Group (as it was originally called) introduced its first proprietary product, a Chinese character system for PCs, the following year. When reduced import tariffs allowed foreign PC makers like IBM and Compaq to enter the Chinese market in 1990, Legend met them head-on by starting to make computers under its own brand. Offering low-priced machines with Chinese characters, Legend steadily won market share, and by 1997 it had met its goal of becoming the dominant player in the domestic computer market.

The company's global aspirations became apparent when it changed its name to Lenovo (loosely derived from Latin *novo*, meaning new) in 2003. The change was necessitated because Legend had already been trademarked (by Acura) in the West, and the West was where Lenovo wanted to go. Still, few people expected the mega-deal with IBM. But from Lenovo's point of view, the strategy made perfect sense. In the first place, the purchase immediately transformed Lenovo from a domestic player into the world's No. 3 PC maker, behind only Dell and Hewlett-Packard. Perhaps more importantly, Lenovo bought a couple of world-class brands: the ThinkPad laptop, and the ThinkCenter desktop. According to the terms of the deal, those high-visibility products would continue to carry the IBM logo for five years, after which time, as Lenovo built its global reputation, they would be sold under the Lenovo brand. As Deepak Advani, Lenovo's marketing director, told the *Christian Science Monitor*, "There will be no doubt that ThinkPad is made by Lenovo, just like iPod is made by Apple."[1]

By the end of 2005, Lenovo chairman Yuanqing Yang was quite clear on the company's goal "to become the most competitive PC company and the most famous PC brand in the world." To that end, he and his board lured William Amelio, who had been president of Dell's operations in Asia Pacific and Japan, to take over as CEO of Lenovo. One of Amelio's first moves was a restructuring that cut 1,000 jobs from the 9,500-person workforce, projected to streamline operations and save the company $250 million a year. As for building the brand, Amelio has taken a global approach. The company worked out a marketing deal to sell and operate Lenovo computers at the 2006 Olympic Winter Games in Turin, Italy, and—needless to say—it plans to have a conspicuous presence at the 2008 Summer Games in Beijing. To help penetrate the Latin American market, the company has hired soccer superstar Ronaldinho of Brazil as spokesperson. In India, Lenovo is working with Bollywood actors and doing product placement on that country's wildly popular game shows. In the United States, Amelio is looking for tie-ins with the National Basketball Association.

However, while both the chairman and the CEO want the brand to be prominent in every corner of the globe, they understand that the key to sales growth lies in emerging markets. As Amelio told the *Wall Street Journal*, "The emerging markets are critical for our success." The model that has led to dominance in China, he says, is being "migrated to India, and we'll do that across many of the emerging markets, whether it's Brazil or Russia."

Amelio unwaveringly describes Lenovo as "a global company," and notes that "we actually rotate the headquarters between Beijing, Hong Kong, Singapore, Raleigh [N.C.], and Paris."[2] But the significance Lenovo's sudden emergence as a global player in a high-profile industry is perhaps best articulated by marketing director Advani, who describes the company as "the poster child of China's move from planned economy to market economy, a market-driven company that is a leader in this transition."[3]

Mittal Steel

India's major companies, no less than China's, have global aspirations. Yet, their strategy is often different. Thanks to the legacy of state-imposed controls over the private sector during the so-called "License Raj," as well to a history of tight-knit family ownership of private businesses, India's private enterprises had been held in check on the domestic front. With growth at home constrained, their strategy had been to expand globally through merger and acquisition.

There can be no better example of this scenario than Mittal Steel. Family patriarch Mohan Mittal was already buying up steel companies in Indonesia in the mid 1970s. In the early 1990s—under the leadership of Mohan's son Lakshmi—the company moved into North America, with acquisitions in both Mexico and Canada. That decade also saw a string of purchases in Western Europe and, in 1998, the acquisition of Chicago-based Inland Steel. In 2004, when the family combined its publicly traded company, Ispat International, with its privately held LNM holdings, it became officially Mittal Steel, the world's largest steel-maker. It strengthened its position the next year with its purchase of the U.S.-based International Steel Group (ISG) for $4.5 billion. Now it owned the coveted title No. 1 steel producer in the United States, too.

But Lakshmi wasn't done yet. In 2006 came the blockbuster—the deal in which, according to *The Times* of London, "the two most acquisitive steel groups in the world became a colossus." Mittal bought Arcelor, Europe's largest steel manufacturer, for $34 billion and thus created the world's first 100-million-ton steel producer. Talk about a dominant player: Arcelor Mittal (as the new company is now called) is three times bigger than its closest rival, Nippon Steel. We should note though that Mittal's expansion is not simply about bragging rights. It's about understanding what it means to be a player in the global economy. As the chief executive of the UK Steel Association told *The Times*, consolidation "is imperative for steelmakers if they are going to work efficiently with large global industries such as car manufacturers.... The steel industry needs to bolster to partner global companies."[4] This "global mindset" of Indian and Chinese companies is a point we'll return to.

The emerging multinationals in China and India will be characterized not only by fast growth but also by deep commitment to R&D. Mittal illustrates this point with the $10 million expansion of its Mittal Steel USA research facility in Chicago. At the 2006 groundbreaking, Mittal USA marketing chief Dan Mull noted that 50 percent of the new steel products used in auto production did not exist 10 years ago and that the steel industry in general is constantly challenged to make steel lighter, stronger, and more cosmetic for use in automobiles and appliances. The state-of-the-art Chicago facility will keep Mittal in the forefront as it researches no fewer than 16 new steel products.[5]

The global highway leading out of India is quickly becoming congested, as IT and pharmaceutical companies follow Mittal's example. This dramatically altered scenario is pointedly described by Manisha Girotra, head of investment banking for UBS India. "Five years ago we were representing multinationals and advising on their entry strategy into India," she tells the *Financial Times*. "Now our biggest business is advising Indian companies to go global.... Every CEO I meet wants to talk about global strategy."[6]

* * *

Watching the rise of multinational corporations in China and India, we might be tempted to understand it as—in Yogi Berra's memorable phrase—"déjà vu all over again." After all, we've seen it before, as first Japan, and then Korea mounted global competitive assaults in the automobile and consumer electronics sectors. But we'll be making a big mistake if we dismiss what's happening in China and India as "same old, same old." The rise of Chinese and Indian multinationals is a new phenomenon and must be assessed as such. The fundamental difference is that the rebirth of Japanese and Korean industry after World War II was export driven, whereas the sudden ascent of Indian and Chinese companies is investment driven. This paradigm shift has such far-reaching ramifications that we might take a few moments to understand *why* it has occurred. The quick answer is: the world has changed.

Let's look at some details.

First, the export model was deliberately created for—and then embraced by—Japan and Korea, because both nations were devastated by war and had no domestic industry upon which to rebuild their economies. In the immediate post-war years, Japan lay in rubble, occupied by a foreign power, its people hungry and demoralized. Thanks to sky-high inflation, goods that were available were unaffordable. The domestic market was in ruins. The United States, as the 1940s ended and the Cold War loomed, came to the realization that it needed a strong ally in Japan, rather than a defeated enemy. To this end, in the famous "reverse course," America initiated the Dodge Plan to promote Japan's economic renewal. With the onset of the Korean War in 1950, Japan's export boom officially got underway—supplying the needs of all the American forces stationed in the Korean peninsula. Once encouraged to adopt the export model, Japan committed to it wholeheartedly. The entire purpose of MITI (Japan's Ministry of International Trade and Industry), which in effect controlled the nation's economy throughout the 1950s, 1960s, and 1970s, was "not only to help firms adapt to world export markets but also to help them take the greatest advantage of them." Starting as an exporter of cheap goods, ignored as an economic force, and protecting its own market, Japan more or less snuck into the global economy.[7]

South Korea followed exactly the same course once the war against the North ended in 1953. It too was devastated; two-thirds of its industrial capacity, not great to begin with, had been destroyed. As in Japan, there was no viable domestic market. It was General Park Chung Hee's decision, when he came to power in 1961, that the Japanese model had to be adopted. Export was the way to go, and the way to get there—to compete in international markets and to withstand foreign imports—was to create a number of big companies. Out of this decision came the *chaebols*, the "national champions," just like the *zaibatsu* in Japan. And like Japan, Korea started at the low end. "Made in Korea" supplanted "Made in Japan" as a source of ridicule. But both nations learned that ultimate success as an export economy depends on moving up the quality chain. As a result, today we have Toyota, Sony, Samsung, and Hyundai.

To Export or Invest

To highlight the contrast between the situation of Japan and Korea a few decades ago and the situation in China and India today, it's worth reiterating a central point: the export-driven model is the *necessary remedy* when there is no domestic market. As we'll emphasize more than once, China and India have domestic markets like nobody has ever had before.

Another important aspect of the economic climate of 50 years ago was the sense of insecurity and protectionism that prevailed after World War II. The weather was bad everywhere, you might say. Among newly liberated nations (including India), anti-colonial sentiment fostered a sense of militant independence—and a reluctance to trade with (or in any way depend on) former colonial masters. Among newly Communist nations (including China), anti-Western sentiment had the same effect. Even the United States tended toward isolationism and the protection of its own industries and markets. The flow of people, of capital, of products, was suddenly curtailed. Trading partnerships were determined by Cold War politics. In such an environment Japan and Korea, "blessed" by Western partners who had a vested interest in their recovery, could focus on "making versus marketing." Marketing—including branding and the creation of distribution and dealer networks—was expensive, certainly too expensive for capital-starved Japan and Korea, so their model was to produce at the low end and turn their products over to import-export specialists who could supply their own capital.

It goes without saying that the weather has improved. The "trade winds" are favorable, as across the globe, a spirit of free-market pragmatism has pushed state control from commanding heights of the economy. The corollary is that, to be successful in the new environment, corporations have to be globally competitive. Today's "investment companies" like Mittal understand that they can't just make steel in one country and ship it out. They look at world resources and world markets. They build facilities or acquire companies where those resources and markets exist. They make steel wherever they can enjoy a competitive advantage.

Another change working in China's and India's favor is that today, capital is available. During the rise of Japan and Korea, unless you were one of the "national champions" favored by the government, you had no access to capital. It seems hard to believe today, but this was exactly the situation Honda found itself in. It was a maker of engines, a supplier to Japan's auto industry, and of course it was being exploited. It wanted to enjoy the valued-added end of the business, which meant becoming a carmaker, but no capital was available to realize this vision. The solution was radical but effective: instead of Tokyo, the company listed its shares in America, the only place where the kind of capital the company needed was accessible. Another surprising example is Sony, which in 1961 became the first Japanese company to be listed on the New York Stock Exchange, thus actually blazing the trail that Honda followed.

Thanks primarily to their positions as leaders in global sourcing, China and India today are awash in a river of capital. In November 2006, the combined activity of the Hong Kong, Shanghai, and Shenzhen stock markets gave China the world's highest IPO total for the month. (Interestingly, the United States fell to No. 3, behind London, where London's "junior" stock market AIM, with its looser regulations and lower market-cap minimums, attracts small-company IPOs from all over the world. In fact, noting that foreign firms are increasingly reluctant to list in the United States because of the strict regulatory environment created by Sarbanes-Oxley, Treasury Secretary Henry Paulson was quick to call for an easing of restrictions in the U.S. market.) In India meanwhile, private equity is making the big plays, attracted to investment opportunities in the booming nation's already publicly held companies. At the same time, Indian interest rates have fallen to half their levels in the mid-1990s, and deregulation has given Indian companies access to cheap money from international debt markets.

Moreover, a deluge of foreign direct investment continues to pour into both countries. According to A. T. Kearney's annual FDI Confidence Index, China emerged in 2002 as the world's most preferred destination for foreign direct investment; the following year, in 2003, India surged from the 15th place to the sixth worldwide. In Kearney's 2005 survey, however, the top three destinations were—in this order—India, China, and the United States. In just one recent example, Switzerland's Holcim Ltd. purchased 67 percent of Ambuja Cement India for $800 million.

Regardless of which country is in first place though, the point remains that the capital is there, big time. And when investment capital is available, you are no longer limited to the export model. If you see an opportunity to acquire a company, or build a new facility, and you have the means to, do it. To illustrate briefly, India's Sona Group, a maker of steering wheels, has Toyota as a key customer. But now that Toyota manufactures in the United States, Sona faced a decision: did it continue to make its steering wheels in India and ship them to Toyota's overseas plants, or did it build its own U.S. facility? Would proximity to the customer be worth the huge capital expense? The analysis revealed all the advantages of building a new plant—not only incentives from the community, like free land and tax breaks, but also an opportunity to upgrade to state-of-the-art technologies. Sona Group took the plunge; but note: if it weren't for available capital, the company couldn't have even considered it.

Yet another cause for improvement in the global business climate is that the clouds of anti-colonialism, protectionism, and xenophobia have lifted.

India, for example, not only welcomes foreign investment, its investments are welcomed in return. In one instance the Indian conglomerate Wipro sought to expand its hydraulics division with the acquisition of a Swedish manufacturer. As the deal was being consummated, the Indian CEO asked the Swedish CEO, "How do your people feel about being bought out by foreigners?" His surprising reply: "We don't care who owns us so long as it's not a U.S. company." (This response, I have to believe, is a measure of European displeasure with America's war in Iraq.) When the Indian CEO asked specifically how the Swedish company would feel about being owned by an Indian entity, the CEO's answer was, "More power to you." This would have been unthinkable 20 years ago.

True, anti-Communist sentiment still impedes China's foreign investment in some security-related sectors, as was shown recently when the U.S. Congress moved to block its purchase of American oil giant Unocal. But these are the last remaining exceptions to the new rule of economic pragmatism. Here in my home state of Georgia, for example, Governor Sonny Perdue has personally been to Beijing to beseech Chinese business leaders to bring their business here. Chinese foreign investment outside of the United States, especially in the ASEAN nations and Africa, is enormous.

Which brings up another significant advantage that China and India enjoy today. As Kenichi Ohmae reminded us in *Triad Power*, the economic landscape into which Japan was emerging was completely dominated by Europe and North America (the United States and Canada). Consequently, following the export model, Japan and Korea were exclusively focused on the advanced markets in the West because that's where the world's buying power lay. Any other nation that might have had a little buying power, as I've mentioned, would have been likely raising tariff walls to protect its own domestic industries. (To sharpen the relevance of this point: China and India are perfect examples of nations that, in the post-World War II environment, would have been too protective of their own domestic industries to welcome imports from Japan and Korea. It's a fine irony that trade barriers have collapsed just in time for China to become "the manufacturer to the world" and to enjoy the world's biggest trade surpluses.)

Going Global

In stark contrast to the experience of Japan and Korea, China and India are by no means limited to exporting to, or investing in, the world's advanced economies. They are free to go global, and that's what they are doing—in South America, in Africa, in Eastern Europe, in Asia. The opportunity that this gives their multinational corporations is incalculable, and all the more so because, today, the world's emerging economies are also the fastest-growing. Goldman Sachs' 2003 report, "Dreaming with BRICs: The Path to 2050," predicted that within four decades (by 2043) the total GDP of the four emerging BRIC nations (Brazil, Russia, India, and China) would likely surpass six of the eight geopolitical giants (G-8): the US, the UK, Germany, Japan, France, and Italy. The fact is that as G-8 domestic markets mature, advanced economies are slowing down. The United States remains the steadiest of the advanced nations with its unspectacular 3 to 4 percent annual growth. Emerging economies are hot, and this development too plays right into China's and India's hands. As the Goldman Sachs report puts it, "As today's advanced economies become a shrinking part of the world economy, the accompanying shifts in spending could provide significant opportunities for global companies. Being invested in . . . the right markets—particularly the right emerging markets—may become an increasingly important strategic choice."[8]

Broadly speaking, the world seems ready for a change, its economic axis shifting from the West to the East. Ohmae's book, published in 1985, needs updating. China and India are now seen as welcome alternatives to the old hegemony of the United States and Europe. The United States, in particular, seems to be losing its popularity because of its often hypocritical tendency to mix economics with social and political issues. The left-leaning nations of Latin America, for example, have clearly lost interest in the United State's old carrot-and-stick approach. Lula in Brazil, Chavez in Venezuela, and Correa in Ecuador—these are some of the leaders thumbing their noses at the United States and doing huge deals with both China and India. In Bolivia, where leftist president Evo Morales has made no secret of his animosity towards the United States, India's Jindal Steel and Power, in July 2007, signed a $2.1 billion deal to mine iron ore. Since 2004 China's largest steel company, the Shanghai Baosteel Group, has been building a $1.5 billion blast furnace operation in Sao Luis, Brazil. But the growing impact of emerging economies on the world's business stage was perhaps best illustrated by this recent news article stating: at the end of 2006, Brazilian steel maker CSN and India's Tata Steel were in a bidding war to take over Britain's Corus Group, the world's eighth-largest steel producer. Who could have imagined, even 10 years ago, that two companies from emerging nations would be battling to gain control of a huge Western corporation?

Moreover, as China and India continue to grow, they'll use their domestic buying power as leverage in bilateral trade negotiations. They'll elbow past the Byzantine process of multilateral negotiations and speak directly to nations that have the desired resources. Often, that will be a

developing nation. Brazil, for example, the world's second-largest producer
of soybean, used to look to Europe as its chief export market. But between
2000 and 2003 China has emerged as the world's No. 1 consumer of soybean,
and in turn, Brazil's soybean exports to the mainland have soared by 70
percent. India too looks with increasing interest at the developing world.
The first official India-Brazil-South Africa (IBSA) economic forum took
place in September 2006, with Indian Prime Minister Manmohan Singh
himself making the trip to Rio de Janeiro.

To reiterate: the rise of Japan and Korea was export driven, and those
exports were largely directed to the advanced markets in the West. The
emerging Chindian multinationals will be investment driven and will
enjoy the whole world as their smorgasbord. It follows that the ascent
of Chindian multinationals will be more rapid than any precedent set
by Japan or Korea, or by any Western company for that matter. In fact,
Indian and Chinese companies will literally leap onto the global stage in
a single bound. Let me explain briefly.

Local Player Today, GIE Tomorrow

Japanese and Korean MNEs, following a model that had been established
in the West, went through a three-step evolutionary cycle. As we've noted,
they began life as export-oriented domestic companies, manufacturing
goods for the domestic market and for export. The second step was to
become "multi-domestic", i.e., you created subsidiaries in countries where
the market was so big that it no longer made sense to export there.
At first you served those constituents by establishing distribution and
marketing networks, but eventually you invested there with the building
of manufacturing plants and corporate facilities, the Japanese auto
industry in the United States being the perfect example. The final stage
was to become a "Globally Integrated Enterprise" (GIE), at which point
the (business or physical?) architecture changed drastically.

Again, this was the model set by American corporations (which,
after World War II, expanded into Europe and then into Asia) and was
subsequently followed by Japanese and Korean multinationals. How
will the Chinese and Indian companies change this trajectory? They will
simply skip the second step ("multi-domestic") and transform themselves,
as it were, overnight into GIEs.

Before examining how this leap is possible, let's quickly identify a few
of the salient characteristics of the Globally Integrated Enterprise. First,

products made by GIEs have the same brand names worldwide: Coca-Cola, Lenovo, Toyota. Second, GIEs avoid the "local manager" syndrome; they hire the best managers from the global talent pool and thus assure themselves of leaders who are loyal to the company rather than to their country of origin. Lenovo's Bill Amelio, recruited from Dell, is the perfect example. Third, quality standards and processes are uniform worldwide. (Products might be tailored to local markets, but processes are standardized.) Fourth, R&D is similarly global, with research centers around the world. More generally, GIEs have a global mindset. The old architecture was to have domestic operations, which received the lion's share of attention, along with an "international division." In American corporations, overseas business had historically been disparaged with the acronym "OUS" (outside the US). The mindset now is radically different.

Now, why do Chindian multinationals get to leapfrog directly into the GIE stature? The short answer, again, is that the world had changed. Let's look at how.

First, today there are fewer restrictions on capital and trade flow than previously, along with fewer regulatory restrictions on the operations of foreign corporations. In the larger sense, the emerging multinationals will benefit from the pro-market global trends we've already noted. Describing how the coming wave of MNEs will be more global, more diverse, and more Asian, a recent report from the National Intelligence Council goes on to say that these large multinationals "will be increasingly outside the control of any one state and will be key agents of change in dispersing technology widely, further integrating the world economy, and promoting economic progress in the developing world."[9]

Second is the emergence of the Internet as an incredible enabler of global business. Not long ago, the global operations of major U.S., EU, and Japanese corporations were impeded by having different IT platforms in different countries. Today, thanks to a company like SAP (itself a GIE, serving 27,000 clients in 120 countries), multinationals can globally integrate back-office functions like distribution, accounting, human resources, and even manufacturing. What's more, SAP's new "mySAP" software products are Web-based, available everywhere at the click of a mouse.

Third, Chinese and Indian MNEs have the seemingly counterintuitive advantage of a shortage of management talent. In other words, because they have a plentiful supply of both entrepreneurs and factory workers but a dearth of senior management, their survival depends on tapping the global talent pool. We've mentioned Lenovo's Bill Amelio, but remember that just a couple of years ago, Sony shocked the business community by naming Welshman Howard Stringer as CEO. Chindian multinationals know they can't wait for a generation of managers to be nurtured indigenously. They need the best guy now.

Fourth, global capital inculcates a global mindset. Not only are Chinese and Indian companies acquiring companies worldwide, but they are also listed on stock exchanges all over the world—which makes them responsible to global shareholders. Global capital also encourages global R&D, which allows Chinese and Indian firms to quickly shore up an endemic weakness. In buying foreign corporations, they are also buying those firms' technological expertise and research capabilities.

And finally, we noted that Japan and Korea built their export-based economies by focusing on Western markets. But another pressure forcing Chindian companies to become GIEs is that their customers are global. Manufacturers like General Electric and Toyota, and retailers like Wal-Mart, Home Depot, or England's Tesco are now GIEs, and companies that sell to those customers will have to serve them globally. Similarly, procurement is global, not just home grown. Your raw material now comes from all over the world—iron ore from Brazil, natural gas from Kazakhstan. In other words, if your whole supply chain is global, you'd better be global, too.

Yet another characteristic of the GIE is that these multinationals tend to be "full-line generalists", as opposed to specialists. We may recall that Japanese and Korean companies entered Western markets as niche players, typically at the low end of the market. The Toyota Corolla, the Datsun 210, the Honda Civic, not to mention the early transistor radios from Sony—all were examples of this strategy. As we know, the real threat (in the auto sector particularly) came when the Japanese began their journey up market by keeping prices low but steadily improving quality. Once entrenched in Western markets, they completed the assault by offering a full line of vehicles, including luxury models like Lexus and Infiniti. We certainly can't say that the strategy was ineffective; after all, look what happened to the American auto and consumer electronics industries. But we can say that the strategy of the Chindian firms—to spring fully armed, so to speak, into the global marketplace, to compete at both ends of the market—will be that much more effective, raising the bar of worldwide competition.

We've looked at Lenovo and Mittal Steel. Now let's briefly introduce a few more of the new players—two from India and two from China.

Tata Tea

Tata Tea, part of India's venerable Tata Group, got its start in 1983 when the now Vice Chairman R. K. Krishna Kumar bought up Indian tea plantations owned by James Finlay, one of the United Kingdom's pioneer tea brokers. Practically as soon as the deal was done, tea-leaf prices crashed, from which Kumar learned a valuable lesson: he needed to move Tata Tea from a commodities business into a branded business. As S. Dinkar tells the story in *Forbes*, six Tata employees in a small room on a tea plantation in Kerala packed the country's first polylaminate tea bags. "The tag line read, 'Blended by nature, packed by Tatas,' and the brand, Kanan Devan, was an instant hit."[10]

That strategy pushed Tata Tea to the forefront of the domestic market. The global play began in 2000 with the audacious acquisition of Britain's Tetley Tea for $425 million. Tetley was the No. 2 brand in the world, after Unilever-owned Lipton, and it was three times bigger than Tata. The move gave Tata not only global presence, but also a two-brand strategy, Tetley at the higher end of the market and Kanan Devan at the lower end. It also gave Tata a strong position from which to compete against global leader Unilever (or, in India, Hindustan Lever), which owns not only Lipton but also a number of smaller niche brands as well. As the *South China Morning Post* reported, the marriage of Tetley's skills in marketing tea bags with Tata Tea's plantation muscle "will enable the Indian brand to storm the North American and European markets for quality and value-added teas, giving Unilever a tough fight for the No. 1 slot in the industry."[11]

Moreover, with the purchase of Tetley, Kumar was just getting started. The $1.4 billion Tata Tea had spent on its quick evolution into a "full-line generalist" included the acquisition of Eight O'Clock coffee (the third-biggest coffee brand in the U.S.) and a 30-percent stake in U.S. flavored water maker Glaceau. Kumar is also working on a joint venture to make and market green tea in China, and a processing business in Uganda to push Eight O'Clock coffee into Europe. "By the end of the decade," Kumar told *Forbes*, "we expect Tata Tea to become one of the largest and most admired beverage players in the world. We want to be a $3 billion company in ten years, and much of it will come from the U.S."

Still, it was Tata Tea's acquisition of Tetley, at that time the largest cross-border deal for any Indian company, which underscored the emergence of Chindian multinationals. After beating out Sara Lee for the deal, Tata chairman, Ratan Tata called an Indian firm buying an overseas company and its global brand a "momentous occasion." Commentators noted that until Tata Tea's move, Indian companies had been the targets. Coca-Cola had purchased Parle Foods for example, and the popular cola drink Thums Up, wounding the nation's pride in *swadeshi*, or self-reliance. Thus Tata Tea's buy-out of the Tetley brand was both smart business and sweet revenge. "To be able to leverage an international brand," as the chief economist at the Confederation of Indian Industry told the *Morning Post*, "that is very important."

Infosys

Given the nature of the business, perhaps all information technology companies are born with a global mindset. Surely this is the case of those in India, as the story of Infosys illustrates. The company's founding is part of Indian industry lore: how in 1981 Narayana Murthy convinced six fellow software engineers to start their own company—with $250 in capital, most of it borrowed from their wives. Business conditions in India in those pre-reform days forced Murthy to seek international clients from day one; after all, it took nine months for the company to get its first telephone line, and three years to get its hands on new computers.

So Infosys' first customers were multinationals like Reebok and Nordstrom, for whom it produced customizable, inexpensive software. A decade later, it was depending on GE for more than 20 percent of its business, but all that business went away when Infosys refused to let the U.S. giant squeeze it into accepting a lower fee schedule. From that experience, Murthy learned never to let one client or product drive more than 10 percent of the business, and he pushed the company to expand its global clientele with customers like Xerox, Levi Strauss and Nynex.

By the late 1990s, as its international business continued to grow, Infosys had established offices in Canada and Japan; in 1999 it became the first Indian company to list its shares on Nasdaq. With the concurrent boom in tech stocks, the company's market cap quickly soared to $17 billion. Today the company operates in 15 countries, offering software development and engineering through its 17 tech centers in Asia and North America; in 2004 it launched Infosys Consulting in North America in order to expand its U.S. business. Its "full line" of IT products includes data management, systems integration, project management, support, maintenance services, and business process outsourcing.

The company continues to grow at a phenomenal pace, with an ever-increasing emphasis on training and retaining a global workforce. Since 1999 it has been running a structured global internship program, called InStep, which helps build the brand worldwide and, at the same time, gives the company a leg up in global recruiting. For the 2006 year, InStep brought 125 interns from top academic institutions around the world to its Bangalore campus, where they were put to work on actual technical and business projects, ranging from application development to business consulting.[12]

At the same time, Infosys' international recruitment efforts continue in full swing. In 2005, for example, the company's efforts on U.S. and U.K. college campuses resulted in the sign-up of 126 American students and 25 more in Britain—kids who would train alongside Indian hires at the software engineering boot-camp at the Infosys facility in Mysore. To make the point that Infosys is "truly global," HR director Mohan Das Pai asks a series of rhetorical questions: "Do we get the bulk of our revenues from the international market; do we have a footprint in various countries across the world; does our board reflect a transnational character, and does the workforce also mirror this?" Pai doesn't mind that the rank and file remain, percentage-wise, largely Indian. After all, India is full of tech talent, "but," he says, "there are areas where we need to cherry-pick global talent"—which explains the fact that the company's international personnel represent no fewer than 59 nations.[13]

Infosys is not alone, by the way. Other Indian IT firms, notably TCS (Tata Consultancy Services) and Wipro, are also speedily transforming themselves from successful export players into full-fledged GIEs.

Haier

The state-owned Qingdao Refrigerator Plant was so abysmally unproductive that when Zhang Ruimin took the reins in 1984 his first act as CEO was to smash 76 shoddily-made refrigerators with a hammer. While he was overhauling the company's procedures, practices, standards, and culture, he went ahead and gave it a new name, too: Haier. Twenty years later, the former "refrigerator plant" is China's biggest appliance maker, producing not only a full array of white goods but also consumer electronics like TVs, mobile phones, and computers. Haier is also now a world-recognized brand, with sales outlets in more than 160 countries.

Like Lenovo, Haier's strategy was to dominate domestically, then expand globally. As Jonathan Story reports, once the company moved to profitability in 1991,

Zhang began acquiring other failing but well-equipped state enterprises. "In nearly 20 takeovers, he used the same tactics: change corporate culture, . . . raise manufacturing products and processes to international standards, and cultivate alliances with foreign companies to license and develop state-of-the-art technologies."[14] But acquisition was only part of the domestic game-plan. Global brands like GE, Electrolux, and Whirlpool were trying to gobble up market share in China, and Haier had to beat them with brains rather than brawn. It applied local knowledge and designed products specifically tailored to Chinese consumers. It redesigned its washing machines to adapt to the use to which rural customers were already putting them—i.e., washing vegetables like sweet potatoes. It designed another washer—tiny and economical—for customers who live in hot, humid cities like Shanghai and Shenzhen and like to change clothes frequently. Haier also captured domestic market share from the big players by creating a distribution and service network that covered not only the urban east coast but also the small-town and rural markets.[15]

Having cemented its position at home, Haier began to go global in the early 1990s. Its expansion illustrates some of the advantages we've been talking about. In the first place, rather than being confined to Western markets, its first ventures were into other emerging economies like Indonesia, the Philippines, Malaysia and Yugoslavia. Moreover, when it began its assault on the West—Germany first, then the United States— in the late 1990s, it had already evolved beyond the export model. Its U.S. strategy included setting up a design center in Boston, marketing operations in New York, and a manufacturing facility in South Carolina— while at the same time establishing partnerships with leading retailers like Best Buy, Home Depot, and Wal-Mart. Zhang, who still heads the company, plans to continue the global expansion. He told the *Wall Street Journal* that the number of his overseas factories should grow from 13 to 20 by 2010, as he adds manufacturing capacity in the Middle East and South Asia. He also plans a second factory in South Carolina, but thore the goal is not so much greater capacity; what Zhang wants in America, he says, is "higher-design level" and the opportunity to produce at the high end of the market.[16]

Speaking of branding, today not only can you find Haier refrigerators displayed right alongside Amana and Whirlpool on the aisles of the world's major retailers, but thanks to a recent sponsorship deal, there's now an Australian pro basketball team known as the Melbourne Haier Tigers. No wonder that as early as 1999 the *Financial Times* had already tapped Zhang for its list of the 30 most respected "global entrepreneurs."

Huawei Technologies

Another Chinese company on the fast track to GIE status is Huawei Technologies, founded in 1988 and now China's largest manufacturer of telecommunications equipment. Having grown by serving domestic customers like China Telecom and China Unicom, Huawei has been steadily expanding overseas operations since 1996. The company reached a milestone in 2005 when it's international sales—$4.8 billion worth—accounted for more than half of its total revenue ($8.2 billion).

It reached a more significant milestone in 2006 when, after posting 50 percent quarter-over-quarter growth, it passed Lucent Technologies to become the world's No. 3 supplier of the networking gear that providers use to deliver bundled services. In fact, some analysts see the fast rise of Huawei as the reason for the impending merger of Lucent and No. 2 Alcatel. (Cisco Systems, of course, remains the global leader.) According to a widely cited report released in July 2006 by telecom market research firm Heavy Reading, the current spate of mega-mergers among the world's biggest telecom companies "is being triggered in large part by the emergence of China's Huawei Technologies as a major force in the global telecom equipment industry." Scott Clavenna, the report's author, writes that "The most game-changing factor in the telecom supply market in the past five years has arguably been the expansion of Huawei outside of China." The emerging giant from China, Clavenna continues, is forcing all the industry's big players—Alcatel, Lucent, Ericsson, Nokia and Siemens—"to merge and realign to better compete." Underscoring his point, Clavenna asserts that "Huawei can no longer be dismissed as a low-price, low-quality imitator in the telecom market."[17]

What has been Huawei's strategy? First, it has developed a full product line, including core voice and data switching platforms, optical networking systems, wireless products, corporate networking equipment, and network management and messaging software. Second, it has moved up the technology chain by means of joint ventures with tech leaders like 3Com and Siemens, as well as manufacturers in Russia and Japan. Third, and perhaps most important, the company allocates a minimum of 10 percent of sales revenues to R&D and, in addition to those at home, it has established research facilities in India, Russia, Sweden, and the United States. In particular, the company has made Ethernet-standard products a research priority. As more and more carriers offer their subscribers the convenience of "triple-play" services—bundled voice, video, and broadband—this Ethernet bet is likely to produce jackpot-sized earnings for Huawei.[18]

With these stories in mind, as well as those of Lenovo and Mittal Steel, let's recapitulate the handful of strategic advantages the rising Chindian multinationals will exploit as they make their global presence felt.

Global Mindset

It's a critical advantage that these fast-growing companies already have a global mindset. Remember that the big companies in Japan and Korea were the so-called "national champions," blessed by government, but burdened with the national agenda to rebuild their post-war economies. In fact, the same phenomenon prevailed in post-war Europe too, where old family companies like Fiat, Olivetti, Philips, Krupp and Thyssen were encouraged by their respective governments to expand and diversify domestically as a way to revivify their moribund economies. In the United States a different scenario was playing out to similar effect. After the war, this nation had such a large and growing domestic market that American companies either didn't have the capacity, or see the need, to go worldwide. Somewhat surprisingly, that parochial attitude still prevails today, as the global share of revenues of major U.S. corporations remains relatively small. Jake Jacobson, at 3M, was among the first to recognize this potential Achilles heel, which is why he mandated that at least 30 percent of revenue had to be generated by international business. (It's my belief that our telephone companies have still not gotten the message, and as the wireless industry goes global, I predict that no U.S. company will survive—just as we saw in the television industry.)

By contrast, the Chinese and Indian companies fully understand that domestic markets were for yesterday and global markets are for tomorrow. No government policy will be discouraging these companies from doing business worldwide. Even in China, where many businesses are still state-owned, global aspirations are endorsed and encouraged. The grand economic dreams of China and India will not be realized by producing technologically inferior products for domestic consumption. They will be realized by dominating their own markets, yes, but also by going head-to-head, and brand-to-brand, against the world's best and biggest.

Human Capital

America's great advantage lay in its seemingly inexhaustible natural resources. China and India possess inexhaustible human resources, and it's worth noting that this resource is renewable and endlessly versatile. Of course, the two nations have always had plenty of people, but the difference today is that their brightest minds now have plenty of reason to stay home. The scientific/engineering brain-drain from East to West is now being reversed, a trend likely to have significant consequences. A couple of decades ago, Chindian engineering students came to America to get their advanced degrees and, often, to pursue their careers. Now those high achievers are headed back home. Among them is Zhang Xiaolin, who, after 20 years in the United States, has returned to China to head up drug-maker AstraZeneca's Shanghai lab, where he expects "to do real innovative research." James Ward-Lilley, president of AstraZeneca China, says, "In 20 years, where do you see new ideas coming from? A significant chunk will be from China." Another example, among the myriad that might be cited, is John Deng, who got his Ph.D. from the University of California and worked for IBM before returning to China to launch Vimicro, a hugely successful designer of chips for PC cameras.[19]

Natural Resources

Both the Chindian nations are also blessed with vast stores of natural resources and, more importantly, the wherewithal to buy more—which they will certainly need. In fact, how the two nations position themselves for access to global resources is such an important question that it's the subject of the following chapter.

Productivity Through Processes

Chindian corporations will enhance productivity not through people but through processes. Productivity-improvement has evolved through three stages: first, getting more work out of more people; second, getting more work out of fewer people through automation; and third (today's model), getting the most out of people and their machines through the best processes. The push to improve processes, associated with the concept of "total quality management" (TQM), is generally assumed to have come from Japan. Actually, the United States exported it to Japan, largely through the work of Edwards Deming, but Japan certainly embraced it, and the concept has achieved its apotheosis in Toyota's "lean operations"— which set the current standard in "best practices." As in so many areas, Chindian companies are benefiting from work already done by the rest of the world. As Zhang is doing at Haier, Chindian companies are putting world-class processes in place without having to work their way through the historic productivity cycle. This advantage will help them remain low-cost producers even as employee wages rise. The best processes guarantee quality and productivity through high efficiency rather than through increased costs.

Global Standards

At the same time, Indian and Chinese MNEs will not only embrace, but increasingly set global standards. Here their respective domestic markets will provide them a huge short-run advantage, because as standards rise to global benchmarks, lower prices will oust competition. In the long run, setting global standards will reverse the royalty flow from East to West and cement the newcomers' position as global players. Take the mobile phone industry. Qualcomm's CDMA standard has been dominant in China, the world's largest cellphone market. For the time being, China has a license and pays Qualcomm royalties. Soon, and with the arrival of new technology, China plans to earn, versus pay royalties.

In August 2006 SK Telecom, South Korea's largest cellphone operator, announced that it was buying a 6.7 percent stake in China Unicom as part of a deal to help the mainland develop its own standard for wireless networks. Up for grabs is the global standard for the third-generation technology known as TD-SCDMA, which promises faster downloads of movies and music onto users' cellphones. Of course, Nokia and Qualcomm are also at work on the technology, which will likely push aside the wideband-CDMA developed by Nokia as well as Qualcomm's CDMA2000. According to China Netcom Group, Beijing may issue its first license for the TD-SCDMA standard by mid-2007.[20]

But that's not all. Yet another battle is brewing to see who will provide the next communications techno-miracle—television service over the cellphone. China has already announced (as of October 2006) that it will offer its own standard for "mobile TV." Chinese regulators did not say that their domestic standard would be the only one allowed in China, but, as the *Wall Street Journal* reports, "the existence of a Chinese standard could ratchet up competition between companies in the scramble to develop a dominant global standard for mobile TV." Nokia and Samsung, for example, are already heavily invested in the technology. The planned Chinese standard, with the working name GY/T220.1-2006, would fulfill China's vow by, in the *Journal's* words, "reducing the amount of money [local telecoms] have to pay in royalty and intellectual-property fees to foreign companies."[21]

High-Priority on R&D

Setting global standards requires deep commitment to research and development, and China and India are making that commitment. According to the Paris-based Organization for Economic Cooperation and Development, China is projected to spend just more than $136 billion on R&D in 2006, moving it ahead of Japan's $130 billion and into second place worldwide, behind only the United States. In reporting this news, the press noted that the Chinese companies and their government are spending heavily on trying to create new technologies and reducing reliance on foreign know-how, which Communist leaders see as a strategic weakness.

At virtually the same time, Business Week announced, "It's the year of innovation in China." According to the article, President Hu Jintao and his government are exhorting China's companies to focus on the lab, not just the factory—and offering financial incentives to make sure the message gets across. In the late '90s, China spent less than 1 percent of its gross domestic product on research and development. That figure is already up to 1.5 percent, but Hu aims to raise it to 2.5 percent by 2020—meaning outlays of $115 billion a year. China's patent applications are also surging—up to 130,000 in 2004 (the most recent year for which figures are available from the World Intellectual Property Organization). That pushes China to No. 5 globally, but perhaps more dramatically, the number of 2004 applications was six times higher than in 1995.[22]

Because India's economic reforms didn't get underway until 1991, India has lagged behind China in emphasizing R&D. As late as 2000, Gurcharan Das was still lamenting that "It is true that when it comes to product development and innovation, Indian companies have clearly failed." India's attitude toward product development and competition, said Das, was epitomized in Nehru's question: "Why do we need nineteen brands of toothpaste?"[23]

But a look at India's pharmaceutical industry (widely considered the nation's next major growth sector, after IT) shows how quickly things are changing. As the industry evolves from reverse engineering and generics to new drug discovery and development, investment in R&D is skyrocketing. In 2005, India's pharma companies plowed about 3 percent of revenues back into R&D, but that figure is expected to triple by 2010. The additional investment is projected to push growth in the sector, already a healthy 9 percent, up to 14 percent before the end of the decade. In the 2005-2006 fiscal year, the R&D expenditure of India's 50 major pharma companies totaled $500 million, up 26 percent from the year before.[24]

Moreover, India's own commitment to R&D will be strengthened as the nation becomes a major hub for R&D worldwide. As the *Economic Times* (India) reports, India's "rich talent base" is attracting 25 percent of "fresh global R&D investment." A few of the big multinationals shifting research work to India are SAP, whose SAP Labs India is its largest development facility outside Germany; GE, whose facility in Bangalore is its second-largest; and Philips, whose campus in India is its largest outside Eindhoven. Other global powerhouses lining up major R&D investments in India include Intel at $1 billion, IBM at $6 billion, Cisco at $1.1 billion, and Microsoft at $1.7 billion. Given that thousands of Indian scientists and engineers will be working in these foreign-owned labs, the spill-over into India's domestic R&D will be incalculable.[25]

Global Brands

Japan and Korea learned this lesson well: nothing is more important than a globally recognized, globally admired brand. Thus we have Toyota, Honda, Sony, Samsung, Hyundai, and many more. The only difference is that China and India will create world-class brands much more quickly than their predecessors. American consumers already recognize Lenovo computers and Haier appliances, just as all global industrial companies now feel the heat generated by Mittal Steel's furnaces.

China and India are beginning to invest heavily in branding, whether it's business to business or in the consumer market. Tata Tea demonstrated the quick way: purchase an international brand (Tetley) and ride it to global renown. Another Indian company Amul, illustrates the incremental method. Starting as an agricultural cooperative producing dairy products, Amul has become the best-known dairy brand in India—and as much a household word among Indians abroad as Land o' Lakes or Kraft. Now the brand's global push is underway. From the "domestic-continental" market (Pakistan, Bangladesh, Sri Lanka), the company moved into China and Hong Kong in 2005. In 2006, it announced plans to expand into Japan, the Philippines, and Africa. From 2004 to 2005, export revenues rose 15 percent.[26]

Economies of Scale

Here is another way in which India's and China's huge domestic markets confer a strategic advantage. Through a combination of scaling up the domestic markets and globalizing through acquisitions, Chindian companies have the potential to grow prodigiously. China Mobile, for example, with close to 150 million subscribers, has surpassed U.K. wireless giant Vodaphone to become the world's largest wireless carrier. Looking to expand through acquisition, it made its first move in June 2006 when it bought a 20 percent stake in Phoenix Satellite Television Holdings from STAR Group for $165 million. More acquisitions are planned.

Mittal Steel, as we've noted, illustrates how Indian companies have historically tended to grow through acquisition first, then focus on the domestic market. Having become the No. 1 steelmaker worldwide, Mittal is now building India's largest steel plant (a 12-million-ton producer) in Orissa, due to come on line by 2010. On the other hand, Mukesh Ambani's plan to open 4,000 Reliance Fresh retail grocery stores across India within three years is evidence that the standard model—domestic first, then global—is now operative in India. In either case, the explosive growth of Chindian companies will demonstrate the full power of economies of scale.

Bankers in Their Pockets

The numbers say it all: Foreign direct investment in China during 2005 was a staggering $72 billion dollars. In India, the 2005 figure stood at $6.5 billion, much smaller than China's, but growing at a much faster rate. In fact, India's total for April-September 2006 was $4.4 billion, a 100 percent jump from the same period a year earlier.

And no wonder. With their GDP growth rates at 8 and 9 percent, who wouldn't want to buy in? China and India are attracting the world's investment capital at an unprecedented rate; indeed, the resulting ripple effect may be their biggest advantage. The FDI inflow produces human resources in the form of talent and expertise. And the financial capital accumulating from FDI and foreign reserves gives the two nations leverage when bartering for the natural resources they will increasingly be consuming. So it's a double whammy: financial resources enhance that access to both human and natural resources.

In Conclusion

To sum it up, our experience with Japan and Korea has certainly not prepared us for Chindia's rising tide. The new Chindian multinationals will not be export-driven niche players. They will be finance-driven, acquisition-minded, full-line generalists. They will be full-fledged members of the global economy—equal partners in the R&D that will drive innovation and create whole new industries, while also being strong competitors in the global consumer marketplace.

In either case, these "multinationals on the move" will provide a powerful new thrust to the world's economy, propelling it forward into the 21st century.

Notes

1. Crowell, Todd, "Ever Heard of Lenovo, Haier, and CNOOC? You Will," *Christian Science Monitor*, Jun 30, 2005, p. 13.

2. Spencer, Jane, "Boss Talk," *Wall Street Journal*, Nov 21, 2006, p. B1.

3. Spencer, Jane, "Lenovo Net Falls 16 Percent," *Wall Street Journal*, Nov 10, 2006, p. B2.

4. Buckley, Christine, "Steel Companies Need Global Base," *The Times* (London), Oct 6, 2006, p. 66.

5. "Mittal Breaks New Ground," *Post-Tribune* (Gary, Ind.), Jul 14, 2006, p. E1.

6. Leahy, Joe and Sundeep Tucker, "On the March," *Financial Times*, Oct 4, 2006, p. 15.

7. Yergin, Daniel and Joseph Stanislaw, *The Commanding Heights: The Battle for the World Economy* (New York: Simon & Schuster/Touchstone, 2002), pp. 144-145.

8. Wilson, Dominic and Roopa Purushothaman, "Dreaming with BRICs: The Path to 2050," Goldman Sachs Global Economics Paper No. 99, Oct 1, 2003.

9. "Mapping the Global Future," Report of the National Intelligence Council's 2020 Project, Dec 2004.

10. Dinkar, S., "Drinking Up," *Forbes*, Oct 30, 2006.

11. Penna, Anil "Tata Tea's Overseas Acquisition May Start a Trend," *South China Morning Post*, Mar 7, 2000, p. 16.

12. "Brand Building Through Interns," *The Hindu*, Sep 19, 2006, p. 1.

13. Babu, Venkatesha, "The Best Companies to Work for in India," *Business Today*, Nov 5, 2006.

14. Story, Jonathan, *China: The Race to Market* (London: Pearson Education, 2003), pp. 187-188.

15. Khanna, Tarun and Krishna G. Palepu, "Emerging Giants: Building World-Class Companies in Developing Countries, *Harvard Business Review*, October 2006 (Online Version).

16. Meyer, Jeff, "China's Haier Group Plans Overseas Expansion," *Wall Street Journal*, May 15, 2006, p. A.2.

17. "Fear of China's Huawei Is Driving Mergers in the Telecom Sector," *PR Newswire*, Jul 20, 2006.

18. Perez, Bien, "Huawei Overtakes Lucent," *South China Morning Post*, Sep 12, 2006, p. 9.

19. Einhorn, Bruce, "A Dragon in R&D," *Business Week Online*, Oct 27, 2006, p. 18.

20. Cho, Young-Sam and Janet Ong, "Mainland to Get Assist with 3G Business Asia," *International Herald Tribune*, Aug 30, 2006, p. 16.

21. Fowler, Geoffrey A. and Jane Spencer, "China Will Set a Standard of Its Own for Mobile TV," *Wall Street Journal* (Asia), Oct 26, 2006, p. 31.

22. Einhorn, Bruce "A Dragon in R&D," *Business Week Online*, Oct 27, 2006.

23. Das, Gurcharan, *India Unbound: From Independence to the Global Information Age* (New Delhi: Pengium Books India, revised ed., 2002), pp. 152-153.

24. "Domestic Pharma R&D Spending to go to 8-9% by 2010," *Hindustan Times*, Dec 5, 2006.

25. "R&D Work Done in India to Touch $27.5 Billion by 2010," *Economic Times*, Nov 2, 2006.

26. "Amul on a Global Trip," *India Business Insight*, July 11, 2006.

2

The Quest for Global Resources

In November 2006, history was made when leaders from 48 African nations came to Beijing for a summit meeting, a meeting unprecedented in size and scope. Its purpose was to forge economic and political links that, in the words of the *Wall Street Journal*, had the potential "to eclipse Africa's historical reliance on Western-led development institutions and former colonial powers."

On the ground, of course, the meeting was driven by China's need for the natural resources that Africa has in abundance, and by Africa's equally dire need for the massive infrastructure improvement and technical expertise that China can supply. As Chinese President Hu Jintao said at the conference, "In this new era, China and Africa share increasing common interests and have a growing mutual need."

The $1.9 billion worth of deals signed during the summit are a boon to Chinese engineering and construction firms: firms that will build a rural telephone system in Ghana, an aluminum factory in Egypt and a highway in Nigeria, among other things. What's more, a much bigger deal—$8.3 billion worth—was signed shortly before the conference: the agreement with China Civil Engineering Construction Corp. to build an 815-mile railway between the Nigerian cities of Lagos and Kano, the most expensive international construction project ever undertaken by a Chinese business. These agreements also promise the kind of infrastructure development that may help Africa emerge from its economic miasma.

Perhaps more important in the long run, this kind of cooperation produces trade between the two entities. Trade, in this case, has already been increasing at 25 percent a year— soaring from $40 billion in 2005 to more than $50 billion in 2006. While China exports its cheap goods and constructions projects, it imports resources and raw material.

Significantly, in 2006 Angola supplanted Saudi Arabia as China's chief supplier of crude oil. Perhaps this explains why, at the Beijing summit, President Hu sweetened the pot by promising to double its aid to Africa, to cancel some of the debt owed to China by Africa's poorest nations, and to offer $5 billion in preferential funding over the next three years.[1]

Less than a month earlier than the Beijing summit, 200 business officials from India and Africa had met in New Delhi, where India announced a new $10 million aid package, along with a pledge for more development funds in the future. It was the latest in a series of loans to African nations over recent years, the sum total of which has risen to $1.37 billion.

Like China, India is bringing its strengths to the huge continent—information technology expertise, inexpensive pharmaceuticals, and low manufacturing costs—in exchange for access to Africa's vast natural resources. For example, India's state-run oil exploration company, Oil & Natural Gas Corp., is investing $6 billion in a power plant and railroads in Nigeria in return for stakes in that nation's rich oil fields.[2]

But Africa is far from the only target of interest. In late November 2006, Deepak Bhojwani, India's outgoing ambassador to Venezuela, declared the oil-rich South American nation to be "the key for us in terms of energy security." Reliance Industries already imports more than 10 million barrels of oil a year from Venezuela, and ONGC Videsh is helping the country certify heavy oil reserves in the Orinoco River belt, a belt that may contain up to 235 billion barrels of heavy crude. Add to the 81 billion barrels already accounted for, the total would make Venezuela the world's richest nation in crude oil reserves. Moreover, ONGC's block is in Junin, the sub-region thought to be the most richly endowed.[3]

Earlier in 2006, ONGC Videsh paid $1.4 billion for ExxonMobil's 30 percent stake in an oil field in Brazil's Campos Basin. Illustrating the growing prevalence of East-West alliances, the deal makes the Indian company partners with both Petrobas, the Brazilian state-owned company, and the Anglo-Dutch Shell, both of which hold 35 percent of the assets. The deal was a coup for India's new energy minister, Murli Deora, who has pledged to continue to strengthen India's energy security through a strategy of aggressive "energy diplomacy."[4]

Post-Colonial Model

Africa, Latin America, the Caribbean, Eastern Europe, Central and Northern Asia—wherever a wealth of natural resources is combined with a dearth of life's other necessities, China and India are racing in. It has to be that way, since the two nations are emerging as not only economic superpowers but also as giants of energy consumption. Just a few years ago a net exporter of oil, China was importing 3.4 million barrels a day by the end of 2005. India imports 70 percent of its crude oil requirements, and its domestic supply is projected to run out within 22 years. Although its stores of natural gas are more stable, it still has to import 19 million cubic meters of LNG every day. As supplies of resources and raw materials run thin, the quest to secure them can only intensify.

But as we saw in our discussion of Chinese and Indian multinationals in the previous chapter, the Chindian quest for natural resources will differ markedly from historical precedent. The traditional model for resource acquisition—whether gold and silver five centuries ago, or oil, iron ore, and minerals in the more recent history—was colonial/military. It was logic of brute force that went something like this: I own your resources because you are my colony, or because I have defeated you militarily. I will, therefore, haul your raw materials back to my country and process them in my own manufacturing plants. I may even turn around and sell finished goods back to you, since I am also in control of your markets. This was the essence of the Spanish conquest of South America as well as of British colonialism.

The new Chindian, postcolonial model could scarcely be more different. Its essence is not power politics but economic partnership, not exploitation but cooperation. Where China and India seek resource assets, they will make economic investments, usually in much-needed infrastructure improvement. Unlike the old "extract-and-run" scenario, the investment model will mean the creation or upgrading of on-site facilities—steel mills, oil refineries—in the owner country, to the benefit of both partners. Perhaps most important of all, rather than seeking to control local markets, China and India will open up their own, allowing their new trade partners access to the world's two largest consumer markets.

The new model is illustrated—albeit on a minor key—by the increasingly warm relations between India and oil and gas-rich Trinidad and Tobago. With one Indian steel plant (Mittal) already in operation there and another (a $1.2 billion investment by the Essar Group) underway, India's then Vice President, Bhairon Singh Shekhawat, visited the Caribbean nation in November 2006 to sign a "bilateral investment promotion and protection agreement." The agreement, as the former Vice President noted in his public address to Trinidad and Tobago's Prime Minister, "will give further encouragement and confidence to the investors from both the countries for investment and joint ventures." As a token of friendship and cooperation, Shekhawat also mentioned the 30 ITEC scholarships being offered to Trinidad and Tobago nationals for IT study in India.[5] Not surprisingly, a few weeks later, ONGC-Mittal Energy Ltd. (or OMEL, the joint venture between the state-owned oil exploration company and Mittal Steel) announced that it had bid for offshore blocks in Trinidad and Tobago.

The old colonial/military model has given way to the investment model for a number of reasons, the most obvious of which is that the old model simply makes no sense any longer. Neither China nor India, both of which are enormous benefactors of the economic pragmatism we described in the previous chapter, is in a position to risk the world's opprobrium by taking a militarist approach to energy and resource security. More specifically, neither can risk the economic sanctions which would surely be imposed by the European Union and the United States.

Today, perhaps more than at any time in history, there is a better way. China and India don't need territory, nor the administrative headache of a colonial empire, nor the enormous costs of suppressing guerilla warfare and insurgency in occupied lands. What they need is oil, iron ore, natural gas—the lifeblood of their surging economies. These things can be had in ways that enhance, rather than endanger, the world's prosperity. Take Turkmenistan, for example, which sits on the world's fifth-largest reserves of natural gas, but lacks the extraction technology to exploit this resource. The recent death in December 2006 of its autocratic ruler, Saparmurat Niyazov, presents an interesting opportunity. Should Chinese tanks roll westward, and flatten Turkmenistan in the process? That won't happen. But if acting president Gurbanguly Berdymukhammedov makes good on his promise to liberalize the nation's closed economy, we can bet that CNOOC—and India's ONGC Videsh, too—will be there in a heartbeat, offering the kind of mutually beneficial partnership that is proving so successful elsewhere around the globe.

Perhaps because both nations were victimized by colonization and occupation, China and India appear to have little appetite for military adventurism. India has its Hinduism, along with its still-pervasive Gandhian legacy, to underpin its longstanding commitment to world peace. On the mainland, PRC has taken on a new meaning: "peaceful rise of China." In his November 2006 address to the Asia-Pacific Economic Cooperation (APEC) summit for example, President Hu Jintao promised more aid to developing nations "with no strings attached" as a way to close the gap between the rich and poor, and thus promote world peace.

Hu emphasized that China now calls for building a harmonious world of "enduring peace and common prosperity," and he noted that harmony was a "defining value of Chinese civilization." Business leaders at the summit understood Hu's message to be that "the peaceful rise of China will bring benefits to the region and the world."[6] More pragmatically, both nations are well aware that peace and stability provide an environment where business can prosper.

Still, the fundamental equation remains. Natural resources are finite, the need for those resources increases more and more rapidly, and energy security is at the top of every nation's agenda. Assuming that pragmatism rather than combat remains the guiding principle, what are the implications, and what might be the consequences of the Chindian quest for global resources?

Strange Bedfellows

First, watch for the development of more, and deeper, government-to-government relationships, putting in place the kinds of "memoranda of understanding" that will push forward the industrial/energy agenda. We've already seen this on the grand scale (the Africa-China summit), and on the small scale (India's Vice President visiting the Prime Minister of Trinidad and Tobago), and it's likely that we'll see more of this with increasing frequency. The paramount boon of economic well-being and stability will make friends out of former adversaries, as China and India seek profitable relations not only with developing but also with developed economies. After all, "resources" include things like brain power and expertise too, and while Chindia seeks oil from Venezuela, it will also need talent and know-how from the West.

Indian Prime Minister Manmohan Singh, speaking at the end of his first year in power, articulated this point: "Our relations with major powers, especially the U.S. and more recently China, have increasingly been shaped by economic factors. Who could have imagined that China would emerge as our second largest trade partner? In the case of the U.S., an acceleration of people-to-people contact and the consequent business-to-business interaction has forged closer state-to-state relations. Shared values and growing economic links have enabled a closer strategic engagement."[7]

The burgeoning Chindian multinationals we looked at in the preceding chapter—Mittal Steel, Infosys, Lenovo, Haier, et al.—could not have succeeded in an atmosphere of political animosity, and the governments of

China and India, as well as those of the nations they seek to partner with, have learned the importance of fostering warm economic relationships. It's the old "stomach and wallet" phenomenon: the government's ideology is less important than the basic needs of the people. Nobody ever said this better than Deng Xiaoping, as he was leading China into its great reform era: "It doesn't matter if the cat is black or white, as long as it catches mice." (Where leaders have still not grasped this truth—for instance, in the Middle East—ideologically-driven strife and turmoil continue to rule the day.)

The point would have been perfectly illustrated in the January 2005 announcement of the first-ever transnational energy link into India—a gas pipeline running from Myanmar to eastern India through Bangladesh. It was one of those deals that could have transformed old antagonisms into win-win partnerships. India would get much-needed natural gas, Myanmar—export revenue, and Bangladesh—transit fees. And since Bangladesh would also get to run pipe to Nepal and Bhutan, the deal would boost trade and investment throughout one of the poorest regions of South Asia. As the *Wall Street Journal* pointed out, "Persuading Bangladesh to allow the pipeline to run through its territory is a big victory for New Delhi in using diplomatic initiatives to business ends." India's oil minister at the time, Mani Shankar Aiyar, described the pipeline pact as "a triumph, as for the first time in 30 years Bangladesh has agreed to its territory being used for transport of a commodity."

What a boon for impoverished Bangladesh. Though the deal eventually fell through (the gas will now be piped to China instead), the spillover effect is that India's industrial houses are beginning to see Bangladesh as a possibility for investment. The Tata group is planning $2 billion worth, including a steel plant with a capacity of 2.5 million metric tons a year, a 1,000-megawatt gas-fired power plant, and a fertilizer unit with an annual capacity of one million tons.

But the biggest benefit in the long run may well be political. India has previously accused Bangladesh of allowing its territory to be used by separatist rebels active in India's northeast, and has also condemned Myanmar's military dictatorship after it crushed a 1988 pro-democracy uprising. Now these strained political relationships appear to be on the mend, and economic pragmatism is beating swords into ploughshares in South Asia.

If that's not remarkable enough, another project under discussion at the same time would bring Iranian gas to India through Pakistan. Could

India be making overtures not only to Iran but to traditional adversary Pakistan? Maybe so. As former Indian Foreign Minister K. Natwar Singh observed, such agreements have the "ability to qualitatively transform the relationships of the countries of the region . . . and set up a new paradigm in regional cooperation and friendship." The *Journal* puts it more succinctly: India's need for energy is "helping make friends out of politically difficult neighbors, both on the east and the west of the subcontinent."[8]

Of course, politics does sometimes still raise its ugly head; the falling through of the Myanmar-India gas pipeline in favor of the Chinese being one example, the love-hate triangle among India, Venezuela, and the United States being another. As we've noted, India looks to Venezuela as a key energy ally and, at the same time, President Bush and Prime Minister Singh have forged close ties between their two nations. The fly in the ointment would appear to be Hugo Chavez, whose animosity toward the United States seems almost pathological. After all, his democratically-elected government had to reestablish itself three years ago after the U.S.-backed Army officers staged a coup. In any case, Chavez believes that the Bush administration wants him assassinated since the United States depends on Venezuela for 15 percent of its daily oil consumption, and would doubtlessly prefer to work with a friendlier regime. Chavez broke off relations with Peru for negotiating a free trade agreement with the United States. Could he turn equally cool toward India?[9]

Brain Gain

Having noted that "resources" include non-tangible assets like brain-power and expertise, let's take a look at the urgency with which China and India are now beginning to develop their human capital.

With a manifest need to "smarten up" in order to compete with developed nations, China has pursued a two-pronged strategy: over the long haul, develop its own "intellectual infrastructure," but in the meantime to buy brain-power from the West as quickly as possible via so-called "technology transfer." As Oded Shenkar points out, even in the early days of Deng's reform, foreign investment was understood as the key to bringing technology to China, and "one of the first things that the reformist leadership did was enact a joint venture law that gave priority to technology-intensive investment and required the taking of a Chinese partner."

China's huge domestic market gave it a strong hand, and the nation played it well. Not only did it pitch one investor against another, China even persuaded investors to agree to multiparty technology exchanges. In the auto sector, for example, Guangzhou Automotive made agreements with both Honda and Toyota, enabling the Chinese partner "to learn 'best practices' from both competitors and be the only one in the three-player network to have access to all others." Of course, foreign companies willing to transfer the most cutting-edge technologies were the most passionately wooed—they were courted with expensive gifts like the best locations, preferential governance and equity terms, tax holidays and duty exemptions, and, perhaps most attractive of all, preferential access to the prized domestic market. As Shenkar notes, "These preferences have survived 25 years of reform, multiple rounds of WTO accession negotiations, and occasional pressure by China trade partners."

The ultimate step in the technology transfer strategy was to persuade foreign multinationals to establish R&D labs in China. In this too, China has succeeded spectacularly. Shenkar reports that a major factor in General Motors winning out over Ford in the hotly contested Shanghai investment was its willingness to establish a large R&D center and transfer up-to-date technology to that center. But that's a small part of a very big picture. Today, more than two hundred such centers have opened up in China, including such notables as Oracle, Siemens, Lucent, Nokia, Nortel, Agilent, IBM, and Hewlett Packard. That's why it's very difficult now to think of a sector—no matter how high tech, from consumer electronics to telecommunications—where China's domestic companies are not already competing successfully.[10]

The other part of the strategy—an upgrade of the educational infrastructure in order to tap China's own vast intellectual reservoir—provides a more daunting but equally necessary task. While Deng's reforms sought, in effect, to purchase Western brain-power and install it in his urban enterprise zones, they neglected China's rural areas. With the advent of reform, writes Ted Fishman, localities had to support their own social services, including school systems. Worse, in 1998, the National People's Congress cut the Ministry of Education in half, "leaving rural education in a free fall." In China's poorest provinces, the situation was dire. "In 35 poor rural areas surveyed for a recent World Bank project, four of ten children ages seven to fifteen had received no schooling whatsoever."[11] Writing in 2002, Jonathan Story agreed that that China's "human capital" was under-developed: while 22 percent of China's population was living on less than one dollar a day, compared with India's 47 percent, China's children were averaging 5.6 years of schooling, the same as in India. Story added that China ranked 119th in the world for per capita spending on education.[12]

Gradually though, this situation is improving. The number of university and advanced vocational students tripled in the four years from 2001 to 2005, surging to 17 million. Most are studying science and engineering, which is why China produced 325,000 engineers in 2005, five times more than did the United States. These impressive numbers reflect China's aggressive commitment to upgrading its higher education facilities, establishing alliances with Western institutions, and even courting foreign-trained faculty.

More important in the long run however, is China's growing resolve to educate its children—rural as well as urban. According to the "Guidelines for the 11th Five-Year Plan for National Economic and Social Development," released in 2006, China plans to increase education expenditures to 4 percent of GDP, up substantially from the 2.55 percent allocated in 1998. A major goal of the program is to promote and consolidate the nine-year compulsory education, "especially in the vast countryside." The increase will add more than $27 billion to the education budget, money expected to benefit some 160 million students in the rural areas, where nearly 80 percent of China's schoolchildren reside.[13]

In yet another effort to bolster its human resources, China is working hard to lure home the thousands of bright young Chinese who immigrated to the United States or to other Western universities to seek the best education—and often the best career opportunities. More than 64,000 students from the mainland were studying in the United States in 2002-2003, writes Shenkar, and the Chinese government has been accelerating its efforts to entice the cream of this crop to return, "offering 'overseas terms' and joint appointments to the most promising prospects." Increasing numbers are returning even without these incentives, thanks to the wealth of economic opportunities back home. These turtles bring with them not only academic knowledge, but also "application know-how and business-related expertise."[14]

So is the "knowledge gap" closing as China seeks to invest in its human capital? Maybe so. As a Beijing consular official told Thomas Friedman, "the hard reality for that [privileged American] kid is that fifteen years from now Wu is going to be his boss and Zhou is going to be the doctor in town. The competition is coming, and many of the kids are going to move into their twenties clueless about these rising forces."[15]

Like China, India has succeeded in luring foreign investment—and with it, brain-power and technological know-how—particularly in the knowledge industries. It has also succeeded in establishing and supporting a handful of world-class institutions of higher education, i.e., the Indian Institutes of Technology, and the Indian Institutes of Management. Also like China, it continues to lag in its efforts on behalf of primary public education, especially in rural provinces.

In *India Unbound*, Gurcharan Das emphasizes this problem repeatedly. In explaining why India has failed to complete its "transformation" since the reforms of 1991, he cites as "perhaps the most important reason" the fact that "it ignored the education of half its children, especially of girls." Elsewhere he writes, "The neglect of primary education remains our single biggest failure" and observes that "the ten most important Indians are the education ministers of the ten largest states; the next ten are the secretaries to these ministers." Das offers as some consolation that Indian literacy "has already risen by ten percentage points in the past six and a half years, from 52 to 62 percent," but adds that this improvement has been the result not of government action but rather "of grassroots pressures from below as social democracy has created upward mobility among the lower castes."[16]

In the half-dozen years since Das's book was published, India has continued to struggle with this seemingly intractable problem, and the most successful efforts remain grassroots, bottom-up rather than top-down. Writing for the *New York Times* in 2003, for example, Amy Waldman sees an "education revolution" underway in India—as hundreds of thousands of schoolchildren, in urban slums and rural villages, abandon the government's public schools in favor of private ones. In one four-mile stretch of road leading toward the capital of the northern Bihar State, Waldman counted 17 private schools, charging students from roughly a dollar a month to just over three (not counting the small outlay for uniforms).

These schools have been packed from the day they were established. The DAV School, outside the Bihar capital, had enrolled 600 students from 27 villages within 11 months after opening. Why? Waldman explains that the founders of these schools—teachers, landowners, entrepreneurs—"have capitalized on parental dismay over the quality of government schools." Even poor parents will pay up because they see private education, especially if instruction is in English, as their children's only hope for upward mobility. In big cities especially, as the number of private academies surges, flight from public schoo's is alarming. "It's more or less over" in cities, said economist Jean Dreze, who helped write a national assessment of education. "Within 10 to 15 years, government schools will be almost wiped out."[17]

It's not that India is not trying. In 2002 the government passed a law that made free and compulsory education a fundamental right for children up to age 14. But the law did not explain how to make the government schools better, which is a most complicated problem. Think of all the hand-wringing that goes on over the state of public education in America, and think of how little progress has been achieved.

If nothing else, the situation has had the attention of India's top leadership. For former President Abdul Kalam, improved education is one of the "ten keys" to realizing India's "Vision 2020." Prime Minister Singh, meanwhile, describes the education system as in such crisis that it threatens the country's growth. He pledges a "massive investment" that will increase education funding to 6 percent of GDP—an investment all the more pressing, he explains, "because we cannot continue to claim to be a rising 'knowledge power' if less than 8 percent of our college-age group is enrolled in the college and university system."

Again, it is a matter of exploiting resources. "India will soon have the world's largest amount of young people," says the Prime Minister. "We must invest in their capabilities so that they can become an asset for the nation."[18]

Fishing Upstream

As the Chindian industry continues to expand, look for a surge in the kind of merger/acquisition and joint venture activity that provides secure access to raw material. Leaving aside petroleum and other energy-related resources, the best example here is the steel industry, which depends primarily on iron ore. In fact, the need for a reliable supply of ore is one of the forces driving a global merger frenzy in the steel industry—in which Indian and Chinese firms are major players.

Today, China is the world's largest steel producer, with a 30 percent share of global production, and 19 percent growth in 2004. But it's also the world's largest consumer—thanks to the rising purchase of washing machines, refrigerators and cars, as well as the massive building projects targeted for the 2008 Olympics in Beijing. So China's steelmakers, like others around the globe, are looking to expand—especially vertically, in order to gain control of raw material facilities.

In late 2003, for example, a Minnesota mine that had been shuttered, was reopened under a new ownership agreement between Chinese steelmaker Laiwu Steel Group and Ohio-based Cleveland-Cliffs Co. The two companies bought EVTAC Mining Co., which had filed for Chapter 11 (American bankruptcy proceedings) and laid off 400 workers. The deal injected welcome new life into Minnesota's Iron Range, which over two decades had faced mine closures and a workforce reduced from 6,200 to 3,700. "Two years ago, it was all gloom and doom in the iron range," says John Rebrovich of the United Steelworkers Association. But with a world-wide shortage of raw material and a reopened mine, small towns in the region are "a little upbeat now."

In Australia, four Chinese steel mills partnered with BHP Billiton, one of the world's largest producers of iron ore, to provide 12 million metric tons of ore annually over the next 25 years for $9 billion. All four mills will get a guaranteed supply of ore during the contract period. Meanwhile, the state-owned mining company China Metallurgical Construction Corp. has agreed to a $650 million investment in a nickel mining project in Papua New Guinea. The deal stipulates that the Chinese company will build and operate the mine, will own 85 percent of the shares, and will garner the entire output of 33,000 metric tons annually of this key component of stainless steel.[19]

In one of China's biggest deals to date, Shanghai Baosteel Group, the nation's largest steelmaker, announced a joint venture with Brazil's Companhia Vale do Rio Doce (CVRD) to build a $1.4 billion steel mill capable of producing 4 million tons of steel slabs annually. The deal would boost Baosteel's global output by 20 percent, but more important, the Chinese company would have an alliance with the world's largest producer of iron ore. Note, too, that this deal illustrates the kind of partnership model we described above. China is not extracting ore; it is producing the steel in Brazil and then shipping it back to China and to other manufacturing plants around the globe.[20]

This is not to say that China does not import iron ore directly. It must, of course, and its steelmakers bring in more every year. In fact, in early 2007, CVRD announced a joint venture with Shougang, China's fifth-largest steel mill, to ship ore from Brazil to a new Shougang plant under construction in north China's Hebei province. Illustrating the pattern of rising global demand, Shougang said it plans to import 15 million tons of ore in 2007, up 20 percent from 2006. China also continues to import ore from North Korea, a practice which was not at all curtailed even when the Mainland was rebuking North Korea for conducting its nuclear test in late 2006. But in a more typical scenario, China's Tonghua Steel announced a long-term agreement to join North Korea in the development of the Musan iron mine, believed to be the biggest in Asia, with estimated reserves of 2.2 billion tons.

More generally, the Chinese government is encouraging consolidation of its domestic steel industry in order to enable its biggest companies to compete worldwide. The stated policy goal is for the top ten companies to control at least half of the Chinese market by 2010, at which point they would be in a position to expand globally through acquisition. Baosteel, in particular, will be a global player, according to a leading industry analyst, as it looks for world markets and secure access to raw material.[21]

India, too, is playing its part in the consolidation of the global steel industry. To take one notable example, Tata Steel's 2006 takeover of the Anglo-Dutch steel giant Corus created the world's fifth-largest steelmaker. It was also India's biggest-ever acquisition of a foreign company (not counting Mittal's acquisition of Arcelor, since Mittal is officially Rotterdam-based). But the interesting thing about this deal is that Corus allowed itself to be wooed by Tata because it sought access to Tata's iron ore resources, not the other way around. In fact, Tata's rival for Corus's hand was Brazil's CSN, another ore-rich company, but Tata was also able to offer access to its huge market.

Indeed, India's low production costs, rich ore reserves, and big market make it an attractive target for global steelmakers, and we may expect to see some acquisition of—rather than by—Indian companies. But India's family-owned firms tend to resist being bought out, just as they resist consolidation, so India's biggest steel companies—the privately-owned Tata and Essar, the state-owned SAIL, and others—will likely follow the pattern and expand globally through investment, merger, and acquisition.

In 2005, for example, India's Jindal Steel and Power agreed to pay Bolivia $2.3 billion to extract one of the world's largest untapped iron ore deposits. The agreement, which marked India's first expression of interest in investing in Bolivia, "highlights the extent to which the quest for natural resources is trumping other considerations," noted the *Financial Times*. Arvind Sharma, Delhi's honorary consul in Santa Cruz, puts his finger on the key allurement for such an investment: Bolivia, he says, "has great natural resources but it lacks the expertise."[22]

We've already mentioned the Essar Group's steel plant in Trinidad. In 2006, the company also bid for the Egyptian government's 83 percent stake in Suez Steel, a major producer of "billets", an important raw material in the steel re-rolling process. As it happens, Essar lost out to a local company, Misr National Steel, but clearly, the impetus for complete vertical integration in the industry continues.

We should quickly note that steel is not the only sector in which the quest for raw material is driving mergers and acquisitions. A frenzy of consolidation has also gripped the generic pharmaceuticals industry, in which India is a huge player. In a few instances (as we saw in the steel sector), India's low manufacturing and raw-material costs are attracting investment from foreign companies. In August 2006, for example, U.S.-based Mylan Laboratories announced that it would spend more than $700 million to acquire 71 percent of India's Matrix Laboratories, the world's second-largest maker of active pharmaceutical ingredients, as well as a manufacturer of finished drugs. The deal was finalized as of January 2007.

More impressive though, is the expansion boom among India's own generics giants. Dr. Reddy's Laboratories moved into Germany with the $572 million acquisition of generics manufacturer Betapharm Arzneimittel. That move was quickly overshadowed by the ongoing buying binge of Ranbaxy Laboratories, one of the world's ten largest generics producers. Since assuming the position of CEO and Managing Director at the beginning of 2006, Malvinder Singh (scion of the founding family) has acquired five businesses around the globe, including Belgium's generics maker Ethimed, divisions of GlaxoSmithKline in Italy and Spain and, most notably, Terapia SA, a $324 million deal that created the largest generics company in Romania.

The young CEO is not done yet. Early 2007 brought word that Ranbaxy would bid for the generics unit of Germany's Merck KGaA, a deal projected to be in the $5 billion to $7 billion range. According to the *Wall Street Journal*, such an acquisition would immediately catapult Ranbaxy into the position of No. 3 in the world in sales, behind only Israel's Teva Pharmaceuticals and Sandoz, the generics arm of Switzerland's Novartis. Though Ranbaxy eventually withdrew its bid because of the high associated costs (and the U.S. based Mylan announced its intention of acquiring Merck KGaA), Singh's expressed ambition is to move his company into the ranks of the top five generics makers worldwide.[23]

Meanwhile, Tata Chemicals, India's biggest fertilizer maker, became the world's third-largest maker of soda ash with its acquisition of UK-based Brunner Mond Group. While it was at it, Tata also bought a 33-percent stake in Morocco-based Indo Maroc in order to bolster its supply of phosphoric acid.

In one sector after another across the global economy, competition will continue to force mergers, acquisitions, investments, and consolidation as companies seek vertical integration, access to worldwide markets, and increasingly, a stable supply of raw material.

Rising Profits in Commodities

As the scramble for raw material continues, of course prices will rise, and so will the profits in commodities markets. Traditionally, profit has come downstream, with value added as materials are shaped into finished goods. But finite resources, and the competition will inevitably lead to upstream profit as well.

Let's again turn to the steel industry, where the demand for iron ore provides a dramatic example. Global need for steel, accelerated by booming industry in China and India, saw the price of iron ore begin to surge in 2004, when it rose 19 percent. In 2005 it soared an incredible 72 percent, and the following year another 19 percent—meaning the price of ore had more than doubled in three years. Shareholders in major producers like Brazil's CVRD were busily adding up their capital gains.

And how about this as a reflection of changing global realities: whereas in the past the major producers had negotiated contracts with Japanese and South Korean steelmakers first, with the rest of the global steel industry falling in line, for 2007 it was China's biggest steelmaker Baosteel, with whom the ore producers negotiated. Baosteel apparently flexed some muscle to hold costs down, but iron ore's price is not exactly falling. At the end of 2006, CVRD, the No. 1 ore producer, and Rio Tinto, No. 3 in the world, signed contracts with Baosteel for an increase of 9.5 percent for the year beginning April 1, 2007. The No. 2 ore producer BHP Billiton, and the other major steel manufacturers are expected to conform.[24]

Iron ore is not the only mineral commodity enjoying a price surge. In mine-rich Australia, Prime Minister John Howard called 2006 a "tigerish" year, thanks to the fact that net profits of the nation's mining companies jumped 74 percent to $11.8 billion—the highest level since records began to be kept 30 years earlier. Shareholders' returns rose on average from an already healthy 15.2 percent to a gaudy 24.1 percent. The outlook for 2007 appeared equally rosy. The Australian Bureau of Agricultural and Resource Economics (ABARE) predicted mineral export earnings for 2006-2007 would rise 31 percent to $69.9 billion, as prices for copper, nickel, and zinc continued to escalate. In fact, the CEO of the Minerals Council of Australia described the current environment as "a super-cycle for mineral commodities" that could last for several more years as supply sought to catch up with demand.[25]

Let's take a closer look at one of those roaring companies, Australian-Anglo BHP Billiton, the world's largest mining company. The fiscal year that ended June 30, 2006, was a good one, to say the least. Net profit stood at $10.2 billion, a 58 percent increase, and the company's third consecutive yearly record. As chief executive Charles Goodyear put it, "The world has rediscovered resources and how critical they are to our daily lives." The surge in iron ore prices in 2005 was more than matched by the rocket-launch of copper prices in 2006, up 100 percent since BHP presciently paid $7 billion for copper producer WMC Resources and expanded its output by 20 percent. Goodyear foresaw demand continuing to grow—and prices continuing to rise—along with the industrial boom in China and India. BHP's sales to China alone were $6.6 billion for the year, up 10 percent from the year before.[26]

What we are seeing, of course, is the other side of the "low-cost" phenomenon. While China and India exert deflationary pressures on the world's retail markets, they exert inflationary pressures on a broad range of commodities: copper, titanium, nickel, rubber, iron ore, steel, coal, oil, and even cardboard. Commodities are known to fluctuate, to cycle up and back down, but Chindia's insatiable appetite may keep demand ahead of supply for the foreseeable future.

Race to Secure

Now let's focus specifically on the energy sector and the natural resources—petroleum especially—most essential to India's and China's continued evolution into economic superpowers. We have already alluded to some of the initiatives the two nations have pursued on behalf of energy security, but more remains to be said—about their rivalry, their potential partnership, and the consequences, for the rest of the world, of energy consumption on such an unprecedented scale.

China has now surpassed Japan as the second-largest consumer of oil after the United States. The 3.4 million barrels a day China imported in 2005 constituted roughly 4.5 percent of global demand, but with Chinese energy use doubling every seven to 10 years, the Mainland will account for some 8 percent of world demand in 2015. As Thomas Friedman observes, "China's foreign policy today consists of two things: preventing Taiwan from becoming independent and searching for oil." If current trends hold, he continues, China will be importing 14 million barrels of oil a day by 2012. "For the world to accommodate that increase it would have to find another Saudi Arabia." Assuming there is not another Saudi Arabia to be found, where will China get what it needs?

The answer is, wherever oil is for sale. In September 2004, *China Daily*, in an article headlined "Cash-Rich, Commodity-Starved Mainland Shopping Spree," made the point that China's nearly $500 billion reserves in U.S. dollars (now closer to $1 trillion) would serve as a bank roll for the acquisition of natural resources. The article reported that Chinese state-owned firms had spent at least $5 billion on overseas oil and gas fields in the previous ten years, and cited a recent $550 million takeover of a South Korean oil refinery as evidence of China's new willingness to buy entire companies abroad.

In an earlier chapter we noted that in June 2005 one of China's biggest government-owned oil concerns, China National Offshore Oil Corporation (CNOOC), bid nearly $20 billion to buy American oil giant Unocal. That bid was withdrawn when the U.S. Congress criticized it as a threat to domestic energy security, but just a couple of months later the nation's biggest oil and gas producer, state-owned China National Petroleum Corporation (CNPC), purchased Canadian oil giant PetroKazakhstan for $4.2 billion. At the same time, representatives from CNPC and CNOOC met with Canadian Natural Resources Minister John McCallum to discuss taking stakes in Alberta's vast oil sands.[27]

Dropping from North America down to South America, we find Venezuela, the world's fifth-biggest oil exporter. Leftist president Hugo Chavez would love to do more business with China and less with the United States (which now takes about 60 percent of Venezuela's oil exports), and he visited Beijing in August 2006 to pursue that agenda. The immediate goal was to increase Venezuela's exports to China of oil and petroleum products from 150,000 barrels a year to 200,000, as well as to strengthen ties between CNPC and Venezuela's state-owned company Petroleos de Venezuela. One deal in the works would have Venezuela buying 12 Chinese-made oil drills and assembling another 12 at a new, jointly owned factory, which would increase Venezuela's output as well as its exports to China. "If China has its way," says Friedman, "it will stick a straw into Canada and Venezuela and suck out every drop of oil."[28]

Hyperbole aside, the fact is that so far, Venezuela represents only a drop in China's bucket of imported oil. Here's the most recent breakdown, according to *China Daily*. In 2006, China imported 136 million tons of crude oil, which was almost half of the amount it consumed (300 million tons). Of the imports, 50 percent came from the Middle East, 25 percent from Africa (with Angola as China's single biggest supplier), 15 percent from Southeast Asia, and 10 percent from Central Asia and Russia. Of these players, it appears that Central Asia and Russia are the most intent on upping their exports to China.

The first crude oil pipeline between Kazakhstan and China opened in July 2006, with a delivery capacity of 10 million tons per year. By the end of the year, however, plans were already underway to double that capacity to 20 million tons annually. The 962-kilometer pipeline runs from Karaganda in western Kazakhstan to the Xinjiang Region in northwest China, and is a joint venture between KazTransOil JSC and CNPC. Meanwhile, a 252-kilometer pipeline from eastern Kazakhstan to Xinjiang had just been completed at the end of 2006 and was scheduled to begin pumping in early 2007.[29]

At virtually the same time (November 2006) Russia's biggest oil supplier to China announced similarly ambitious plans. State-owned OJSC Rosneft said it would increase exports to China of crude oil and oil products by 65 percent in 2007, from 12 million tons to 20 million. The announcement came as the Russian company opened its first office in Beijing, from which it will oversee a growing number of projects in 22 locations across Southeast Asia. Rosneft and CNPC have been partners since the Chinese company bought a $500 million piece of Rosneft's $10 billion public offering in mid-2006. Now the joint venture is working on a deal to explore for and develop oil in Russia for a proposed refinery in China with a capacity of close to 10 million tons annually.[30]

Not that China is ignoring its other suppliers. As we noted at the beginning of the chapter, China's need for Africa's resources was the reason it feted 48 of the continent's leaders at that unprecedented Beijing summit in November 2006. Also in late 2006, China expressed its desire to initiate "direct negotiations" with OPEC. Speaking at a conference of oil ministers in Dubai, China's assistant minister of foreign affairs, Zhai Jun, said his country hoped to establish "a negotiating mechanism" with OPEC in order to "participate as much as possible in some of the big decision processes on the world stage."[31]

All of which raises some interesting political questions. We looked at the pipeline from Myanmar to India as a palatable—and perhaps even peace-promoting—case of "strange bedfellows." Can we say the same of China's deals? Friedman points out that China's priority is to secure oil supplies from countries that would not retaliate if China invaded Taiwan, which means "getting cozy with some of the worst regimes in the world." He cites as an example the Islamic fundamentalist government in Sudan, which supplies China with 7 percent of its oil imports and in which China has invested $3 billion in oil infrastructure projects. China is thus put in the position of having to vote against sanctioning Sudan for its genocide in Darfur. Along the same lines, 13 percent of China's oil supplies come from Iran, so how meaningfully can China protest against that nation's nuclear proliferation program?[32]

On the other hand, what choice does China have? As Zhang Zhongxiang, senior fellow at the East-West Center in Hawaii, told the *Wall Street Journal*, "China's options are limited. As a late entrant to the international oil game, China has little choice but to strike deals with what the U.S. and others call rogue states to secure oil supplies."[33]

The situation in India is much the same, if on a slightly less dramatic scale. Government officials predict that by 2025 oil demand will double and natural gas demand will triple. Already the nation's energy bill is high. It spent $39 billion on petroleum imports in 2005, as opposed to $29 billion a year earlier. Overall, imports supply about 70 percent of the nation's petroleum needs. Former oil minister Mani Shankar Aiyar couldn't have put it better: "We need energy and we don't have enough of it."

India's search for energy security is complicated by the fact that it often finds itself in competition with China. In September 2005, ONGC Videsh lost out to several Chinese companies when trying to buy oil reserves and a pipeline in Ecuador. A month earlier it had lost the bidding war for Canada's PetroKazakhstan. A year earlier it lost to a Chinese rival in a bid for an oil block in Angola. And now the Chinese have snagged the Myanmar piped gas deal by pulling the rug from under India's feet. To India's disadvantage, China has deeper pockets and a clearer resolve to spend whatever it takes. "China has three companies that are bidding for stakes overseas," explains Indian energy analyst Ketan Karani. "India has only ONGC Videsh, [and] raising big-time money is always a problem because approval of the cabinet is needed and we lose out often due to delays in getting approvals."[34] The reluctance of the Indian government to finance the Indian Oil Corporation's bid of $2 billion to set up a huge refinery in Nigeria resulted in the project falling in the CNOOC's lap (for a price tag of $ 2.3 billion).

Still, as we've noted, ONGC Videsh has had some notable successes—acquiring oil stakes in Brazil, Venezuela, and Trinidad and Tobago, along with the pipeline deal with Iran. The company also has interests in Sudan, Libya, Burma, and Syria and is pursuing deals in Colombia, Cuba, Ecuador, and Argentina. In late 2006 ONGC teamed up with its private sector rival Reliance Industries to develop the Tuba oilfield in southern Iraq, with each party holding 30 percent of the venture and the other 40 percent going to Algeria's Sonatrach.

So, like China's quest for fuel, India's quest is also a global enterprise. What's interesting though, is that several of India's recent energy deals have come with China as a partner, in spite of China as a competitor. The stage for cooperation was set in November 2005 when India's then-oil minister Mani Shankar Aiyar visited Beijing to explore ways for the state-owned energy companies of the two countries to bid jointly for energy exploration and production rights wherever it is in their mutual interest. After all, why compete? As Aiyar noted, in their search for energy assets the two nations are often "pitted against each other to the advantage almost always of the third country." As a result, their rivalry raises fuel prices for both nations. China spent more than $50 billion on oil imports for 2005, not far ahead of India's $39 billion.

The two countries' first successful joint investment was the Greater Nile Oil Project in Sudan, and Aiyar noted that "This model of cooperation can be replicated in Iran, sub-Saharan Africa, Central Africa, Latin America and North and Central Asia." By purchasing stakes in fields where they can produce oil and gas at cost plus the expense of extraction and transport home, they would spend much less than the international market price for oil (around $70 a barrel at the time of Aiyar's remarks). Plus, if they are not bidding against each other, they won't have to resort to expensive deal-sweeteners like government-backed aid and preferential lending rates.[35]

Aiyar's pledge "My ambition is not to compete with China, but to explore ways and means of partnering with it", bore fruit in 2006 when ONGC teamed up with China's Sinopec to buy a 25 percent stake in Omimex de Colombia, a subsidiary of Omimex Resources, a U.S.-based oil explorer and producer. The two partners paid $800 million for their share, making it their biggest joint investment to date. Later in 2006, China's President Hu Jintao visited New Delhi, the first visit to India by a Chinese head of state in 10 years. He was joined on the journey by foreign-trade officials and executives from some 50 Chinese companies, but the centerpiece of the talks was the establishment of an "energy-investment alliance" to acquire for overseas oil and increase their bargaining power in bidding for foreign energy assets. As China's ambassador to India, Sun Yuxi, put it, "We will put this partnership in real terms."[36]

China and India working together to acquire energy assets around the world is a fascinating prospect indeed. However, if China and India are going to partner up in the quest for resources, and if both are equally willing to invest in exploration in countries like Sudan, Syria, and Iran, fairness compels us to look again, briefly, at "the politics of oil." Should

India be congratulated for "boosting trade in Southeast Asia" via its pipeline deal with Myanmar, while China is excoriated for "cozying up" to rogue regimes? Maybe the answer to that question lies in who's doing the congratulating and the criticizing. Some much-needed perspective on the issue was supplied by Ted Koppel, in a *New York Times* op-ed piece in early 2006.

Taking as his starting point President Bush's rebuke of the "partisan critics who claim that we acted in Iraq because of oil," Koppel reminds readers that, as a matter of fact, keeping oil flowing out of the Persian Gulf and through the Strait of Hormuz "has been bedrock American foreign policy for more than a half-century." Executing that policy, moreover, has not always been pretty. In 1953, when duly elected Iranian Prime Minister Mohammed Mossadegh announced plans to nationalize Iran's oil industry, he was promptly ousted by a military coup orchestrated by U.S. and British intelligence officers. Power was transferred to Shah Mohammed Reza Pahlavi, who kept the oil flowing to the West and used his billions of "petrodollars" to buy weapons from the United States.

Today Iran may be maligned as a "rogue nation," but as Koppel points out, U.S. interests in the region have not changed. In 1990, when Saddam Hussein threatened to follow his invasion of Kuwait by crossing into Saudi Arabia, Dick Cheney, then Secretary of State, expressed America's concerns: "We're there because the fact of the matter is that part of the world controls the world supply of oil, and whoever controls the supply of oil, especially if it were a man like Saddam Hussein, with a large army and sophisticated weapons, would have a stranglehold on the American economy and—indeed—on the world economy." While stopping short of saying that the United States invaded Iraq to take over its oil supply, Koppel notes that "the construction of American military bases inside Iraq, bases that can be maintained long after the bulk of our military forces are ultimately withdrawn, will serve to replace the bases that the United States has lost in Saudi Arabia." Our continued presence in the country serves primarily to forestall the "power vacuum and regional instability, and the impact this would have on oil production."[37]

Certain countries have the resources. Other countries need them. The Chindian policy, like the U.S. policy, will be to do the deals necessary to acquire these assets. There's reason to hope that good will follow. Writing in the *The New Yorker*, James Surowiecki notes that, despite all the America-bashing on the part of Hugo Chavez, America remains Venezuela's largest oil customer, and trade between the two nations increased 36 percent in 2006. In a similar vein, despite their bitter history, Japan is now South Korea's second-largest trading partner, and the animosity between China and Taiwan is belied by their $65 billion in annual trade. Surowiecki says he doesn't necessarily agree with Enlightenment thinkers like Thomas Paine, who believed that trade could be counted on to bring peace in its wake, "operating to cordialize mankind." But, he writes, "the benefits of trade often excuse even the most grievous of sins. Sometimes, it just makes sense to deal with the devil."[38]

Environment: The Show Stopper

A final topic remains to be considered—one that eventually must transcend politics. Given what we know today about the myriad dangers of environmental contamination (and what we suspect about the connections between fossil fuel consumption, global warming, and climate change), it now behooves us to turn our attention to the environmental consequences of Chindia's race for, and consumption of, natural resources. It's a discussion that invites the full range of opinion, from stone-faced denial to wild-eyed alarmism. Let's steer a middle course, beginning with a small sampling of the data.

First, relating to China:

- According to the World Bank, 16 of the 20 most polluted cities in the world are in China, and China's three largest cities have about three times the level of suspended particulates deemed safe by the World Health Organization.

- An estimated four hundred thousand Chinese die every year from air-pollution related illnesses such as lung and heart disease.

- Thirty thousand new cars appear on the streets of Beijing every month and, within a decade, the nation will be adding 8 million new cars to its roads every year. It's not just the numbers that make cars the country's chief source of pollution; it's also the fact that China sets weaker pollution standards for automobile emissions than do the United States and Europe.

- Over the next two decades, roughly half of China's 700 million rural citizens are expected to move into the cities, creating an unprecedented demand for even more cars, houses, power, steel, sewage control, and infrastructure.

- In the Yellow River, China's second longest river, 50 of the 150 fish species have been killed, and many of those that remain are unfit to eat. Along the river's 5,464-kilometer course across northern China, two-thirds of the water is no longer drinkable.

- China's marine ecosystem continues to deteriorate, thanks to pollutants filtering from the land into the sea. In 2006, a total of 149,000 square kilometers of coastal sea failed to meet acceptable standards, an increase of 10,000 square kilometers from the year before.

- In 2006, China reported 161 pollution-related hazardous accidents, a rate of close to one every other day.

And with respect to India:

- · India's capital, New Delhi has been the world's most polluted city prior to its recent clean-up act. This clean-up has not addressed the issue of cleaning-up the Yamuna River, the city's sole source of fresh water, which receives 630 million liters of untreated sewage as it passes through the city each day, so that, except during the monsoon, its flow consists entirely of industrial effluent and sewage.

- India's sacred river, the Ganges, is just as bad, with its toxic brew of industrial chemicals, pesticides, heavy metals, trash, animal corpses, and of course, raw sewage. The 2007 purification festival in the city of Allahabad drew some 75 million pilgrims. At this festival, where pilgrims have traditionally bathed in and sipped the river's soul-cleansing water, hundreds of Hindu holy men threatened to commit mass suicide to protest the condition of the river and the government's failure to improve it.

- As in China, automobile use is exploding. The Asian Development Bank predicts that while the number of vehicles in China could grow by 15 times in the next 30 years, the number in India may grow by 13 times. Corresponding carbon dioxide emissions will rise by a factor of 5.8. Tata Motors' new "ultra-low-cost" car, decried by environmentalists as "a total disaster," may quickly bring auto ownership to tens of millions of additional citizens.

- The brown cloud of pollution—one of the world's largest, formed from the soot from factories and tailpipes—that hangs over much of India, has been blamed for stifling the growth in the country's critical rice harvest and helping curtail the beneficial effects of the Green Revolution.

We noted at the beginning of this chapter, and of the previous one, that the rise of Chindia is abetted by a "postcolonial" mindset. That is, both the success of its multinational corporations and its acquisition of resource assets are to be achieved not by colonial-style exploitation but rather by global partnerships and "mutual interest" investments.

In this light it's quite interesting to note China's reaction to a November 2006 report from the International Energy Agency that the Mainland would probably surpass the United States as the world's largest contributor of the greenhouse gas carbon dioxide by 2009, more than a full decade earlier than anticipated. The response has, in part, taken the form of an information campaign that seeks to blame foreigners—in particular, multinational corporations—for the country's mounting environmental problems. The nation's top environmental official Pan Yue accused the developed countries of "environmental colonialism." Multinationals like 3M, Panasonic, PepsiCo, and DuPont, according to Pan, are guilty of transferring resource-intensive, polluting industries to China without regard to their environmental consequences.[39]

That may be true, and India may make the same claim. It's certainly true that the West has been instrumental in China's ongoing power-plant-building binge, and it plans to build an astounding 30 more plants by 2020. Since the job is too big for Chinese construction firms alone, as Ted Fishman reports, the world's major industrial construction firms, like Bechtel, are already at work there. Many plants already operational are being run by international firms like American giant AES, which manages five power plants in China, including the country's biggest. China constitutes a billion-dollar market for General Electric's giant turbines, while Japan's Mitsubishi Heavy Industries and Germany's Siemens are also big players. "The price tags are enormous and represent the sort of big-ticket, high-tech trade that America, Europe, and Japan most hope the Chinese will engage in," writes Fishman. "Nothing moves trade officials in world capitals faster than the chance to place their biggest companies into the development of China's cities."[40]

To the extent that these foreign corporations take the money and run, without regard to the environmental consequences of China's over-heated industrialization, the specter of colonialism may be discerned. Moreover, such a scenario fosters in China itself the old colonial agenda: develop now, clean up later.

However, to Pan Yue's credit, and despite his finger-pointing at foreign multinationals, he and his State Environmental Protection Administration (SEPA) seem determined to change that mindset.

Interviewed in *China Daily*, Pan explained that, even if it wanted to, China could not follow the old model. Once the Western nations "completed their capital accumulation" at the expense of the less developed world, they "established a series of international rules in their favor" which make it "impossible for China to transfer the cost of pollution to the rest of the world." Moreover, he adds, China's "culture of harmony" means that the nation "will never practice any form of eco-colonialism." China's path will be sustainable development, "namely a path of peaceful and environment-friendly development."

Platitudes? Maybe. China certainly has its environmental work cut out for it. But the good news is that Pan's actions reinforce his "Green GDP" message. In January 2007, SEPA cited 82 projects (with a total investment of $14.44 billion) that failed to pass environmental appraisal. It also suspended appraisals for all new projects in four cities and for four of the country's major power groups. The media described the measures as an "environmental protection storm." Moreover, China's government at the highest levels has given SEPA its endorsement. The 11th Five Year Plan calls for a compulsory 10 percent reduction in major pollutants across the board. As is always the case in China, enforcement at the local level will be problematical, but Pan is pushing regulations that will tie local officials' evaluations and promotions to their environmental performance. "Only by doing this," says Pan, "can we change the officials' 'economy-overriding-all' perspective to one of low energy consumption, high utilization and low emission."[41]

India's efforts on behalf of environmental regulation appear less focused. In Pondicherry, battery-operated three-wheelers are increasingly replacing gas-powered vehicles. Bangalore, at the end of 2006, got its first state-of-the-art EMD (electro-magnetic display) to measure air quality and pollution levels. Orissa has followed West Bengal's lead in implementing "cost of pollution" mechanisms to force industries to pay for the damage they inflict upon public resources like water and air. For the long term, India's most significant move so far may have been its 2006 agreement to acquire civilian nuclear technology from the United States in an effort to break its dependence on power generated from coal and oil.

But the Indian government, as a whole, appears typically ineffective. Its inability to address itself to a national problem like environmental degradation is typified by the 20-year, $100-million Ganga Action Plan, whose purpose was to clean up the Ganges River. Leading Indian environmentalists call the plan a complete failure, due to the same problems that have always beset the government: poor planning, corruption, and a lack of technical knowledge. The river, they say, is more polluted than ever. As Gurcharan Das puts it, "We [Indians] have realized that our great strength is our people. Our great weakness is our government."[42]

In Conclusion

China and India have tremendous opportunity and tremendous responsibility. Both nations appear committed to peaceful prosperity, and when the two most populous nations on earth opt for a postcolonial model of global cooperation and comity, the earth stands to benefit.

The quest for resources will test their resolve. Can they work together to acquire diminishing resource assets? Can they strike deals that benefit rather than exploit owner nations? Most important, can they use those resources wisely, conserve them where possible, and lead in the development of alternative energy sources? If they fail in this task, the world will pay a heavy price. If they succeed, Chindia's rise will lift people everywhere.

Notes

1. Batson, Andrew, "China and Africa Strengthen Ties," *Wall Street Journal*, Nov 6, 2006, p. A2.
2. "Business Officials from Africa, India, Discuss Ways to Boost Trade, Investment," *International Herald Tribune*, Oct 9, 2006.
3. Shreeharsha, Vinod, "India and Venezuela: A Success Story," *The Hindu*, Nov 25, 2006, p. 1.
4. Merchant, Khozem, "ONGC Set to Buy Stake in Brazil Oilfield," *Financial Times*, Jan 31, 2006, p. 27.
5. "India Should Step Up Investment in the Caribbean," *Hindustan Times*, Nov 14, 2006.
6. Sun Shangwu, "Hu Urges More Aid to Developing Countries," *China Daily*, Nov 18, 2006.
7. Singh, Manmohan, "Facing India's Challenges," *Wall Street Journal* (Asia), May 19, 2005, p. A11.
8. Bhattacharjee, Ashok, "Focus on Energy," *Wall Street Journal* (Europe), Jan 25, 2005, p. A5.
9. Varadarajan, Siddharth, "Chavez is India's Passport to Latin America," *The Hindu*, Mar 4, 2005, p. 1.

10. Shenkar, Oded, *The Chinese Century: The Rising Chinese Economy and Its Impact on the Global Economy, the Balance of Power, and Your Job* (Upper Saddle River, N.J.: Wharton School Publishing, 2006), pp. 66–71.

11. Fishman, Ted, *China Inc.: How the Rise of the Next Superpower Challenges America and the World* (New York: Scribner, paperback ed., 2006), p. 55.

12. Story, Jonathan, *China: The Race to Market* (London: Prentice Hall, 2003), p. 118.

13. "China to Raise Education Expenditures to 4 Percent of GDP," Xinhua News Agency—CEIS, Mar 6, 2006, p. 1.

14. Shenkar, pp. 4–5.

15. Friedman, Thomas, *The World Is Flat: A Brief History of the Twenty-First Century* (New York: Farrar, Straus and Giroux, 2005), p. 264.

16. Das, Gurcharan, *India Unbound: From Independence to the Global Information Age* (New Delhi: Penguin Books India, revised and updated ed., 2002), pp. xii, 76, 352, xviii.

17. Waldman, Amy, "India's Poor Bet Precious Sums on Private Schools," *New York Times*, Nov 15, 2003, p. A1.

18. Mills, Don, "Education System Failing India's Youth," *National Post*, Jul 26, 2006, p. WK7.

19. Glader, Paul, "China's Steel Industry Looks Abroad," *Wall Street Journal*, Mar 31, 2004, p. A6.

20. McGregor, Richard, "Baosteel Forges Links with Brazil," *Financial Times*, Feb 4, 2004, p. 32.

21. Ping, Yin, "Steelmakers Get Ready to Go Global," *China Daily*, Nov 3, 2006, p. 10.

22. Weitzman, Hal, "Bolivia Attracts Fresh Investors to Mining Assets," *Financial Times*, Jul 18, 2006, p. 10.

23. Zamiska, Nicholas and Eric Bellman, "Heard in Asia: Ranbaxy Unveils Its Ambition," *Wall Street Journal* (Asia), Jan 10, 2007, p. 19.

24. Gibbens, Robert, "Surge in Iron Ore Prices Expected to Slow in 2007," *The Gazette* (Montreal), Dec 23, 2006, p. C3.

25. "Super-cycle for Mining Likely to Continue," *Gold Coast Bulletin*, Dec 27, 2006, p. 45.

26. Arnold, Wayne, "BHP Profit Rises in Year of Copper," *International Herald Tribune*, Aug 24, 2006, p. 11.

27. Fishman, pp. 294–295.

28. Friedman, p. 410.

29. Ping, Yin "Kazakhstan to Double Oil Supply," *China Daily*, Dec 8, 2006, p. 2.

30. Fangchao, Li, "Russia Firm to Increase Oil Supply," *China Daily*, Nov 11, 2006, p. 1.

31. "China Eyes Talks with OPEC," *The Globe and Mail,* Dec 5, 2006, p. B9.

32. Friedman, pp. 409–411.

33. Oster, Shai, "In Beijing, a Gala Summit Takes Aim at Africa's Resources," *Wall Street Journal* (Asia), Oct 30, 2006, p. 12.

34. Kumar, Himendra, "India Increases Search for Oil," *Wall Street Journal* (Asia), Sep 16, 2005, p. M3.

35. Richardson, Michael, "Oil Fuels Regional Rivalry," *South China Morning Post*, Sep 2, 2005, p. 19.

36. Wonacott, Peter, "How Beijing and New Delhi Are Moving Closer," *Wall Street Journal* (Online), Nov 16, 2006, p. A4.

37. Koppel, Ted, "Will Fight for Oil," *New York Times*, Feb 24, 2006, p. A23.

38. Surowiecki, James, "Synergy with the Devil," *The New Yorker*, Jan 8, 2007, p. 26.

39. Economy, Elizabeth, "China Must Clean Up What It Messed Up," *Atlanta Journal-Constitution*, Dec 6, 2006.

40. Fishman, p.113.

41. "'Pollute, Then Treat Is Not the Right Model," *China Daily*, Jan 18, 2007, p. 12.

42. Das, 346.

3

The New Innovation Imperative

Diminishing supplies coupled with increasing need for natural resources is one of the obstacles to Chindia's rise. Others include massive poverty, substandard education among the rural poor, and environmental degradation. To face these daunting problems, Chindia must heed the call of "the new innovation imperative."

Indeed, the journey upstream toward knowledge creation and innovation is well underway. Let's begin our analysis with a couple of stories.

Suntech Power Holdings

Shi Zhengrong happened to be in the right place at the right time to take full advantage of the Chinese government's willingness to underwrite both advanced education abroad and technology startups at home. Raised on a farm and the oldest of four children, he was the one to shoulder the family's hopes for a better life through education. He headed to college in 1979, just as the universities were emerging from the chaos of the Cultural Revolution, and as Deng was opening up the nation's economy. After studying optics at Jilin University, he entered a Master's program at the Shanghai Institute of Optics and Fine Mechanics. He won one of the institute's coveted government-sponsored grants to study abroad, but a bureaucratic foul-up sent him to Australia instead of the United States. No problem. At the University of New South Wales he ended up studying under Martin Green, a prize-winning specialist in solar power.

Zhengrong is the classic "turtle." Following the typical pattern, upon completing his Ph.D. he took a good job in Sydney, as research director of a company that marketed some of the new solar technologies. He bought a house, got Australian citizenship, and started a family. But he heard that China had changed, that it was booming, that foreign investment was pouring in, and in 2000 he went to see for himself. He was quickly convinced that the time was right for the creation of a China-based solar power company.

In Wuxi, a suburb of Shanghai, he secured $6 million in start-up investment, which gave 75 percent of his company to the government and state-owned companies who put up the money. He put in $400,000, plus his technology know-how, for 25 percent and a free hand to run the company. Registered in January 2001, Suntech Power Holdings quickly became one of the world's largest producers of photovoltaic equipment, the equipment that converts sunlight into electricity. As the *Wall Street Journal* puts it, "The company's combination of first-world technology and developing-world prices has helped it gain market share from more-established, and expensive producers."

Production began in September 2002. Within six months, the entire inventory was gone and the need to expand was obvious. A second production line was ready in December 2003, just in time to hit soaring demand. From a revenue of $14 million in 2003, the company exploded to revenues of $226 million in 2005. First-half revenue in 2006 was $218 million. No wonder Suntech sold solar modules for $3.78 per watt, beating by far the global average of $4.30.

Zhengrong next step was to buy out his investors and take the company public. The state shareholders didn't want to go, but Shi argued that the move would allow the company to grow faster, hire more people, and pay more taxes. That convinced government officials, who helped craft the buy-out. Besides, having to get out wasn't all bad. The investors took away 20 times the money they had put in. Dr. Shi did even better. On December 14, 2005, Suntech debuted on the NYSE. Its value soared to a peak of $5 billion, though it has come down since. Dr. Shi's own stake is valued at somewhere between $1 and $2 billion, depending on stock price. In any case, some experts call this the largest private fortune of anyone living in mainland China. On a list of the 500 richest people in China, compiled by the Chinese-language New Fortune magazine, Shi debuted at No. 1 in 2006.

Dr. Zhengrong has since purchased a company in Japan and now plans to turn Suntech into a true multinational entity. "The time is right," he says. "The soil is rich."[1] Thomas Friedman, writing in the *New York Times*, agrees that Zhengrong has got a tiger by the tail: "[Zhengrong] thinks . . . that renewable clean power—wind, solar, bio-fuels—is going to be the growth industry of the 21st century, and he wants to make sure that China and his company are the leaders. . . . [Zhengrong] hopes to do for solar energy what China did for tennis shoes: drive down the cost so that millions of people who could not afford solar photovoltaic panels will be able to do so."

Though right now most of the solar business is abroad, Friedman continues, as Zhengrong brings the price down, the Chinese market will open up, bringing much greater scale and driving the price of his solar modules down further. "Now we are at about $4 per watt," says Zhengrong. "In 10 years time, I'm pretty sure we will be below $2 per watt," which would make solar competitive and scalable.[2]

Not surprisingly, Dr. Zhengrong was selected as the recipient of the Top 10 Entrepreneurs Award for 2006 by CCTV, the largest official TV station in China. It's considered the most important award recognizing individuals who have made outstanding contributions to China's economic development. In accepting the award, Zhengrong noted that it has been his ambition "not only to create a leading global solar company, but also to make an important contribution to China's overall economic and social development. . . . This award also demonstrates the importance China's government and society places on developing clean, alternative energy sources such as solar to ensure China's sustainable development."[3]

Dr. Reddy's Laboratories

Even when it was focused on making "copycat" drugs, Dr. Reddy's Laboratories was an innovative company. When it found out that Prozac users typically took two 20 mg tablets a day, it came out with 40 mg tablets of Fluoxetine, a generic version of the Prozac anti-depressant. Not only was the innovation accepted and patented by the U.S. Food and Drug Administration, but Dr. Reddy's was given six months exclusivity to sell it, netting a handsome $60 million.

Manufacturing generic versions of branded drugs has long been a key strategy of Indian pharmaceutical companies—and one that made a lot of sense. In the first place, with hundreds of millions of people too poor to afford branded prescription drugs, Indian law long refused to recognize foreign drug patents. It was this situation that motivated K. Anji Reddy, a government scientist specializing in pharma research and production, to start his own company in 1984.

Wanting to make drugs less expensive and more accessible to the poor, Dr. Reddy's company specialized in the manufacture of bulk active ingredients as well as finished dosage forms. The problem was, a lot of Indian pharmaceutical companies had the same idea. The business was becoming "commoditized." Dr. Reddy's solution, according to company spokesman Rammohan Rao, was to separate itself from the competition by producing "the difficult-to-manufacture" drugs. Pouring money into research and development, the company took on drugs like the German-made antibiotic ciprofloxacin, for example, which heretofore had had to be imported from Europe.

But even that kind of work is just basic apprenticeship for Dr. Reddy's researchers. Their holy grail is new drug discovery. In 1997, the lab discovered a new anti-diabetes molecule. Without the financial resources needed to take the drug's trials through the final stages, the company licensed its discovery to Danish pharmaceutical giant Novo Nordisk—and in the process became the first Indian pharmaceutical company to win recognition of its intellectual property abroad.[4]

The push into drug discovery was well timed. In May 2002, the Indian government approved a revised patent law designed to bring India into compliance with the World Trade Organization. What that meant, in part, was that as of 2005 Indian pharma companies, like all others around the world, were prohibited from copying patented drugs. Of course, the plight of the "copycat" producers had long been evident. In one typical scenario, Dr. Reddy's applied to produce a generic version of Plavix, the blockbuster stroke treatment. Predictably, lawyers for Sanofi-Synthelabo, the French maker of the multi-billion-dollar seller, accused Dr. Reddy's of patent infringement and threatened to take action.[5]

Producing generics continues to be Dr. Reddy's bread and butter (and the way it pays for research into drug discovery), but the company was one of the first to see the writing on the wall. Its drug-discovery program actually dates from 1993, making it India's oldest. By 2002, it was spending more than 6 percent of revenues on R&D, three times the Indian average. Two years later, Dr. Reddy's sponsored "Pharmacophore 2004," the largest-ever international symposium in India to focus on drug discovery research. In 2005, Anji Reddi formed a separate company called Perlecan Pharma to fund drug development, naming it for a protein that the company's researchers suspect causes hardening of the arteries.

Today, Dr. Reddy's is concentrating on four areas of original research: metabolic disorders like diabetes, cardiovascular diseases, inflammation, and infections. The molecule it discovered in 1997 was the first of several. There are now nine potential new drugs in the company's pipeline, the success of any one of which would catapult Dr. Reddy's into the top ranks of global pharmaceutical companies. Which is where the founder wants it: "I want to see one of my products being taken by people across the world," Anji Reddy told the *International Herald Tribune*. "I want to see them improving and leading a better life."[6]

The roughly 12 percent of adult Indians who suffer from diabetes may constitute the market for Dr. Reddy's first original product. Balaglitazone, a drug the company developed to sensitize the body's ability to use insulin, entered the final stage of human testing in 2007 and could be available by 2011. Since the WHO estimates that a low-income Indian family with a diabetic adult may well spend a quarter of its income on diabetes care, Anji's vision, and determination to innovate, may prove especially rewarding.[7]

★ ★ ★

Solar power and pharmaceuticals are but two of the many industries that highlight the advancing wave of Chindian innovation, and we will look at several others. But first, let's consider the innovation phenomenon in light of China's and India's on-going economic evolution.

The Rationale for the New Innovation Imperative

The journey of industrialization inevitably leads up the value chain. So it was in Europe in the 19th century, then later in America, then in Japan and Korea. And now we begin to see it in Chindia. We must not expect China and India to remain content as the world suppliers of low-cost manufacturing and low-wage IT services. That was merely the beginning of their journey, and it behooves us to pay attention to how that journey proceeds.

As China's economy matures, it's quite natural that workers there will demand higher wages. Like every industrial nation before it, China will respond by outsourcing manufacturing to less developed economies—in Southeast Asia, in the Caribbean, in Africa, in Eastern Europe. Indeed, this process is already well underway. Haier is now building appliances in Indonesia, Malaysia, Yugoslavia, and elsewhere in the developing world. Shanghai Baosteel is operating blast furnaces in Brazil. Textile manufacturing is being outsourced to Africa.

As for India, the call center business at the heart of its IT services industry is already going away, for a number of reasons. First, the workday in America is the graveyard shift in India, which is difficult to manage, and gives the advantage to competitors in the western hemisphere. Second, Canada, which is taking much of this business now, is subsidizing the industry so as to minimize the wage difference. Also, Nortel and Cisco, suppliers of the dominant platform, can install their systems more cheaply in Canada than in India, which further mitigates the wage disproportion. In addition, call center training in Canada takes two to three weeks, less than half the training cycle in India. At the same time, Latin American nations like Costa Rica and El Salvador have come to the realization that India's English-language advantage is counterbalanced by their Spanish-language advantage—given that, by 2020, a quarter of the U.S. population will be of Hispanic heritage.

The competition is not hurting India, just as low-wage manufacturing in Vietnam and Africa is not hurting China. The two nations are simply continuing their journey—up the value chain—toward their destination as producers of knowledge rather than of goods or services. The West, Japan, and Korea have already felt the innovation imperative. Chindia is now beginning to experience what I call "the new innovation imperative."

India is already on the cutting edge in pharmaceuticals, and China is a telecommunications leader. Commentators in America who still wring their hands over U.S. jobs outsourced to China and India have some catching up to do. It's time to turn our attention, not to the low-cost phenomenon, but rather to the knowledge phenomenon.

Traditionally, it is in the "knowledge" area that Chindia has lagged, and experts inside China and India readily concede that, in both nations, traditional pedagogy has not fostered creativity. "Students cram and recite," says Shen Baiyu, director of curriculum development at the Education Ministry in Beijing. "They remember, but they don't understand." Shen sees this lack of creativity as "a fatal disadvantage of Chinese education." Similarly, says Anil Gupta, who directs a center for agricultural innovation at IIM-Ahmedabad, "We are producing followers, not leaders. Indian society makes people fit into a groove."[8] Given this assessment, and given also the vital link between education and innovation, let's take a minute to consider how education in Chindia is changing, how both nations are bringing innovation into the classroom so that more innovation will flow out from it.

In the first place, where government has fallen short, industry is stepping in. Corporations understand that government is too slow, too bureaucratic to respond with urgency to what is needed now in educational innovation, so we are seeing the rise of close partnerships between industry and institutes of higher learning. Corporations need a global talent pool, so they are helping to create it. A good example is India's Manipal Academy of Higher Education, a network of 53 private professional colleges sprawling across the country's southwestern coast. The Manipal network includes the Manipal Institute of Technology, one of India's 2,240 "second tier" engineering schools that graduated more than 200,000 engineers in 2005 alone. Like other highly regarded schools, MIT brings the real world onto the campus by inviting corporations to recruit its students at the end of their next-to-last year. For students who accept offers, the school creates senior-year electives geared to the work they'll be doing. Companies like Infosys, Tata Consultancy, and Wipro go further: they provide course material and even train professors in subjects like chip design and network management. Such collaboration allows the corporations to spot and nurture the talent they need while significantly reducing in-house training after graduation.

To stay on the cutting edge, Manipal's current CEO Dr. Rangan Pai (the grandson of founder Dr. T. M. Pai) is investing $23 million in new facilities, including a $7.6 million "innovation and incubation" center that will house labs from major multinationals like HP, Philips, EMC, and Infosys. Other schools at the top of the second tier are following suit. PSG College of Engineering in Tamil Nadu is developing a "play and learn" approach, where classes are broken into 20 minutes of lecture and 30 minutes of hands-on experimentation. The Dean of the school's Mechanical Engineering Department emphasizes the importance of "real-life situations"; he makes sure that students meet customers, and pushes faculty to spend summers in the field, helping companies solve their problems.

Meanwhile, what's going on at the "top tier"? Across the nation at the IITs, students and faculty are working together to "incubate" start-up companies. With the schools providing office space, labs, and a little seed money, innovation and entrepreneurship are redefining the classroom. A team of engineers at the IIT-Kharagpur campus is working on a next-generation BlackBerry; at IIT-Bombay, an earth sciences professor is launching a company that will use the vapor from geothermal springs to drive turbines; at IIT-Madras, students and faculty are working on building a computer for the Asian markets that is expected to sell for a mere $100. Recreating the kind of symbiosis evident in the relationship between Stanford and Silicon Valley, the IITs have created some 50 viable companies.'

An even more sweeping change to the education paradigm is the e-learning phenomenon, which best represents the global need for alternatives to the traditional classroom. One of the first models was the U.S.-based University of Phoenix, which recognized early-on the growing demand for further education on the part of working people, single parents, and the millions of others who weren't in a position to "go to college." Long scoffed at by "traditionalists" (who fail to realize that nowadays only 27 percent of college students are "traditional"), the University of Phoenix now offers on-line classes and flexible schedules at 250 campuses serving roughly 300,000 students. It is, in fact, the largest institution of higher learning in the United States.

The potential for this [educational/academic] model in Chindia is limitless. Researchers estimated that by the year 2020, 100 million people around the world will be demanding higher education, but won't have access to traditional programs. Half of these people will be in Asia, and 20 million will be in China, which explains why the University of Liverpool opened a university in China in 2006, the first such venture between the UK and China.

Located in Suzhou, about an hour outside of Shanghai, Xi'an Jiaotong-Liverpool University will help meet China's need for tech professionals by specializing in programs in computer science, electronics, and IT. However, its off-campus capabilities and suite of e-learning programs will give it global reach, enabling students from all over the world to get a degree on-line. The fortuitous conjunction of China's huge market and e-learning's potential also explains why China Education Alliance, one of the nation's leading e-learning enterprises, announced that 2005 earnings were an incredible 5,920 percent greater than the year before. According to company's president Xiqun Yu, "We expect to continue building on this momentum in 2006 and well into the future."[10]

In India, the e-learning phenomenon is represented by companies like Tata Interactive Systems. Founded in 1990, this global pioneer demonstrates e-learning's applicability not only in the education establishment but in business and government as well. Its client list includes more than 50 Fortune 500 companies from every corner of the globe; it includes cutting-edge educational institutions (including the University of Phoenix, the University of Maryland, and the Florida Virtual School), and education-oriented publishers like McGraw-Hill and Pearson Education. It counts among its clients even foreign government organizations like the British Educational Communications and Technology Agency (BECTA) and, in the United States, the Department of Defense Education Activity (DODEA), the civilian agency that manages all the schools on overseas military bases. With close to 1,000 multidisciplinary specialists developing curricula on everything from simulations and systems training to K-12 math, TIS suggests the vast range of e-learning's capabilities.[11]

So, yes, China and India may still lag behind the West as knowledge producers, and the blame may rest with their traditional educational institutions, but as these examples show, innovation will not wait for government reform of education. Instead, it will transform education into a laboratory where Chindian genius and creativity can be nurtured. This education revolution results from the same pressures that are turning Chindia into the world's R&D capital, a theme I've touched on before. I'll elaborate on that point a little further, and then take a look at the three major forces—affordability, scarcity, and environmental health—that will drive Chindian innovation in the decades to come.

The World's Laboratory

In Chapter 1, I made the point that both China and India understand that their continued growth depends on their commitment to R&D. I noted that, in terms of percentage of GDP, President Hu has called for an R&D investment of 2.5 percent—or, roughly, $115 billion a year—by 2020; in addition, according to the *Economic Times*, India's high tech industries are attracting "25 percent of fresh global R&D investment." Now let's observe that China and India are not merely going to put more into R&D, they're going to get more out of it.

According to the traditional formula from Western research, one dollar spent in R&D yields 20 cents worth of innovation. The other 80 percent is not wasted; it is simply not turned into commercially viable products. This is because much of this research is conducted on behalf of the government, especially the Department of Defense, or conducted by university research facilities seeking agricultural or biochemical miracles. In other words, this is the kind of long-cycle research whose goal is the Nobel Prize, or a medical breakthrough, or a missile defense system, rather than a marketable consumer product. Instead of knowledge-driven, R&D in Chindia will be product-driven, business-driven, with investors demanding accountability and watching their ROI. My research indicates that the rate of return will be 60%, rather than 20%

A perfect example is mobile telephony, where the pace of innovation remains breathtaking as producers race to the market with the latest upgrade. In late January 2007 came word that Shanghai had launched a trial run, not of the anticipated third-generation mobile technology, but of 4G technology in what it called the world's first rollout of the wireless application. Leaping beyond 3G, 4G technology offers much faster speeds, sharply improved high-quality images and data services, and whiz-bang features like multi-channel high-definition TV broadcasting. Seizing the moment, Chinese engineers moved directly into the development of 4G technology even while repeated delays have prevented 3G from becoming available to consumers. Korea's Samsung has also been working on 4G and plans to put the technology into commercial use by 2010. China hopes to beat that deadline.[12]

I also noted the zeal with which foreign multinationals are seeking to establish a presence in Chindia—often entering into technology-sharing agreements, and in many cases setting up state-of-the-art research laboratories. Exemplifying the kind of industry-education partnership we discussed above, a new initiative was announced in early 2007 when IBM and the Indian School of Business (ISB) signed a memorandum of understanding to create a first-of-its-kind "Research on Service Science, Management and Engineering" (SSME) program in India. Responding to the new global reality that services now accounts for more than 50 percent of the labor force in Brazil, Russia, Japan and Germany, and more than 75 percent of employment in India, the United States and Great Britain, the IBM-ISB partnership intends to produce cutting edge research and develop case histories/studies to improve service processes across key industries. The new interdisciplinary program will foster and coordinate innovative research in computer science, operations research, industrial engineering, business strategy, management sciences and related fields. As Nick Donofrio, IBM's executive VP for innovation and technology, summed up program status, "We are at an incredible tipping point for the world economy, and it's all around innovation."[13]

Yet another point worth reiterating is the huge number of scientists and engineers now flooding the Chindian talent pool—even at a time when engineering appears to be of declining interest to Western university students. This is one of the reasons why Palo Alto-based Accelergy Corp., which does contract research in nanotechnology for mostly Western clients, opted to locate its R&D operations in Shanghai. Part of the company's rationale is that the Mainland is seeking to become a nanotech powerhouse. Adjusted to reflect purchasing power parity (PPP), China's 2005 investment in nanotechnology was second only to the U.S.—\$1.11 billion compared to \$1.57 billion. But more specifically, Accelergy CEO Vic Sprenger offered two reasons for the move: "The first is to tap into China's rapidly growing pool of world-class scientists. The second is a trend of scientific innovation and creativity." Confronted with the traditional wisdom that China excels as a manufacturer but lags as an innovator, Sprenger says, "We believe conventional wisdom is about to change." In fact, China's sizable investment in nanotech is going not only to centers already in operation, like the National Engineering Research Center for Nanotechnology in Shanghai, but also toward the construction of 33 nanotech centers across Asia.[14]

Clearly, the trend will continue—indeed, will become an expanding cycle. As more foreign multinationals (not just Western, but also Japanese and Korean) shift R&D to Chindia, Chindia's "R&D infrastructure" will rapidly improve, thus luring yet more foreigners into the game.

As an aside, it might be noted that not every industry will be indiscriminately interested in both countries. As a lingering effect of Cold War animosity, some Western nations (including the United States) are leery of trading arms technology with China. Long-term, this may work to China's advantage, since it will continue to focus its R&D effort on consumer-product sectors like autos, electronics, and telecommunications and thus leverage its huge domestic market.

On the other hand, India isn't likely to complain about all the high-tech weapons technology it will be acquiring from around the world—not only from the United States but from the U.S.' military partners like Israel, Japan and Singapore. Of course, India used to depend on the Soviet Union for its military arsenal, but the new friendship between Washington and New Delhi has drastically changed that scenario—witness the recent agreement to share civilian nuclear technology. Another sign of the times was the biennial air show in Bangalore that took place in February 2007. Executives from more than 50 U.S. companies, along with aircraft makers from around the world, came to exhibit their jets, explore partnerships with local firms, and lobby Indian defense officials. With the Defense Ministry planning a significant expansion of its Air Force, Lockheed Martin and Boeing were there, hoping for their first-ever sales to India, along with GE, Raytheon, Honeywell, and Bell Textron, among others. As the Associated Press pointed out in covering the event, "A key factor for India in choosing new planes is the supplier's commitment to share technologies to make spare parts, and to develop and produce aircraft in India."[15]

Now, given Chindia's continued emergence into a global research and development hub, let's turn to those three major forces that will drive the coming wave of innovation.

Affordability: The Father of Innovation

It's important to acknowledge, first, that the technologies that came out of the industrial revolution failed to benefit most of the world. They were Western, for the most part, and elitist—for the benefit of the relatively small consumer class. Even today 50 percent of the world's population has never turned on an electric light, or enjoyed running water, or made a telephone call. Research and development—and the society-improving inventions that flow from it—are targeted to markets where money is to be made, which constitutes approximately 15 percent of the population. Even in the most developed economies, a huge gulf still exists between rural and urban populations—witness Appalachia or portions of the Deep South in the United States.

In *The Fortune at the Bottom of the Pyramid*, C. K. Prahalad shows with startling clarity the distribution of purchasing power across the world's population. At the top tier of the pyramid are 75 million to 100 million people who live on more than $20,000 dollars a year (figures adjusted to PPP). These people constitute the world's consumer society. But at the bottom of the pyramid are the approximately 4 billion people who live in poverty, who live on less that $2 a day.

Chindia is in a unique position to transform this dismal ratio. In the first place, these two most populous nations also are home to most of the world's poor, so the problem is at their doorstep. Second, poor people today are more aware of their poverty, relative to the more affluent, and less inclined to accept it. The enormous democratization of wealth creates aspirations where none existed before. Thirty years ago, as Deng's reforms got underway, a few farmers were allowed to sell some of their produce and keep the profit. Now all of a sudden there are 250,000 Chinese with incomes of more than $1 million a year, and the number is rising by 15 percent a year. Such aspirations of course are fueled by knowledge and, like never before, knowledge—via television, mobile telephony, and the Internet—is penetrating into rural and impoverished regions.

In short, the gap between the haves and the have-nots, which historically was assumed to be the "natural state of affairs," is no longer so easily tolerated. It is now acknowledged as a problem—by government agencies, by NGOs, and certainly by the poor themselves. Importantly, knowledge is increasingly seen as boundless opportunity. Again, we're talking about a market of four billion people, people who need, and will purchase, products and services, once innovation makes them affordable and accessible. Indeed, as affordability becomes the father of innovation, as those at the bottom of the pyramid are transformed into part of the consumer society, Chindia's growth will be sustained over the coming decades. Let's keep in mind that affordability is less about creating new products than about innovatively rethinking the ways in which current products are made and distributed. This phenomenon is illustrated by Prahalad who writes about "the single-serve revolution sweeping through bottom-of-the-pyramid (BOP) markets." For example, thanks to the availability of single-serve sachets, the penetration of shampoo in India is now at 90 percent, including name brands like Pantene.

Cell phones provide a particularly striking example. We know that China is now the largest cell phone market in the world by far, with close to half a billion subscribers. However, in September 2006, India overtook China in the number of new subscribers per month. Amazingly, in a single month, January 2007, seven million Indians signed up for cell phone service—a new world record. And though it will still trail China, India too will have a half-billion subscribers by 2010.

Given such numbers, it's clear that cell phone use is penetrating the BOP, that the "mobile miracle" is empowering the less fortunate. People, who not long ago couldn't even have dreamed of being on India's years-long waiting list for telephone services, are now the newest beneficiaries. To illustrate, Prahalad writes of the Kerala fishermen who, until recently, would haul their catch ashore and sell at the price the local market offered. Today, at the end of the day's toil, they use their cell phones to contact multiple markets along the Kerala shore and sell to the highest bidder.[16] Naturally, these fishermen will now have more money to spend on the increasing number of products which innovative entrepreneurs will make affordable and accessible.

Affordability is also pushing innovation in the PC industry. In March 2007, Michael Dell announced the unveiling of the EC280, a computer targeted specifically to the Chinese market. Created at Dell's Shanghai design center, the new model comes with a monitor and runs Microsoft Windows XP, but it's smaller and uses less electricity than standard desktop PCs. The price? From $336 to $517, depending on upgrades. "China is the center of growth and innovation that we're seeing in the technology industry right now," said Dell, and for the vast number of Chinese computers trying to buy their first computer, "affordability matters."[17]

Another interesting aspect of this innovation is that it will be "trickle-up" rather than conforming to the standard "trickle-down" model. Historically, the prime mover of innovation has been survival, and as societies and then nations evolved, innovation-producing R&D still to a considerable degree fell under the purview of the military-industrial complex. It was centered on developing the weaponry (from gunpowder to bombs to nuclear missiles) necessary for national defense, or for conquest. Since the most potent weapons conferred the most power and security, governments became the primary sponsors of scientific and technological research. We see this in NASA, Reagan's Star Wars, and other so-called strategic defense initiatives. This is long-cycle research, primarily intended to produce breakthrough knowledge, but what has happened in many cases is that innovative products developed for military-industrial use have subsequently "trickled down" to commercial application.

Once again cell phones provide an excellent example. The technology was originally developed by the military for battlefield communications. Now it has trickled down to some two billion cell phone subscribers in the consumer market worldwide. To take another example, air filtering technology was developed for industrial power plants; today there is a vacuum cleaner in every western home. BF Goodrich's first radial tires were too expensive for the consumer market, but they were perfect for the aircraft industry. Later, with economies of scale and lower costs, radials were embraced by the consumer market. So the trickle-down model typically progresses from military to industrial to commercial uses, where the consumer market awaits.

On the other hand, innovation spurred by affordability, innovation targeted to the bottom of the pyramid, will increasingly be "trickle-up." For a good example, let's look at electronics, whose economics are uniquely suited to this model. In the industries that produce mechanical products—automobiles, for example—fixed costs are approximately 30 percent, while the other 70 percent goes to procurement. Consequently, economies of scale are gradual, a slow curve. But in electronics there are only two basic components—software and chips—and virtually all costs are fixed. If, for example, it cost $1 billion to develop Windows Vista, then we might say that our first Vista software product will cost $1 billion. But the cost of the second is virtually nothing. Now we are talking about immediate and spectacular economies of scale. The higher your volume, the lower your costs, and the more affordable your product. It's the same with chips. The cost of a wafer factory is so immense that the first chip costs $2 billion. But, again, the cost of the second is minimal. Of course, you've still got to amortize that $2 billion investment, so you need a lot of volume; you need worldwide markets. And the biggest worldwide markets exist at the bottom of the pyramid. So look for trickle-up innovation in electronics and other industries—like generic pharmaceuticals, for example—where fixed costs are high, procurement is low, and volume is more important than margin. It doesn't hurt that, with their legacy as old-world traders, Chindians are comfortable with the concept of thin margins.

In addition to being "trickle-up," innovation driven by affordability will also be "price-minus." Cost-plus won't work for the BOP. Forget determining a retail price based on the traditional formula of costs plus desired margin. For the BOP, we have to start with an affordable price, then figure out how to make and distribute the product for less than that. "Price-minus" has driven the cell phone revolution. It took 12 and a half years for the first billion customers to sign up for GSM cell phone service. The second billion subscribers will sign up within 18 months. Why? Because the carriers like China Mobile and Reliance have told the manufacturers like Motorola and Nokia, that they want a handset for less than 50 dollars. And the manufacturers have come through. Price-minus innovation is now driving the pharmaceuticals industry in India. The cost of developing a new drug in the United States is estimated to be $900 million. In India the cost is estimated at $20 million to $30 million. Admittedly, part of the difference is explained by the lower wages of the Indian scientists and by lower regulatory costs, but the overriding fact is that in India today affordable drugs are a mandate. It is the innovation imperative.

It might be noted that price-minus innovation—making existing products more cheaply—has not historically been the "high calling" of science. Western scientists, with their sights always on breakthrough technology, might not want to be bothered with such simple work. Fortunately, Chindia has the advantage of not being burdened with such a legacy. It hears the call of affordability.

Finally, look for affordability to spur an increase in Chindia of "technology fusion." This trend, spotted by the *Harvard Business Review* in the early 1990s, gives less emphasis to R&D's "breakthrough approach" and more to the combining of existing technologies into hybrid technologies. The basic principles underlying technology fusion are first, "intelligence gathering" to keep tabs on technology developments both inside and outside of the given industry, and second, long-term R&D ties with a variety of companies across different industries. The *Review* observed that this trend had developed in Japan in the 1960s and 1970s, when MITI estimated that Japanese manufacturers were devoting more than one-fourth of their R&D investments to "digesting" imported technologies.[18] Today we see examples everywhere: in automobiles, for example, where mechanical and electronic technologies are increasingly combined; or radio frequency identification (RFID) technology being incorporated in industrial uses from agriculture to biomedicine to transportation.

The point to emphasize is that technology fusion is the perfect solution to Chindia's technology needs. It is, in fact, what technology sharing is all about; and technology sharing, as I've noted, is the route Chindia must take as it plays catch-up to the West in tech development. The global R&D labs sprouting like daisies in China and India will prove an enormous boon to this trend, as Chinese and Western scientists and engineers cross-fertilize each other's curious minds. Clearly, fast-growing but not yet fully advanced economies like China's and India's are less in need of miracle breakthroughs than of affordable technology developments that get desirable consumer products to more and more people, thus tapping the deep well of the BOP market.

Now let's take a look at a few of the innovative ideas spawned by affordability.

Microlending

In a little village in Bangladesh in 1976, Professor Muhammad Yunus founded the Grameen Bank with the idea of offering "microloans"—small, high-risk, unsecured loans—to poor individuals and small businesses that would have had no chance for credit from mainstream banks. Today, with a loan recovery rate of 99 percent and a healthy balance sheet, Grameen has more than 7 million customers and 11,000 employees in more than 43,000 villages. What's more, microlending has spread around the world; according to UN estimates, somewhere between 700 million to 750 million microloans were offered by thousands of lenders worldwide in 2005. That same year, which was declared the Year of Microcredit by the UN, Professor Yunus was awarded the Nobel Peace Prize.

Grameen Trust, the non-profit arm of Grameen Bank that conducts training and workshops in microfinance, now operates in 37 countries— including, as of January 2007, India. But Grameen's fame—and philosophy—preceded it into India. Most of the nation's commercial banks, including SBI, ICICI and HDFC, have extensive microfinance divisions, while others, like Basix in Hyderabad, specialize in the micro sector.

In a typical scenario from the northern state of Uttar Pradesh, an impoverished farm family might borrow $130 from ICICI to buy a buffalo and sell its milk. The deal represents a tiny increment of what is becoming a huge business. Since 2003, ICICI has doubled the size of its rural micro-banking to about $3.4 billion and has outstanding microloans totaling some $538 million. The CEO of Basix points out that given the 100 million Indian households that still have no access to credit, the microlending market could easily reach $30 billion. Bankers are now even talking about bundling microloans into larger bond issues and selling them to Indian and global investors.[19]

Microlending, of course, is not high technology. It's innovative thinking spurred by poverty, by the need to make an existing product or service affordable to the masses. As Professor Yunus told the *Sunday Times*, "I found it difficult to teach elegant theories of economics in the university classroom in the backdrop of a terrible famine in Bangladesh. I wanted to do something immediate to help people around me."[20] Now bankers throughout the developing world are recognizing that need creates opportunity.

Thinking Small

Talk about price-minus! It was India's CavinKare that got shampoo to the nation's rural poor, but the guys in accounting must have been shaking their heads. The company's research showed that in the 1980s, rural Indians were just beginning to take to the notion of using shampoo for their once-a-week hair-washing. The problem was cost. The typical sachet priced at 2 rupees (4 U.S. cents) would mean a lay-out of 8 rupees for the typical month's four washings. That was too much. The company's surveys showed that customers couldn't afford to spend more than 2 rupees on hair-washing for the whole month, so, working backward from that price, it launched its Chik brand in 50-paise (1 cent) sachets in 1983. The brand sold 1 million sachets that year in Tamil Nadu, and it's been spreading across the nation ever since.

But the small-size phenomenon is about more than the affordability of the product in question. It's about innovative marketing that considers the way life is lived at the BOP. Hindustan Lever, for example, sells three-inch square packets of margarine that don't require refrigeration. It's not just that Chindia's poor can't afford refrigerators; they're not likely to have room for such an appliance either. At the BOP, living space is at a premium. While a U.S. family of four might live in 1,600 square feet, a family of nine in China will typically occupy 600 square feet, and a family of six in India will live in 344 square feet.

As Vijay Mahajan and Kamini Banga point out in *The 86% Solution*, developing-world consumers prefer a "just-in-time" approach to purchasing life's necessities, whether food or fuel or household goods. Their small pantries have no shelf space for "economy size," nor are they enticed by "buy one and get one free." One of Haier's first successful innovations was a refrigerator-freezer that could be separated into its two components, making it easy to move in and out of tiny apartments. Another was a single appliance that doubled as both a washing machine and a drier.[21]

Pooling Demand

When a savvy entrepreneur buys a two-liter bottle of Coke and sells it by the glass to neighbors who can afford only an individual serving, or when a cell phone customer sells service by the call to her women friends, the demand from a group of mini-customers is being pooled to form one significant customer.

There's no better example of this trend than the *e-choupal* project happening now in India's rural agricultural villages. The project places a single solar battery-powered Internet terminal with satellite access in the home of a central farmer, and all the surrounding farmers use the system to check on grain prices, track weather, purchase supplies, and sell their products. Launched in 2000, the project had connected 3.1 million farmers through a network of 5,000 *e-choupals* (choupal means village square) by 2003, handling $100 million in transactions. With 30 new villages "coming on line" every day, that number is projected to triple—to 10 million farmers—by 2010.[22]

The *e-choupal* project is the innovation of Calcutta-based ITC (Indian Tobacco Co.), best known as a hotelier and as India's largest producer of cigarettes. The company also sells fertilizer to farmers and buys their grain, business it used to conduct through a complex maze of inter-mediaries. But then S. Sivakumar, the company's head of international business, had the idea of using e-commerce as a way to break the stranglehold of the middlemen. He started the experiment in 20 villages in the state of Madhya Pradesh, giving farmers a chance to check grain prices in the local market, in the state capital, in New Delhi, and even on the Chicago commodities exchange—and then compare those prices to ITC's own offer. Typically, a direct sale to ITC nets the farmer 5 to 15 percent more than selling in the traditional marketplace. More remarkable, thanks to the host of benefits conferred by the *e-choupal* system (including saved time and increased productivity), it's estimated that farmers incomes have risen 25 to 30 percent.[23]

Here again we see the upward spiral. Innovation on behalf of affordability brings a service to those who couldn't pay for it before. That service, in turn, brings to its new users a higher level of prosperity.

Health Solutions for the Poor

The Annapurna Salt story illustrates, once again, that innovation aimed at the BOP is often more about new ideas in marketing and distribution than about high-tech science and engineering. It also shows that improving the health of millions of people can be a profitable proposition.

Iodine deficiency is the world's leading cause of such mental disorders as retardation and sub-normal IQ. The well-balanced diets of affluent societies supply plenty of iodine, but the poor remain alarmingly susceptible to iodine deficiency disorder (IDD). In India, where almost 90 percent of the population earns less than $3,000 a year, over 70 million people already suffer from IDD, and another 200 million are at risk. Since even the poor eat salt, the solution to IDD is iodine-enhanced salt, requiring neither great know-how nor tremendous expense. Bowing to necessity, China in 1995 and India in 1997 outlawed the sale of non-iodized salt. In India, though, the law was vehemently challenged by the 300 or so small, local producers who claimed they couldn't afford the iodine, the machinery, or the new packaging they would need. Their lobbying worked, and the law was repealed in 2000.

Even though large-scale manufacturers continued to voluntarily add iodine to their salt, the national campaign against IDD was failing. Hindustan Lever took on the challenge with the creation of Annapurna Salt. The company's first step was to create an utterly original marketing program. Unlike other iodized salts, Annapurna advertised itself as healthful. It was the first to directly address IDD-related health problems and to promote its brand of iodine-enhanced salt as the solution. As a result, it won the endorsement of the International Council for the Control of Iodine Deficiency.

Next, Annapurna purposefully targeted the BOP, setting as its primary goal convincing unrefined salt users (75 percent of the market) to use iodized salt and as its secondary goal winning over the 25 percent who were already branded consumers. That meant new, smaller packages—200g and 500g rather than the less affordable 1kg bag. It also meant innovative ways of getting its health message to the 50 percent of the population beyond the reach of the normal mass media. To address this problem the company developed Project Shakti (meaning "strength" in Sanskrit), a direct-to-consumer marketing campaign to reach the rural poor. The heart of the program was women's self-help groups (SHGs), in which women with an entrepreneurial bent were trained to sell door-to-door, while also educating consumers on the health benefits of Annapurna, and nurturing loyalty to Annapurna and Hindustan Lever.

Hindustan Lever faced yet another problem: iodine loss during storage and transport, as well as from traditional Indian cooking. To address the first part of the problem, the company reworked the supply chain, using more rail and less roadway to mitigate the inevitable problems with truck transport, and at the same time decreased transport time by increasing the number of consumer purchase points. To address the cooking problem, the company retreated to the research lab and created a proprietary product, K15, a stable iodine released only in an acidic environment—like the human stomach—rather than in the cooking pot. Not miracle science, to be sure, but a timely innovation spurred by BOP thinking.

Thus, as C. K. Prahalad writes, Hindustan Lever is proving that "the bottom of the pyramid can serve as a profitable impetus of innovative technology and marketing savvy, and that corporations . . . can address social problems at affordable costs."[24]

Scarcity: Replacing, Reusing and Renewing

In an editorial in *The Hindu*, B. S. Prakash, India's Consul-General in San Francisco, looks at what India needs to do to maintain growth and create employment, and asks whether the nation can in fact aspire to be a hub of innovation on a global scale. The answer, he says, is yes. India is uniquely positioned on the crest of innovation because, if for no other reason, "some of the conditions that foster out-of-the-box solutions include scarcity and need."[25] As I see it, scarcity will drive a more profound and fundamental innovation. Where innovation for affordability was about making existing products less expensive and more accessible, the innovation spurred by scarcity will require new products, new technologies, whole new industries.

In both China and India, there's plenty of scarcity to go around—and more is looming. As I pointed out in Chapter 2, China and India are well on their way to becoming the world's most voracious consumers of virtually every kind of resource—natural, human, and manmade. Not only are their domestic markets fueling such consumption, but as they become manufacturers and producers for the rest of the world, their appetite for resources will increase all the more. Where resources are finite, or unavailable, or difficult to access, innovation must seek to fill the gap. As Chindia seeks to secure continued growth and prosperity, the threat of scarcity will be a mighty spur to innovation.

We may define "scarcity of resources" as broadly as we like. For example, we may argue that scarcity is a function of inaccessibility and look for innovations in distribution. A promising development along these lines (as noted above) is distance learning via the Internet, bringing everything from basic literacy to nuclear physics to areas or institutions where such study was not feasible before. Remote medical diagnosis is another example. Doctors in the world's most far-flung regions are now having x-rays read and symptoms analyzed by sophisticated laboratories thousands of miles away.

Or we may consider a looming shortage of human capital. Development and industrialization tend to bring about decreasing birth rates, which explains the aging populations in the West. Spain and Italy, though largely Roman Catholic, have among the world's lowest birth rates today. In purely economic terms, children in post-agricultural economies are no longer an asset, but rather a liability—a source of "headaches and heartaches." The same scenario will eventually unfold in China and India—and will be exacerbated by China's "one-child" policy. In the meantime, continued development in Chindia will mean that farm and factory workers will migrate up the value chain to higher-value-added jobs, creating scarcity at the bottom of the labor pool. This trend will spur further innovation in automation, especially in robotics, where new high-tech assembly-line miracles seem to occur every day.

Of course, the problems of scarcity that absorb—the pocket-book—have to do with natural resources, especially the raw material that provides the energy we use every minute of every day. Looking at the energy challenge, Daniel Yergin points out that rising prices, increasing demand, and supply worries "are stimulating the most widespread drive for technological innovation this sector has ever seen." OPEC's current target range—$50 to $55 a barrel—is double the price band of just a few years ago, and the cartel's revenue has tripled over the past four years, from $199 billion in 2002 to $600 billion in 2006.

Consequently, writes Yergin, "there is a bubbling and brewing of technological innovation along the entire energy spectrum—from conventional supplies and renewables and alternatives, to efficiency and demand management." Renewables like solar and wind, alternatives like biomass and natural gas in place of diesel power—all are coming in to their own, thanks to a potent combination of government mandate and private investment. Yergin reports that venture capital investment in energy reached $1.7 billion in the first three quarters of 2006, almost five times what it was in the same period in 2004. Ironically, the boom has led to a shortage of turbines and blades for windmills.[26]

Then there's water, perhaps the most precious of all natural resources, where the problem of scarcity is compounded by that of contamination, and where the need for innovative thinking is critical. The good news is that in all these areas Chindia's—and the world's—scientists and engineers are responding. Let's look at a few examples.

Solar Power

At the beginning of the chapter we told the story of Suntech Power. But China's insatiable need for electricity, along with the host of environmental problems associated with producing electricity from coal, has spurred plenty of competition for Dr. Zhengrong company. Trina Solar Limited became the second Chinese solar energy firm to have its shares traded on the NYSE, raising $98 million with the initial offering. LDK Solar Hi-Tech Co., with a Nada listing planned for 2007, aims to become a world-class supplier of high quality multi-crystalline solar wafers. Already it considers itself the fastest-growing player in China's photovoltaic industry.

In Xi'an, the capital of the northwestern Shaanxi Province, BP announced in late 2006 that it would invest "many million dollars" to quadruple the current capacity of its solar energy joint venture there. BP Sunoasis Co., a partnership between BP and Xinjiang Sunoasis, plans to up production from 25 megawatts to 100 megawatts by 2010, according to Mark Twidell, regional director of BP Solar's Australian and Asian business. The company manufactures both panels and panel automation equipment for the use of solar power generation. The venture "represents a strategic move by BP Solar to bet on China's booming new energy market," says Twidell.[27]

The poor in rural China probably don't care much about the IPOs, but they're the benefactors of innovative technology these companies produce.

Solar energy is bringing the unheard-of idea of regular hot bathing to the provinces. For a fee of one yuan (12.5 cents) per head (or 1.5 yuan in winter), more than 1000 villagers can bathe in the solar bathhouse in Zhuangke village in Dezhou city, in east China's Shangdong province. In all, more than 100 solar bathhouses have been established in and around Dezhou. Solar energy experts report that more than 150 million Chinese people are now using solar energy water heaters, over an area of 75 million square meters. That area is increasing by 15 million square meters a year.

Meanwhile, in India the traffic lights are going solar. Eight states have applied to the Ministry of Non-conventional Energy Sources (MNES) for subsidies to install the solar-powered signals, all part of a national energy policy that is pushing the use of renewable energy sources. Once the subsidies come through, the work will be contracted out to companies in India's fast-growing solar sectors like Luminelle, Bharat Electronics, and Tata BP Solar. As of late 2006, the state of Karnataka was leading the way with a total of 160 solarized traffic lights.

Why focus on the traffic lights? To avoid the nerve-wracking traffic snarls that result from the frequent blackouts caused by India's woeful electricity infrastructure. Indeed, India's chronic power shortages make the nation an ideal market for solar energy—which explains why California-based SolFocus is delighted by its deal with Indian optics giant Moser Baer to build a production facility in India and distribute its products there. When skeptics point out that the price of solar can't yet compete with national electricity grids, SolFocus's founder, Gary Conley, points out that when the grid goes out, companies have to fall back on diesel electric generation. "Compared to diesel electric," he says, "our systems are quite attractive."

Conley also likes India because the nation as a whole gets 50 percent more direct sunlight than California, which is already one of the world's leading solar markets. Entire villages can be powered "from just a few small arrays," he notes, and solar-powering those villages is finally cheaper and more practical than extending the existing grid to far-flung locations. Conley is also encouraged by a report from the European Photovoltaic Industry Association predicting that 40 gigawatts of solar capacity will be installed in developing nations by 2020, bringing electric power to some 950 million new customers.[28]

As for Moser Baer, its solar-focused subsidiary, Moser Baer Photo Voltaic Ltd. (MBPV), has bought equity stakes in two other high-tech

California firms also—Solaria and Stion—as it pursues its strategy of taking over the tech leadership in the fast-growing PV industry and positioning itself as a major provider of solar photovoltaic power. As MBPV CEO Ravi Khanna explains, the investments are "in line with our strategy to reduce the cost of solar power generation significantly . . . and emerge as an engineering and technology driven company. We are decisively responding to the rapidly expanding solar PV market, where worldwide demand far outstrips supply."[29] In plainer language, what we have is a company on the cutting edge of innovation bringing electric power to places it's never been before.

India's "Wind Man"

Like sunlight, wind power is another alternative energy source attracting the attention of Chindia's scientists and entrepreneurs.

Until the mid-1990s, Tulsi Tanti and his brothers ran a textile manufacturing business in Gujarat, in northwestern India, but rising energy prices and undependable supply led them to investigate the possibility of running their factory on wind power. He quickly decided that manufacturing power was a more promising business than manufacturing textiles. In 10 years' time, Tanti has built his company, Suzlon, into the largest manufacturer and developer of wind turbines and wind farms in Asia, and the fifth-largest worldwide. When the company went public in 2005, the run-up of its share price on the Bombay Stock Exchange pushed Tanti's personal net worth to $3.7 billion, making him India's eighth-richest man. The company is now expanding into Eastern Europe, China, Australia, and North America, but India's domestic market itself is substantial.

The nation currently generates about 120,000 megawatts of power, which is about 10 percent less than it needs during periods of peak demand. What's more, experts predict that over the next five years an additional 100,000 megawatts will be required. Those figures are an invitation to Tanti. "We want to fill up the gap in the current energy deficit," he says.

Still, wind power remains more expensive than electricity from coal-fired plants, so Tanti's real innovation is in his business plan. For example, some customers, like motorcycle maker Bajaj Auto, invest in Suzlon wind farms. In return they get a break in their energy prices over the 20-year life of the turbines, and are also excluded from scheduled weekly power cuts because of their contribution to the electricity grid.

More generally, rather than simply selling electricity to its customers, Suzlon offers them "end-to-end" wind power service. It not only manufactures all the components for its turbines, it also develops the wind farm sites and operates them for its customers—usually industrial companies or investors. Tanti calls it "single-window shopping." The customers "invest, they get their energy, and they get their money. It's a good business model."

And while he looks at "high-growth" countries for expansion, he's busy constructing a giant 1,000-megawatt project in the state of Maharashtra, which he describes as "the single largest wind park in the world." Former Indian President Abdul Kalam wanted wind to supply 16 percent of India's electric power by 2030, and Tanti likes where his company is positioned. "It's a good beginning," he says.[30]

Other Renewables

China too hopes to harness the power of the wind. Wind turbine installations on the Mainland grew by 65 percent in 2005—compared to 48 percent in India. At the same time, it should be noted, China accounted for 79 percent of the world's growth in coal consumption, with predictable consequences in terms of CO_2 emissions, acid rain, and respiratory ailments. Responding to the plague of coal consumption, China's government has officially required that power companies generate at least 20 percent of their electricity from renewable resources by 2020.

That's why, in addition to solar and wind power, China is also steadily increasing the generation of power from bio-fuels like marsh gas. In north China's Hebei Province, for example, the use of marsh gas, combined with solar and wind, is cutting standard coal use by approximately 10 million tons each year. Nearly 153,000 marsh gas stations using crop stalks as raw material have already been erected to help meet Hebei's 600,000 farmers' domestic power needs.

Looking at the big picture, in October 2006 the National Development and Reform Commission (NDRC), China's top economic planner, released its latest targets for renewable energy production: renewables are to constitute 16 percent of total energy use by 2020, compared to 7.5 percent now. The government plans an investment of $187 billion in the sector, to be used to construct hydroelectric dams, wind farms, and bio-fuel factories. Also, a special fund will be directed toward renewable R&D, backed up by favorable tax policies. These policies, says Ye Dong, CEO of China Environment Fund, "will mean huge growth prospects for enterprises in the renewable energy sector." According to China Venture Capital Research Institute, a Shenzhen-based research firm, 33 percent of 126 venture capital funds it surveyed in April 2006 said the renewable energy sector would be the most promising investment area in the coming two years, replacing biotech and the Internet.[31]

Then there are the "clean alternatives," like dimethyl ether (DME), which are also attracting the attention of innovators and the interest of investors. A gas under normal pressure and temperature, DME can be compressed into a liquid and used as an alternative to diesel, as well as a blendstock (sub-octane gasoline that is intended to be blended with an oxygenate) for liquefied petroleum gas (LPG) or liquefied natural gas (LNG). Its low emissions make it an increasingly promising alternative fuel, and experts predict that DME may eventually replace a significant amount of petroleum in the Chinese economy. Shanghai Municipality opened the first DME-fuelled bus line in 2006 and announced plans to operate 1,000 such vehicles before the World Expo in 2010.

As for that investment opportunity, China Energy, China's biggest DME producer, sees the alternative fuel as its main growth driver, and has therefore been increasing production exponentially: from 50,000 mtpa (metric tons per annum) in 2004, to 150,000 in 2006, to 600,000 mtpa during first half of 2007. The ramp-up comes in conjunction with a successful IPO in late 2006—at which the sale of 248 million shares netted the company $171 million.[32]

The Water Crisis

While the need to discover alternative sources of energy is certainly spurring Chindian innovation, finding solutions to Chindia's water problems are providing the paramount challenge.

The situation is particularly severe in China, where in recent years chronic water shortages and chemical spills have even stirred public unrest and caused riots in various parts of the country. "The nation faces the toughest challenge in the world over water resources, which on the whole are polluted," Vice Minister of Construction Qiu Baoxing told the 5th World Water Congress, held in Beijing in September 2006. Some 20 billion tons of industrial and residential wastewater is released into rivers and lakes annually in China's cities, and 90 percent of the urban sections of rivers are polluted. In 2006 the government pledged to spend $125 billion to improve water quality and build sewage treatment systems, but the nation knows it needs help.

Enter Hyflux, from Singapore, a world leader in water use innovation. Proprietor of a reverse-osmosis technology that produces drinking water from the sea, Hyflux is building a desalination plant in the city of Tianjin, in Bohai Bay. And in the western province of Ningxia, Hyflux is developing another project, which uses a membrane-based technology to produce clean water from treated wastewater. Indeed, Hyflux is one of the companies that have made Singapore world-famous for its ability to manage its meager resources by recycling wastewater and desalinating seawater. And China, where urbanization and industrialization have increased demand for clean water even as those same forces have polluted fresh water supplies, is desperately in need of such innovative technologies.[33]

Additional help is on the way from Canada, where water treatment company Zenon has also developed a membrane technology that makes water reusable. The 2003 winner of the Stockholm Industry Water Award, Zenon, according to CEO Andrew Benedek, has been recycling wastewater for reuse for the last decade and claims the title of "technology leader for water reuse."

The company is working on two projects in China. One is in the coal-mining city of Datong, in Shanxi Province near Inner Mongolia, where 40 percent of China's coal is produced, but which faces critical shortages of groundwater and surface water. In the newly constructed power plant there, Zenon's "ZeeWeed" membranes are treating municipal wastewater for a second use as "cooling tower make-up water" and "boiler feed water". The other client is Beijing Yanshan Petrochemical Co. Ltd., located in the water-hungry capital. In the case of the latter, membrane technology is being used to produce a high-quality effluent that can be reused as "process water" and "boiler feed water", thus adding to the chemical company's water supply and drastically reducing its discharge costs.[34]

We can bet that China's scientists will be quick to adopt and build upon such technologies, but in the meantime there's plenty of home-grown innovation going on in Beijing, where the water situation is especially dire. In the past 15 years, the municipal government has raised water prices nine times, and the current price—46 cents per ton—is 30 times what it was in 1991. The city exists in a state of constant shortage; according to the municipal water authority, each Beijinger has access to less than 300 cubic meters of water a year, one-eighth the national average and one-thirtieth the world average. A five-year drought hasn't helped. For 2006 alone, the city was short by 794 million cubic meters.

Beijing is trying to respond with a combination of regulation and innovation. New factories are now required to install water-recycling facilities, hotels are converting to water-conserving shower heads and toilets, and car washes must use recycled water. By 2010, all businesses and 90 percent of families will be engaged in the city's water-saving regimen.

The upgrades are costly, but today's pain is tomorrow's gain. For example, the Swiss Hotel in Beijing spent $250,000 to switch out all its bathroom hardware and install water recycling devices. Discarded water from the air-conditioning system, baths, dry cleaning and boilers in the hotel is now collected, cleaned, and recycled to flush toilets and water lawns. As a result, the hotel's water use dropped from 316,000 tons in 1994 to 170,000 tons in 2005, a decrease of 40 percent. As a hotel spokesman noted, "On one hand, we are responding to the government's call for energy conservation. On the other hand, it is also in the interests of the hotel itself."

Yuan Lisong, an enterprising carwash owner, notes that recycling allows one ton of water to wash 15 cars, compared to only 4 cars if the water is not reused. Moreover, Yuan has gone the next step: he has invested $125,000 to open four carwashes that collect rain water to wash cars. The rainwater is stored in tanks and filtered before use, a process that costs only 12 cents per ton. Moreover, the used water is collected and recycled. Yang Guichun, a Beijing retiree who collects rainwater for watering flowers, mopping floors and washing clothes, captures the new spirit of resource awareness: "Energy conservation is both wise and a duty," says Yang.[35]

Innovations in water use are also getting the attention of China's farmers. For instance, in Xinjiang's Uygur Autonomous Region, "drip irrigation under plastic film technology"—is saving both water and manpower. A 20-acre cotton field can be irrigated with just two-thirds of the water needed in traditional irrigation. Increasingly in use for the past several years, drip irrigation is already saving more than 600 million cubic meters of water every year.

Such innovations are all the more important because China's farms account for more than two-thirds of the nation's consumption of water. Most of this agricultural use is for irrigation, but the problem is that 55 percent of irrigation water is wasted, twice the rate of most developed nations. Here's where the new technologies add value. Drip irrigation and similar innovations that prevent waste from run-off are now in use on more than 6 million acres of Chinese farmland.

How rapidly that figure grows depends to a large extent on the government. Because water is cheap and farmers are poor, they are reluctant to pay for the new technologies themselves. Moreover, the government can see much more clearly than the poor farmer the potential uses of conserved water: it can be diverted to households and industrial uses; it can be used to irrigate additional farmland and thus increase grain yields and ensure food security; and it can increase the amount of water in downstream water courses, thus preserving ecologically sensitive desert areas. More generally, such conservation promotes sustainable development, the government's current mantra. Presently, the government invests 2 billion yuan annually on water efficiency. With China's prosperity in the balance, we can expect that figure to increase dramatically.[36]

India faces the same problems, aggravated by poverty. For struggling farmers, water is too scarce; for the poor everywhere, it is too dirty. Anji Reddy (of Dr. Reddy's Laboratories), who has been on what he calls a "crusade" to solve India's water problems, is convinced that innovation has already supplied the answers—if those answers can be adopted by the communities rather than imposed by the government.

The solution for farmers, he writes, is Lift Irrigation, which was brought by the government to farming regions in Andhra Pradesh. But when the machines wore out or broke down, there was no cohesive community or State action to get them running again, and the farmers fell back upon the ruinously expensive option of borewells. The exception, says Reddy, was in the village of Korampally, where, with the help of the Naandi Foundation, the farmers took over the irrigation project themselves. They ran the installations "more as professional business units—with water management, distribution, utilization, and cess guidelines—and less as Government handouts" and in the process tripled their incomes.

As for water sanitation, Reddy believes that the government is again the problem rather than the solution. "Water is every political party's favourite flogging horse during elections," he writes; "I do not see [the problem] being solved in a hurry." Yet the innovative technology is already available, thanks to the pioneering work of Indian scientist Dr. Ashok Gadgil, who works with the Lawrence Berkeley National Laboratory at the University of California-Berkeley. Dr. Gadgil created UV Waterworks, which Reddy describes as "a low-cost water-purifying model guaranteed to destroy pathogens and bring good health back to families at less than 5 paise a liter"—and which won for Dr. Ashok the Discover Award of 1996, for the most significant environmental invention of the year.

"Once such innovations become the property of communities, once solutions are brought down to the village level," says Reddy, "I will have had a successful crusade. There will be no war for water because India will have enough."[37]

The Environmental Challenge

China and India don't have the luxury that was afforded to the West during the 19th and early 20th centuries. For two hundred years Europe and the United States proceeded on the assumption that they could "industrialize now and clean up later." For Chindia, after just 20 years that option has been exhausted. The world's ecological conscience has been awakened, and, these days, no environmental damage goes overlooked.

Even more compelling than international censure, however, is Chindia's own enlightened self-interest. China and India realize that the environmental issue—that is, both environmental degradation and global protest against that degradation—could become the "the show-stopper" that disrupts worldwide economic growth, including their own. I can discern four developments that, in confluence, could threaten to bring the curtain down on Chindia's march to prosperity.

The first is the unfettered industrial growth that continues to produce spectacular technological breakthroughs—in medicine, in aerospace, in weaponry—even as the world becomes increasingly worried about the environmental consequences of such advancing technologies. America's rise to dominance has abetted the industrial juggernaut and has set a perhaps dubious example for the rest of the world. The United States produces and consumes a disproportionate share of the world's manufactured goods, while at the same time resisting pressures to slow down, to take the earth's temperature, or to sign earth-friendly treaties (like the Kyoto Protocol) that might be burdensome to its global corporations. The crux of the problem is that we don't fully know the range of side-effects of global industrialization—the effects of, say, agricultural chemicals or nuclear waste—on essential elements of life like air and water. When we do ascertain those side-effects, and if they are as severe as some would have us believe, then there will be enormous pressure to shut down the engines of economic growth.

Along with industrialization has come increasing global inter-dependence—another mixed blessing. Trade drives economic growth, and liberalizing trade policies produce an ever freer flow of products, people, money, and information. Don't get me wrong: trade is good. But the rising tide that lifts all boats gives more nations and more people a stake in the industrial enterprise. The same is true of the economic pragmatism through which nations find common ground and mutual interests. Dollar diplomacy is certainly an improvement over gunboat diplomacy. But although free-market philosophy may well be a force for peace, historically it has not had much of an environmental conscience.

The third development comes as an inevitable response to the first two: the anti-globalization movement gaining force around the world. Wherever the world's industrial powers convene these days, whether it's the G-8 or the WTO, mass demonstrations take place in the streets. Protesters are marching against global warming caused by industrial smokestacks, against the noxious influence of the West's consumption society on the developing world, against trade policies that encourage economic and industrial growth at the expense of workers and the environment, against the marginalization of voices and institutions that question what they see as a global corporatocracy. As the debate over environmental policy intensifies, it's getting harder to dismiss protesters as leftist kooks.

The fourth development is the subject of this book: the rise of Chindia. I have repeatedly emphasized that the rise of Chindia represents the emergence and convergence of the world's two largest consumer markets, and I've discussed in detail the race for global resources that will necessarily follow. But can we even begin to predict the environmental consequences?

These four developments, as I see it, are pushing toward a climax. Is it an either-or proposition? Either economic growth and prosperity, or environmental health? No, we can have both, but it will take a combination of political and social will, individual and collective sacrifice, and incisive, innovative thinking. China and India have lagged, but that must change. They will have to lead the developing world toward the goal of sustainable development. They will have to be equal partners with the West in a broad program for environmental protection that includes positive action in three key areas: consumption, production, and policy enforcement. Let's look quickly at all three.

Smart Consumption

Part of the problem is that we consume too much. A greater part of the problem is that we consume unwisely; we consume the wrong things.

Consumption seems to race ahead of awareness. We demand products that appear to make our lives easier or happier, and scientists come along afterward, slapping on warning labels and cleaning up the mess. The good side is that with knowledge comes innovation and improvement. Think of how long we burned leaded gasoline.

But we must make smarter choices and—with or without the help of government agencies. One answer here is the global boycott. It has worked with cigarettes, which turn out to harm not only the smoker, but, in the form of second-hand smoke, anyone in the smoker's vicinity. Mandatory smoke-free environments (including public facilities in entire cities) have become so prevalent that tobacco companies have had to diversify in order to stay alive. Pesticides like DDT were also effectively boycotted and banned but were subsequently reversed for malaria control.

Now an interesting scenario is developing with regard to genetically modified (GM) foods. In India, several large farmers associations are urging the boycott of Bt brinjal, the nation's first GM food crop. After staging a demonstration in Chennai, the farm leaders presented a petition to Prime Minister Manmohan Singh demanding a total ban on open-air, large-scale field trials of GM foods. In addition to the bio-safety issues, the farmers argued that GM technology was unsuited to an agricultural economy like India's where 80 percent of farmers are small and marginal. On the other side of the debate are Monsanto (which owns the patent on the Bt bacterial gene) and its Indian subsidiary Mahyco, which are pressuring the Genetic Engineering Approval Committee (GEAC) to allow trials to continue.[38] Meanwhile, the European Union continues to resist trade deals with the United States that would allow for the import of GM foods and hormone-laced beef.

Whichever way this particular issue is settled, it's clear that people across nations can be mobilized to take action on behalf of environmental health. Consider Earth Day, April 22, which not only has formal U.N. sanction but is now celebrated by 500 million people and 175 governments.

A second way to encourage smart consumption is to impose economic disincentives. Merely asking people to cooperate in conservation efforts doesn't seem to work. We all remember when President Carter put on his cardigan and asked everyone to turn down their thermostats. Since nobody will volunteer to pay more for products or services than they already do, here is where governments need to force change. As Europe has shown, when taxes are added to gasoline, consumers respond. The streets of Europe are full of cars that look to be half or a third the size of American sedans and SUVs. Meanwhile, the added tax revenues can be earmarked for environmental innovation like hydrogen fuel-cell technology. Similarly, increased taxes or surcharges could be levied upon industries—or even communities—based on the volume of waste they fail to recycle. As we've seen, new recycling technologies are coming to market every day that make waste water reusable, and the same goes for paper, metals, plastics, and a host of other industrial goods. Big fines for big hazards, like nuclear waste, will discourage dependence on such technologies while encouraging innovative alternatives.

Yet a third way to reform consumption is to move in the direction of a post-industrial consumption model. Progress along this path is already rapid, as we see in the on-line shopping phenomenon. Of course, consumers are still buying things—often too many things—but the on-line model conserves vast transportation resources that would have been consumed in brick-and-mortar shopping. The vision of deserted stores or empty mall parking lots may seem emblematic of economic decline, but it's not. It's all part of the natural evolution from a manufacturing/industrial economy to a knowledge economy. Here is where we need to reinvent our own lives as we live them every day: shop at home, work at home, swap your car for a bicycle. This is the post-industrial model of smart, sustainable consumption.

Smart Production

Again, it's not just that we produce too much; in our pursuit of industrial progress we have produced many of the wrong things. Some, like asbestos, we have already stopped producing. Because of its effectiveness as a fire-retardant, it seemed like a good idea at the time. But then we discovered that breathing asbestos fibers could cause mesothelioma and lung cancer, and production was banned in 1978 (though installers were allowed to use up their inventories until 1986). Some people, especially asbestos producers, argued against the ban, saying the cure was worse than the disease, but the ban spurred innovation. There are now fire-retardants that use organic fibers instead of asbestos, and a team from Brookhaven National Lab and W. R. Grace & Co. has developed a foam that can remove the asbestos from a wall or ceiling while preserving its fireproof capabilities. This award-winning innovation eliminates the considerable expense of tearing out walls or ceilings in which asbestos has been mixed with cement or other building material.

What happened in the case of asbestos needs to happen elsewhere. As harmful materials and products are phased out of production, alternatives must be developed. As we noted earlier in this chapter, tremendous innovation is now taking place in the energy sector—in solar, wind, biofuel, and other power sources. But at the same time both China and India are embarking on huge nuclear power programs, despite the fact that there is as yet no safe disposal method for radioactive waste. There's a challenging project for tomorrow's scientists and engineers.

In other areas, environmentally unfriendly production can be reduced or curtailed by innovative approaches to production strategies. Organic farmers, for example, know that our foods do not have to be chemically protected or genetically modified. Right now their food is more expensive to produce, but prices would go down if organic farms could enjoy economies of scale. This means more land converted from conventional to organic production, a path Europe and Scandinavia have been following for two decades. There, farmers are granted generous subsidies to convert to organic production, money that keeps them in business during the complicated process of soil reconstitution. Now America may be getting the message. The 2006 farm bill (which spends $87 billion over the next five years) earmarked more money than ever to organic production, particularly to California's specialty crops like vegetables, fruits, and wine grapes. Moreover, rapidly growing consumer demand for organic may have the same effect. In 2006, Wal-Mart announced that it would begin selling organic produce for 10 percent above the cost of conventional food, a move that will surely increase the amount of acreage devoted to organic farming.

Then there's Whole Foods, which recognized the genius in bringing the supermarket concept to organic food retailing. Specializing in foods that are free of pesticides, preservatives and sweeteners, CEO John Mackey has built the world's largest natural foods chain. Himself a vegan, Mackey has helped transform what used to be a niche—natural and organic foods—into the fastest-growing segment of the grocery business. With close to 200 stores that need to be supplied, Whole Foods is certainly adding to the pressure to make organic farming scalable. Plus, Whole Foods' effort to stock its shelves with local produce illustrates another element of smart production.

How to curtail harmful production, and encourage smart production will provide one of the fascinating challenges of the 21st century; meeting that challenge will require a new mindset, a new leadership culture. We can see the new culture emerging in leaders like John Mackey, who not only redefined organic food retailing but, in the face of rising competition and dropping share price, cut his annual salary to $1. We see the new culture in initiatives like GE's "ecoimagination" project, which began in 2005 when the company hired consulting firm GreenOrder to conduct an environmental analysis of a range of its products from appliances to building materials. Products that meet GreenOrder's high standards qualify for the GE's ecoimagination stamp of approval.

Smart Policy

Environmental policy can be encouraged, and encouragement can sometimes be effective. A good example is public-private partnerships dedicated to conservation programs. We've seen governments successfully partner with corporations, or even individuals, on land preservation deals, for instance. On a large scale, the national government and forest products companies have worked together to add to the acreage of protected national forests. On a smaller scale, local governments are offering to work with landowners to protect their property in perpetuity from development. Non-governmental organizations (NGOs) are also great vehicles for showing the way to environmental consciousness. Philanthropic trusts and foundations—the Rockefeller Foundation, the Ford Foundation, Ted Turner's Better World Foundation, Ben & Jerry's Social Mission, and Google.org, to name just a few—are donating millions and even billions of dollars to environmental causes. At the same time, literally dozens of environmental non-profits lobby governments for greater preservation efforts and stricter pollution guidelines. All these efforts are laudable. It may even be true, as Gary Wockner (somewhat facetiously) writes in the Denver Post, that "Billionaire philanthropy is the only thing that can save the Earth."[39]

My own belief, though, is that we need smart policy, and we need enforcement, from the top down. China perfectly illustrates the difference between conventional policy and smart policy. Grasping the gravity of the environmental situation, the nation is now revising its environmental laws to maximize the efficient use of resources, minimize waste, and curb pollution. The difference between the old laws and the new (smart) laws is that the new has teeth. Under the old system, pollution penalties were capped at 200,000 yuan ($25,000), so many businesses found it cheaper to pay the fine and keep polluting than to retrofit and comply. Under the new law, polluters will be fined daily until the problem is fixed. Mao Rubai, chairman of the Environmental and Resources Protection Committee, articulates the growing spirit of enforcement: "The penalty should be calculated from the day that factory is found guilty of pollution discharge until the day its emissions meet environmental protection requirements."[40] And of course, policy enforcement spurs innovation like the "scrubbers" that dramatically cut the pollution from coal-burning smokestacks.

China's initiative is good. Even better (because 27 nations are involved rather than just one) is the new initiative from the European Union. Issuing a challenge to the United States, India, and China, German chancellor Angela Merkel announced the EU's commitment to reduce greenhouse gas emissions by 20 percent from the 1990 level, by the year 2020. Going further, she said the EU would commit to a 30 percent reduction if other nations would follow suit. The "groundbreaking" deal, said Tony Blair, "gives Europe a clear leadership position on this crucial issue facing the world." EU lawyers would be responsible for drawing up the rules for compliance and the penalties for noncompliance, but the bloc's officials said they were prepared to levy the ultimate sanction: "prosecution at the European Court of Justice and the imposition of heavy fines."[41]

Now, let's go global. How about UNEDO (United Nations Environmental Development Organization) instead of—or along with—UNIDO (United Nations Industrial Development Organization)? How about a global environmental organization along the lines of the International Labor Organization? How about global compliance standards? Indeed, the time is right for a global compliance network, and the technology is certainly available. If Interpol can fight international crime, then Inter-EPA should be able to track international crime against the environment. What's needed is a non-aligned, politically neutral, global oversight body. Call it GEHO: the Global Environmental Health Organization. The EU is showing the way. If its 27 members can agree on an emissions-reduction document, there's no reason other nations can't join in. Nobody doubts the urgency of the issue.

To reiterate, in the absence of decisive action now, the continued expansion of the global economy, and the rise of Chindia in particular, will be threatened by environmental instability. Meeting the environmental challenge calls for a three-point program that includes

- smart consumption—through global boycotts, economic disincentives, and the adoption of a post-industrial model of consumption;

- smart production—through phasing out harmful materials and products, encouraging innovative alternatives, and injecting a new leadership culture; and

- smart policy—through public-private partnerships, strict government oversight and regulation of environmental guideline, and the creation of a global compliance network.

This three-part strategy adds up to a holistic solution to a complex problem. Nothing less is needed. The stakes could not be higher.

In Conclusion

China and India launched their economic take-off as low-cost producers of service products and manufactured goods. The launch proved phenomenally successful and propelled the kind of growth that made the rest of the world, especially the West, sit up and take notice. What Chindia has now learned is that growth on that platform is ultimately not sustainable, and the time is right to take on the next challenge: to become producers of knowledge.

The evolution is well underway, and Chindia is steadily advancing toward its place as Asia's bulwark, and the West's equal in global economic power, reach, and influence. How soon the evolution arrives depends on its response to the innovation imperative. Can it make the necessary goods and services affordable and accessible to consumers at the bottom of the pyramid? Can it invent and create new technologies to overcome the scarcity and shortages that are bound to threaten its people and resources? And, perhaps most important, can it commit to the kind of smart consumption, smart production, and smart policy that will allow for continued growth without disastrously compromising the environment?

We know this much: A vast army of Chindian scientists, engineers, and entrepreneurs will be working hard to answer those questions in the affirmative.

Notes

1. Batson, Andrew "Rising Son: For Chinese Tycoon, Solar Power Fuels Overnight Wealth," *Wa l Street Journal*, Nov 12, 2006, p. A1.
2. Friedman, Thomas "China's Sunshine Boys," *New York Times*, Dec 6, 2006, p. 29.
3. "Suntech CEO Receives CCTV's Top 10 Entrepreneurs Award," *PR Newswire*, Jan 22, 2007.

4. Chin, Koh Lay, "Pioneering Spirit of a Drugmaker," *New Straits Times*, Dec 9, 2003, p. 7.

5. Merchant, Khozem, "Drugs Innovation Is Just What the Doctor Ordered," *Financial Times*, Jun 7, 2002, p. 28.

6. Singh, Abhay and Mrinalini Datta, "Indian Drug Maker Struggles in Move from Copycat to Originator," *International Herald Tribune*, Dec 6, 2006, p. 18.

7. Singh, Abhay and Mrinalini Datta, "Indian Drug Maker Innovates in Diabetes Trials," *International Herald Tribune*, Sep 27, 2006, p. 24.

8. Engardio, Pete ed., *Chindia: How China and India Are Revolutionizing Global Business*, New York: McGraw-Hill, 2007, pp. 240, 253.

9. Engardio, pp. 255–256, 258.

10. "China Education Alliance Announces a 5,920% Increase in Revenue," *PR Newswire*, May 23, 2006.

11. "Tata Interactive Systems," *M2 Presswire*, Aug 15, 2006, p. 1.

12. "Shanghai Trial Run Lifts 4G Hopes," *The Standard*, Jan 30, 2007.

13. "IBM, ISB Launch Major Services Initiative in India," *Hindustan Times*, Feb 7, 2007.

14. Wolfe, Josh, "Nanotech Gets Big in China," Forbes.com, Feb, 1, 2007.

15. Mahapatra, Rajesh (for AP), "U.S. Aeronautic Firms Court India," *Atlanta Journal-Constitution*, Feb 6, 2004, p. D3.

16. Prahalad, C. K., *The Fortune at the Bottom of the Pyramid: Eradicating Poverty Through Profits* (Upper Saddle River, N.J.: Wharton School Publishing, 2006), pp. 4, 17, 15.

17. Simons, Craig and Dan Zehr, "Dell Tries to Win Over Chinese with Scaled-down PCs," *Atlanta Journal-Constitution*, Mar 22, 2007, p. C1.

18. Kadama, Fumio, "Technology Fusion and the New R&D," *Harvard Business Review*, Jul/Aug 1992, pp. 70–78.

19. Lakshman, Nandini, "Indian Banks Are Big on Microfinance," *Business Week Online*, Aug 23, 2006.

20. Smith, David, "Financial Seed Corn Grows into a World Poverty Beater," *Sunday Times*, Dec 24, 2006, p. 7.

21. Mahajan, Vijay and Kamini Banga, *The 86% Solution: How to Succeed in the Biggest Market Opportunity of the 21st Century* (Upper Saddle River, N.J.: Wharton School Publishing, 2006), p. 115–118.

22. Mahajan and Banga, pp. 126–127.

23. Engardio, p. 91–92.

24. Prahalad, pp. 213–219.

25. Prakash, B. S., "India As a Hub for Innovation?" *The Hindu*, Feb 2, 2007.

26. Yergin, Daniel, "A Great Bubbling," *Newsweek*, Dec 18, 2006.

27. BP to Quadruple Capacity of Xi'an Solar Energy Facility," *Financial Times Information / Global News Wire*, Oct 19, 2006.

28. Krauss, Leah, "Solar World: SolFocus Looks to India," *UPI Energy*, Oct 12, 2006.

29. "Moser Baer Photo Voltaic Invests in Stion Corporation in California," *Hindustan Times*, Nov 16, 2006.

30. Kirby, Jason, "Where Business Is a Breeze," *National Post / Financial Post*, Sep 27, 2006, p. FP8.

31. "Venture Capital Firms Search for Next Suntech," *Financial Times Information / Global News Wire*, Nov 20, 2006.

32. Gan, Audrina, "China Energy Launches IPO in Singapore," *The Edge* (Singapore), Dec 18, 2006.

33. Bezlova, Antoaneta, "Beijing Turns to Singapore to Help Solve Its Water Crisis," *Inter Press Service / Global Information Network*, Sep 21, 2006

34. "Chinese Market Responding to Growing Need for Water Reuse," *PR Newswire*, Nov 11, 2003, p. 1.

35. Dingding, Xin, "Water Conservation Helps Stop Money Going Down the Drain," *China Daily*, Sep 12, 2006, p. 1.

36. "Saving More Water from China's Agriculture," *Financial Times Information / Global News Wire*, Nov 13, 2006.

37. Reddy, K. Anji, "The War for Water," *The Hindu*, Sep 11, 2004, p. 1.

38. "Manmohan Urged to Ban Field Trials," *The Hindu*, Jul 11, 2006, p. 1.

39. Wockner, Gary, "Can Billionaires Save the Earth?" *Denver Post*, Jun 5, 2005, p. E4.

40. Xiaohua, Sun, "Laws Tighten Screws on Polluters," *China Daily*, Mar 8, 2007, p. 7.

41. Bilefsky, Dan, "Europe Sets Ambitious Limits on Greenhouse Gases," *New York Times*, Mar 10, 2007, p. A5.

4

Chindian Hegemony: Economic Power, Geopolitical Clout and Cultural Diffusion

Of course, the rise of Chindia is not just a story about scientists, engineers, and entrepreneurs. Nor is it only about government and business leaders. Chindia's ascent is cultural as well, so the story also includes leaders in the arts and entertainment, in food and fashion, and in religion and philosophy. When we draw this broad, all-inclusive picture of Chindia on the rise, what are we looking at? Can we appropriate the term that has been exclusively applied by the West and call the phenomenon "Chindian hegemony"?

First, let's disassociate the word "hegemony" from some of the negative connotations that have attached to it. The hegemony of the West, basically unchallenged for five centuries, came to be bound up with conquest, colonialism, even slavery. The Western European civilization that pushed outward beginning in the late-15th century, implicitly, the doctrine of white supremacy. Consequently, the West's hegemony came to imply, in its relations with the rest of the world, arrogance, superiority and, indeed, racism.

Chindian hegemony won't be rooted in either conquest or pseudo-genetics, but rather in numbers. Yes, the word will still imply dominance, but dominance without the attitude. A few historical, economic, and demographic trends are converging—to Chindia's apparent advantage. I've mentioned them earlier, but a quick recap might be helpful. First, economic power continues to shift from governments to free markets, at the very time that China and India are beginning to tap the potential of the largest domestic consumer markets the world has ever seen. Second, Western nations—along with Japan—are aging, and their populations are in decline. Some analysts go so far as to say that Europe and Japan are "shutting down." Third, led by China and India, developing nations are experiencing the world's fastest rates of economic growth.

These numbers will translate into Chindia's emerging economic hegemony, and economic hegemony will be followed—as it was in the West—by growing geopolitical and cultural influence as well. But before we get to those implications, let's take a closer look at Chindia's economic power, specifically in three areas: international trade and business, the push for a pan-Asian currency, and the trade-off of markets for resources.

Economic Hegemony

International Trade and Business

It is impossible to overestimate the eagerness—even the anxiety—of Western corporations to grow their businesses in Chindia. Business at home is slowing down, sales are stabilizing, markets are saturated. But Chindia represents a veritable utopia: business is booming and its markets are insatiable. Multinational corporations must either ride this wave or be drowned by the competition. Of scores of examples that might be cited, let's look at a handful.

Starbucks opened its first store in tea-drinking China in 1999. Today there are about 200 stores on the Mainland and 430 in Greater China, employing some 4,000 people. But 200 stores in seven years is a snail's pace compared to what the company is planning. Martin Coles, president of Starbucks Coffee International, indicated in late 2006 that 20,000 international stores are on the drawing board and that half of those will be in Asia. Though he did not offer a country-by-country breakdown, he suggested that 100 new stores a year in China was a conservative estimate: "We see China as a strategic market for many years ahead." After all, China now has 660 cities with more than a half-million citizens, and Starbucks considers them all as potential sites for store locations.[1]

As an interesting aside, Starbucks ran into something of a pothole in busy Beijing. For six years the company had operated a small, intentionally inconspicuous store inside the Forbidden City, Beijing's vast imperial palace. Then in early 2007 Rui Chenggang, a news personality on China Central Television, wrote a blog entry suggesting that, as a sign of cultural respect, Starbucks should withdraw from the revered location. It seems that the Chinese, perhaps because they lack other means of free expression, have taken to the Web—especially in the case of the 20 million or so active bloggers. Consequently, Mr. Rui, though far from an extremist himself, incited such a storm of protest over Starbucks' "cultural aggression" that Starbucks opted to close down the location.

Despite setbacks / opposition, the juggernaut charges ahead, especially in big cities like the capital. In fact, to increase its control over its China operations and smooth the way for the planned expansion, Starbucks has been buying out its Asian partners like H&Q Asia Pacific, which had an investment in 62 outlets in Beijing and Tianjin. A similar buy-out is in the works in Shanghai. In the short term, Starbucks is not disclosing China sales or profits, but CFO Michael Casey has made it clear that the company is "willing to sustain losses" to pursue the vast growth opportunity that China represents.[2]

When IBM returned to India in 1992 after a 15-year hiatus, it returned with a vengeance. Local companies like Wipro, Infosys and Tata Consultancy Services had taken advantage of Big Blue's absence to grow into serious IT players, and IBM was determined to reassert itself. Since 2000 IBM India has gone off like a rocket. The company's Indian staff exploded from 9,000 at the end of 2003 to almost four times that number just two years later, and in the process it blew past Japan to become the company's second-largest operation, after the United States. Apparently, the company was just warming up. "What you have seen in the past five years is nothing compared to what you will see in the next five or 10," says Mats Agervi, vice-president for global delivery at IBM Global Services, India.

Part of the activity is a massive restructuring, and migration of the workforce to take fuller advantage of India's lower costs. For example, 14,000 service employees were let go in Western Europe, the United States, and Japan, while hiring proceeded apace in India and Eastern Europe. However, as I noted in another context, Chindia is moving upstream, and IBM India is leading the way. At its major research lab in Delhi, the company develops software and services for worldwide consumption, not just for local projects. For instance, engineers there created "e-Coupon" technology, which distributes electronic coupons to consumers and helps them manage and use them before they expire. In addition, IBM India has software labs in Bangalore and Pune, engineering R&D in Bangalore, and two brand-new data centers, one of which matches the capabilities of the company's III data center in Boulder, Colorado—absolutely state of the art.[3]

For calendar year 2006, VP Agervi's prediction was on target. IBM India reported 37 percent growth for the year and added another 10,000 employees to the payroll, bringing the total to 53,000. Its six straight years of double-digit growth makes IBM India the best-performing unit in all of IBM's worldwide operations. Considering past performance and future potential, maybe it's not surprising that at the end of 2006 IBM chairman Sam Palmisano announced plans to invest another $6 billion in India over the next three years.[4]

Wal-Mart can't afford to let the China opportunity slip from its grasp. Not only is the nation's economy growing 10 percent a year, the retail sector is growing even faster, with sales increasing about 15 percent a year. Back in the United States, meanwhile, growth has slowed, and same-store sales are lagging. As a Deutsche Bank Securities analyst puts it, "China is the only country in the world that offers Wal-Mart the chance to replicate what they have accomplished in the U.S." Of course, other multinational retailers, like England's Tesco and France's Carrefour (the international leader in China), are also fighting for market share, as are China's own major retailers like Lianhua. Not surprisingly then, Wal-Mart's progress has been slower than it hoped. After 10 years of operations on the Mainland, Wal-Mart has only about 70 stores up and running (compared to Carrefour's almost 200), and has not yet cracked the list of the nation's top 20 retailers.[5]

The solution? A major acquisition. In early 2007 came the announcement that Wal-Mart had paid close to $1 billion for 35 percent of Taiwan-owned Bounteous Company, which operates more than 100 retail outlets in China under the Trust-Mart brand. The 35 percent stake was sufficient to give Wal-Mart controlling interest in Bounteous and, more important, to immediately extend its reach into 34 Chinese cities. The Trust-Mart stores—so-called "hypermarkets" because they sell everything from groceries and clothing to home appliances—will almost double Wal-Mart's China payroll to approximately 65,000, and will also put Wal-Mart in position to challenge Carrefour as China's dominant foreign retailer. It's a critical foot in the door, according to George Svinos, KPMG's Asia retail expert. "You can see why Wal-Mart is looking to invest in a country that by 2015 could have the largest economy in the world."[6]

If one huge Asian consumer market is good for Wal-Mart, two are even better. At roughly the same time Wal-Mart's deal for Trust-Mart was announced, the company also reported a major initiative in India by means of a joint venture with Bharti Enterprises, the country's leading cellphone operator. With the help of Bharti's chairman, Sunil Mittal,

Wal-Mart found two loopholes to work around government regulations prohibiting foreign retailers from opening their own stores in India. First, foreigners are allowed to operate through franchisees, and second, they can invest their own capital in wholesale stores. Thus, the huge deal provides for "hundreds" of Wal-Mart branded retail stores—under Bharti ownership—to open across India beginning in 2007. It also marks the first significant penetration by a foreign retail giant of this heretofore well-protected consumer market. "It is the last and a very big frontier," Mittal told an interviewer at the World Economic Forum conference in New Delhi. "Brazil is done. China is done. This is the last Shangri-la of retail."[7]

If you're Nokia, the world's No. 1 maker of cell phones, you've got to love Chindia. Emerging markets—particularly those in China and India—account for roughly 1.6 billion cellphone subscribers. That's 59 percent of the global market, a percentage that's certain to keep on growing. Here's why: In the United States, cell phone saturation has reached 70 percent of the population; in Western Europe it's even higher. But only a third of the people in the developing world have cell phones, and in Chindia the percentage is much smaller still. Just 15 percent of Indians are mobile subscribers, but India has now become the fastest growing cell phone market in the world with 7 million new subscribers every month—compared to China's 5 million.

Nokia is right there. Its successful and innovative push into Chindia is a primary reason for its dominant 40 percent share of the global cell phone market. For Chinese consumers Nokia was the first to come through with a unit capable of both English and Chinese text recognition. Overall, its phones now offer user interfaces in about 80 different languages, including nine of the officially recognized languages of India. For customers who can't read, it offers features like an icon-based contact list and a speaking clock; for rural areas, its phones have dust-proof casings. For the poor, it is shaving margins to make phones affordable.

Looking at the Indian market specifically, Nokia opened a new $150 million manufacturing plant in Chennai in January 2006. It hired 550 people at start-up, expecting that number to rise to 2,000 by year's end. Instead, the plant's payroll shot up to 3,800 as demand from the Indian market—and other markets in Southeast Asia—continued to surge. Before 2006 was over, the new facility had produced 20 million handsets. "On every metric," says Jukka Lehtela, director of operations for Nokia India, "we have seen tremendous growth." Encouraged by this success, and abetted by government policy that allows telecom manufacturers 100 percent foreign direct investment, Nokia now plans a "special economic zone" near Chennai—a "Telecom Industry Park", that will attract component suppliers and service providers. While creating 20,000 jobs, the park will keep costs down and streamline service to this all-important market.[8]

Nokia's Chindian strategy appears to be working. In the last quarter of 2006, profit was up 19 percent, based largely on increasing sales in emerging markets. Sales increased 13 percent to $11.7 billion, and with a total of 106 million units sold, it exceeded the 100-million mark for the first time. Chief executive Olli-Pekka Kallasvuo predicted that continued growth in the developing world would bring the total number of cell phone subscribers to 4 billion by 2010—a rosy scenario indeed for the global leader.[9]

It's arguable that no multinational has conducted more business in China, over a longer period of time, than General Electric. CEO Jeff Immelt traveled to Beijing in May 2006 to mark the 100th anniversary of GE's presence in China. The number of GE enterprises on the Mainland, whether solely-funded or joint-venture, has now surpassed 30. Immelt took the opportunity to tell reporters in Beijing that GE would be expanding its research facility in Shanghai, which already employed 2,000 engineers, in order to develop the next line of power generation, and water filtration products. He also touted the launch of GE's "ecoimagination" program in China—an initiative designed to explore new environmental protection and energy-efficient technologies with Chinese businesses and research institutes. With his company's China revenues having hit $5 billion in 2006, Immelt declared, "We think business could double again in the next four or five years."[10]

Where will the growth come from? Some, certainly, from its Consumer Finance unit (GECF)—as illustrated by its 2005 Strategic Cooperation Agreement with Shenzhen Development Bank, China's first publicly traded bank. But where GE hopes to find unlimited growth in China is in the nation's vast infrastructure needs—in transportation and power and water. With the coming of the Summer Olympics to Beijing in 2008, the World Expo to Shanghai in 2010, and the Asian Games to Guangzhou that same year, some of these needs are immediate and critical. Beijing's plans to spend $40 billion in Olympics preparation—new stadiums, subways, and an airport terminal—provided GE the motive for ponying up $200 million to become an Olympic sponsor. More generally, China puts the price tag for the infrastructure improvements it needs by 2010—including airports, roads, water systems, and other public works—at a whopping

$400 billion. GE intends to enjoy a slice of that pie. It had already won more than $1 billion worth of Olympics-related projects as of mid-2006 and was bidding on 25 to 30 contracts a month. Nobody expects business to dry up after the games, either. "The Olympics effort is an opportunity for all of our businesses to create new relationships, expand on the ones we had, and take our effort in China to the next level," says GE Vice Chairman John Rice, who's in charge of the $42 billion infrastructure group.[11]

Indeed, GE is well positioned to capitalize on "what could be trillions spent in infrastructure in the developing countries in the coming years," observes Nicholas Heymann, a GE analyst with Prudential Equity Group. Heymann also predicts that as GE meets the developing world's needs in sectors like power generation, oil and gas equipment, rail and airplane engines, and water processing technology, the company's overseas revenues will climb to 60 percent of total sales by 2010. Overall, GE seems to have a pretty clear vision of economic trends in emerging nations like China and India, and it likes what it sees. As GE International CEO Ferdinando Beccalli-Falco puts it, "The international picture at this point is particularly favorable to us."[12]

So, where does all this leave GE's venerable appliance business—the unit with which middle-class Americans most closely associated the name with throughout much of the 20th century? Let's recall that in July 2005, Whirlpool offered $1.4 billion for a struggling Maytag—a month after a group of investors led by China's appliance leader Haier offered $1.3 billion. Maytag chose Whirlpool, and when the deal was consummated in March 2006, Whirlpool had consolidated its position as No. 2 in the world, after Sweden's Electrolux. GE's appliance unit (GE Consumer and Industrial) was No. 3. Given former CEO Jack Welch's famous directive to exit any business his company was not No. 1 or No. 2 in, it's time to ask whether white goods is still a business GE wants to be in—especially with developing-world players like Haier driving down prices. Perhaps the company will divest, or perhaps it will acquire another appliance maker in order to bolster its global position in the sector. In any case, GE will be a major player in China for the foreseeable future.

Global Growth from Chindia Consumers

The full significance of the size of the Chindian consumer market is difficult to grasp. The world economy has never seen such a phenomenon. Name a sector, and the Chindian market for it is probably the largest in the world—or soon will be. Cell phones, cars, consumer electronics, microwave ovens, tea, beer, cigarettes, financial services—the list goes on. The math is very simple: As the purchasing power of more and more millions of Chindians continues to rise, so will the demand for more and more thousands of products.

To reiterate, multinationals from advanced countries including Japan and Korea will be forced to seek their growth in these markets. This situation gives Chindia enormous advantage and enormous power; indeed, it confers economic hegemony. After all, it's not easy for foreign multinationals to succeed in Chindia. The competition is fierce. They have to shave their margins. They have to negotiate regulatory hurdles (which have naturally been erected to protect domestic enterprises). They have to do better than their international rivals—all while playing by the rules Chindia dictates. Particularly with respect to China, the situation now is that the world needs it more than it needs the world. The *Wall Street Journal* described this scenario at the end of 2006: "The growing scale and sophistication of its domestic economy has made the outside world less important to China now than it was during the early years of the country's export boom." Thus it will seek to an even greater degree to nurture its own companies; it will become more selective in approving foreign investment and increasingly dispense with give-aways like tax concessions and land.[13]

Meanwhile, China and India are inundating advanced markets with their low-cost manufacturing and services products, and China in particular is running global trade surpluses that are making Western economies nervous. Much of the imbalance is blamed on the low value of the yuan, or on China's intellectual property violations. But where is the WTO? What happened to the Doha round?

It may be that, in the face of Chindia's growing clout, the WTO is now following rather than leading. The July 2006 summit in Hong Kong that intended to complete, at last, the Doha round of negotiations, was a failure. WTO director-general Pascal Lamy despaired that "we are now seeing more protectionism and scapegoating." And he blamed the West: "The process of economic de-colonialization is not yet complete," he told an interviewer, and the "reality" is that the global trading system "disfavors the developing world. . . . On agriculture, on footwear, on coffee, there remain in the system rules which work against developing countries."[14] Since now-powerful economies like China and India refuse to be treated unfairly, the WTO's work is at an impasse. Lamy was somewhat more optimistic in early 2007, suggesting that Doha might yet be completed if there were a "breakthrough" in the negotiating positions of the United States, the EU, and India.

But the question remains: Does Chindia need Doha (the WTO's attempt at lowering trade barriers around the world, permitting free trade between countries)? Neither China nor India appears to lack for bilateral trading partners. In January 2007, China's trade surplus grew to $15.9 billion, and its export gain was the highest in 17 months. Exports were up 33 percent from a year earlier, but, importantly, imports were up 27 percent.

One of those bilateral partners is Australia, whose trade with China has tripled over the past 10 years. In fact, China is expected to surpass Japan as Australia's leading trade partner in 2008, and relations between the two nations are more than cordial. Chinese tourists are flocking to the island nation (1 million are expected in 2010, four times more than in 2004), and its partnership with China is offered as one of the main reasons for an "Australian Revival" that has seen steady economic growth for 16 straight years.[15] Another partner is South Korea, whose trade with China in 2006 increased 20 percent from a year earlier. While South Korea is now China's fourth-largest trade partner (after the United States, Japan and Hong Kong), China is South Korea's most important trade ally—its largest export market and second-largest import source.

Meanwhile, both China and India, independent of one another, are negotiating bilateral trade deals with the European Union, as well as with the Association of Southeast Asian Nations (ASEAN). As the *Wall Street Journal* reports, these efforts to create trade pacts in Asia "reflect a broader trend to push for more trade liberalization independently of the World Trade Organization."[16] Bilateral trade between China and India and individual nations in South America and Africa is also growing.

This is not to mention the massive growth in trade between China and India themselves. In 2005, China and India signed an agreement pledging to increase trade between them to $20 billion by 2008. As it turns out, they hit that target two years early, when they announced 2006 trade volume of $24.9 billion. Even more remarkable, in 2000, trade between the two nations had amounted to only $2.9 billion, meaning that the annual increase since that time has averaged 45 percent. According to a "joint declaration" issued during Hu's visit to New Delhi in November 2006, an "India-China Regional Trading Arrangement" is on the drawing board.[17] But maybe it's not necessary. In January 2007 alone, trade volume between the two hit $2.63 billion, a 63 percent increase over January 2006.

Pan-Asian Currency?

Surging bilateral trade is fueled, in large part, by the rest of the world's desire for low-priced Chindian exports, whether in manufacturing or service industries. Imports into both countries are rising, but exports from them are rising faster, leading to growing trade surpluses. The surpluses result in growing piles of foreign currency holdings. In the case of India, the total is just under $200 billion; in China, it's a staggering $1 trillion. Almost all of this money is in U.S. dollars, since the dollar is the world's reserve currency. As the balance of economic power shifts from the West to the East, this scenario takes on heightened interest. The question right now is: to what extent does the dollar's strength depend upon the support of foreign investors like China and India? What if China and India decided to cash out? What if they started looking for other assets?

In assessing the aborted Dubai port deal in 2006, the *Wall Street Journal* noted that, like China's attempt to buy Unocal a year earlier, it was an example of "purchases by emerging nations trying to recycle their dollar-based wealth—whether from selling toys, electronics or oil—into something other than U.S. Treasury securities." After all, as the *Journal* noted, assets held by foreigners were disproportionately liquid: "At the end of 2004, foreigners held $1.9 trillion in U.S. corporate stocks, $2.2 trillion in government securities, $2.1 trillion in private bonds and $2.9 trillion in debts owed to banks and other lenders." During the first 11 months of 2005, Chinese investors plowed another $81 billion into U.S. bonds. The point of the article was America's fiscal vulnerability. On the one hand, it insists on the right to tell foreigners where they can and cannot invest, but on the other hand, it can't afford to incite the displeasure of those investors: "While lawmakers may fight to keep out certain foreign investments, they know that the economy would likely descend into a deep recession if foreign investors as a whole lost interest in U.S. factories, companies, stocks and bonds."[18]

Looking 50 years into the future, *The Guardian* imagines a scenario that magnifies the point: It's 2056, and after a coup in Saudi Arabia, the new government announces that it is cutting off oil supplies to the United States. The White House threatens to send in troops to keep supply lines open, but Beijing steps in to say that it will cease shoring up the dollar unless the military action is called off. This not-so-fanciful vision reminds us we can't assume the dollar will be shored up forever. The history of the British pound shows that currencies don't necessarily maintain their dominant positions forever. Actually, writes Larry Elliot, *The Guardian's* economics editor, we might not have to wait 50 years to witness a currency revolution: "In my lifetime, the dollar will start to lose its reserve currency status, not to the euro but to the renminbi or the rupee. This would clearly have massive economic and geopolitical consequences." Elliot then quotes financial expert Avinash Persaud, "There will be an avalanche of cheques coming home to be paid when the dollar begins to lose its status."[19]

Some analysts believe the future is now. With America mired in wars in Iraq and Afghanistan, in a dangerous confrontation with Iran, and embroiled in the global war on terror, it may already be time for Asian central banks to reconsider their support for the dollar. China and India, with their huge foreign exchange reserves, can't risk waiting until some new setback triggers a panic flight from the dollar. That's why, over the past decade, ASEAN, China, and India have been working on the basic infrastructure for Asian economic and monetary integration on the EU model. That's why Indian Prime Minister Manmohan Singh, at the Asian summit in Kuala Lampur at the end of 2005, called for the launch of the Pan-Asian Economic Community.

According to Middle East specialist Anthony Cordesman, one of the early fruits of this pan-Asian initiative might well be an Asian Monetary System (AMS), perhaps based on the internationalized yuan (or "Asyuan"). Cordesman reports that the Asian Development Bank has already laid the groundwork by developing the concept of Asian Currency Units (ACUs), which Gulf oil producers could legitimize by oil sales "denominated by destination in ACUs, dollars, or euros." Such a move would give the ACU "corporate liquidity for world trade and clear the way for the launch of the AMS."[20] I must concur that a single, major Asian currency seems an inevitability. As economic power continues to shift from West to East, it is no longer practical for the dollar and the euro to dominate international currency markets. The central banks in America and Europe are no longer in a position to dictate monetary policy to the East. Nor should Chindia be at the mercy of currency fluctuations in the West. Just as the European Union produced the euro, so Asia will produce its own currency. And as the euro is anchored to the German mark, Asia's new currency will likely be tied to China's yuan, and Japan's yen.

Two questions remain: What will the new currency be called? And, considerably more important, how long will it take to eclipse the dollar as the world's most coveted money?

Markets for Resources

Chapter 2 was devoted to Chindia's growing need for resources and its global quest to acquire them. Now let's briefly emphasize the point that China's and India's vast consumer markets will constitute an unparalleled bargaining chip in this high-stakes game. In effect, the two nations will be in a position to say, "You're welcome to come in. Just bring an oil lease with you."

Of course, America operated the same way, but always with an ideological slant: "Come in, as long as you're anti-Communist." Politics dictated that the United States could do business with Taiwan but not Cuba, for example (a prohibition that seems increasingly silly in the 21st century). Sometimes, as we know, America has even been willing to abet a "regime change" in order to have a government suitable for doing business with. Only recently has the United States decided to forgive India for trying to remain non-aligned during the Cold War. What motivated that forgiveness? India's huge market.

China and India have made it clear there will be no ideological hurdles in their game of markets for resources. China is not likely to roll back the clock to the Maoist era and start waving the Little Red Book. And why would it? Consider Australia again. In 2006, the resource-rich nation began a $25 billion long-term contact to export liquid natural gas to China. And since Australia holds 40 percent of the world's uranium deposits, it will also be a major supplier of the uranium China needs for its nuclear power binge. China will no more refuse to deal with Australia because it is a pro-Western democracy than it will refuse to deal with Iran because it is an anti-Western theocracy. Similarly, India has already shown itself perfectly willing to deal with Myanmar, Iran, and even problematical Pakistan.

To sum it up: Chindia has become the location of choice for global business. The largest consumer market the world has ever seen gives Western corporations their best opportunity for growth; they, in turn, give Chindia tremendous bargaining power in the quest for resources to keep its economy growing. Meanwhile, trade surpluses have resulted in such a vast hoard of foreign exchange reserves in Chindia that the reign of the dollar as the world's standard currency may be coming to an end. When a pan-Asian currency takes its place beside the dollar and the euro, we will have reached another benchmark of Chindian economic hegemony.

Geopolitical Muscle

Economic power confers geopolitical influence. The rise of Chindia is like a temblor reconfiguring the geopolitical landscape. What kind of influence the two emerging powers exert is a question that no one can fail to be interested in. Will Chindia be a force for peace, a diffuser of global tension? Today, leaders in both nations are offering welcome reassurances and steering clear of overt confrontation with the other players on the world stage. But the world is perhaps a more fractious place that it's ever been before, and who knows what provocation might loom? In any event, the tilting fulcrum is already causing considerable maneuvering.

In February 2007, the foreign ministers of Russia, China, and India—the three giants of the Asian landmass—met in New Delhi to work toward a trilateral alliance "promoting international peace, prosperity, and parity." According to Madhav D. Nalapat, director of the School of Geopolitics at India's Manipal Academy of Higher Education, the alliance's three principal objectives would be to ensure that:

- all Asian countries are allowed to pursue their own paths to political, economic and social development, without outside pressure;

- no single country can dominate Asia or any corner of the continent, including the three trilateral partners; and

- a worldwide balance is established so that healthy cooperation rather than confrontation becomes the norm in relations between countries.

Nalapat is at pains to emphasize the peaceful intentions of the alliance, a point he makes via a sharp contrast to Western aggression. China and India, he notes, have historically relied on "soft power." Russia, too, has avoided all military conflict since its "disastrous intervention" in Afghanistan in 1979. By contrast, writes Nalapat, "the European powers all won special advantages in the rest of the world not by peaceful cooperation but by conquest," and the West "has relied on tooth and claw to establish and retain its supremacy." The India-China-Russia alliance, says Nalapat, "would act as a check on such action."

Ultimately, Nalapat sees the alliance as the necessary response to Western hegemony. "The refusal of the West to acknowledge the equality of China, Russia and India with themselves is the reason that the years ahead are likely to witness the birth of a possible India-China-Russia alliance." Its extension to Africa and South America is also possible, he writes, but in any case the alliance "would become the biggest geopolitical factor in Asia."[21]

Nalapat's rhetorical slant makes the proposed alliance sound pro-peace and anti-West, and his argument raises the fundamental question: can West and East be equal partners? Much of the developing world harbors resentment against the West, and the extent to which new geopolitical alignments are shaped by this animus remains to be seen.

Consider the Shanghai Cooperation Organization, an organization that includes Russia, China, Kazakhstan, Uzbekistan, Tajikistan, and Kyrgyzstan; India, Iran, Pakistan, and Mongolia can soon expect an invitation to join. At the organization's June 2006 meeting, China proposed increased military cooperation, and Russia floated the idea of an "energy club" that would exclude the United States. Clearly, the group's embrace of Iran at the very time the United States was trying to outlaw the nation's nuclear program would have to be viewed as yet another slap at American authority. No doubt with a smirk in the direction of the United States, Iran's Ahmadinejad said at the summit, "We are on the right track for expansion of relations and ties, and the SCO can play a very important role in promoting peace, tranquility, and sustainable security in the region." The United States, it hardly needs to be added, has been denied admission to the organization.

In response, the United States has established new military bases in Tajikistan, Uzbekistan, and Kyrgyzstan. And while securing major energy deals in the region, reports the *Boston Globe*, the United States also worked to establish the Baku-Tbilisi-Ceyhan pipeline, which allows Western nations to get at the Caspian Sea's energy reserves without having to go through Russia or Iran. Finally, according to Shi Yinhong, director of American Studies at the People's University in Beijing, the United States is blamed for supporting revolutions that toppled pro-Russian and pro-Chinese allies in Ukraine, Georgia, and Kyrgyzstan, and replaced them with pro-Western leaders.

The SCO has flexed its muscles in response. After granting India, Iran, and Pakistan "observer" status in July 2005, the organization formally requested that the United States withdraw its troops from member states, and Uzbekistan asked the United States to close down an air base it established after the attacks of 9/11. Also, both Russia and India have set up military bases in Tajikistan, not far from the U.S. base there. India's and China's efforts to divert the Baku-Tbilisi-Ceyhan pipeline into a feeder for Asia are also stepping on Washington's toes.[22]

However, the new Asian geopolitics is too complicated to be explained merely by anti-Western bias. India and the United States are on friendly terms at the moment (a point we'll return to below), and the European Union is looking to bolster ties with both China and India.

This maneuvering became evident at the bilateral EU-India "summit" in Helsinki in late-October, 2006, at which Finland's Prime Minister (and acting EU president) Matti Vanhanen, European Commission president Jose Manuel Barroso, and Prime Minister Manmohan Singh of India met to endorse the recommendations of year-long negotiations between India and the EU. While "an ambitious free trade agreement" between the two entities headlined the agenda, discussions covered the complete array of global interests.

Overall, the summit was described as "an opportunity to review the progress of bilateral cooperation in the context of the EU-India action plan with a view to enhancing the strategic partnership between the EU and New Delhi, especially on scientific and technological cooperation." The negotiations had been the work of the EU's High Representative Javier Solana, Finnish Foreign Minister Erkki Tuomioja, EU External Relations Commissioner Benita Ferrero-Waldner, EU Trade Commissioner Peter Mandelson, and Indian Trade Minister Kamal Nath, whose discussions ranged far beyond trade to encompass ongoing international concerns like climate change, energy security, combating terrorism and nuclear proliferation.[23]

Much the same language could be heard in January 2007, when China and the European Union announced the start of negotiations on a new agreement to expand their 20-year-old trade pact. The so-called Partnership and Cooperation Agreement (PCA), a revision and enlargement of the 1985 Trade and Economic Cooperation Agreement, will include 22 sectors of mutual interest, including energy, the environment, agriculture, transport, education, and science and technology.

The change in terminology is illuminating, as comments from the representatives indicate. According to EU External Relations Commissioner Benita Ferrero-Waldner, the new agreement is needed because the existing one has not kept pace with "our rapidly expanding partnership. Twenty years ago, we were only trade partners, but now we are strategic partners, which means broader and deeper cooperation." Chinese Foreign Minister Li Zhoaxing agreed that the two nations are now "all-round strategic partners. We share broad common interests and common positions."[24]

G7 to G10

It should be noted that one reason why China and India are negotiating bilateral "partnership" agreements with the EU is that, to this point, they have not been invited to join the G7 (or G8 if you include Russia). This seems unwise, as an increasing number of commentators are pointing out. The make-up of the G7 continues to reflect a set of post-World War II realities that are no longer realities and are no longer relevant. "It is a remarkably lopsided gathering," Roger Bootle, managing director of Capital Economics, opined in the *Daily Telegraph* after the G7 meeting in Essen, Germany, in February 2007. The group consists of four members from the EU, two from North America, and one from Asia (Japan). China and India remain excluded, along with all nations from Africa, the Middle East, and Latin America. "This is hardly representative of the world as it is now," writes Bootle, "never mind how it will look in 10 years' time."

Bootle recommends that global economic reality would be better reflected by a G5—the United States, Japan, China, India, and a single Euro-zone delegation—or a G6 if you wanted to include Britain plus a Euro-zone delegate. But the exact constituency of world bodies like the G7 or the IMF or World Bank—or even whether they continue to exist—is not the issue. "The most important thing," says Bootle, "is to recognize how the world is changing and to make sure we embrace its new multi-polar—and increasingly Asian—nature."[25]

Noted financial journalist Hamish McRae, writing in *The Independent*, also attributed the G7's ineffectuality in Essen to its antiquated make-up. How could China and India remain excluded, he asks, when they are clearly more important to the world economy than any individual nation in Europe? China is investing more in Africa, he points out, than all of the West's aid programs added together. And in terms of the global environment and climate change, everything pales in comparison to what's going on in China and India. It's not that the West should give up its role in world governance. "Rather," writes McRae, "it is that we should seek in everything we do to set our policies within the new realities of shifting economic power."[26]

When will China and India get their seats at the table? History teaches us emphatically that people in power don't like to share, so it wasn't surprising to find Germany's representative, Bernd Pfaffenbach, saying that there was "no chance of agreement on enlarging the group." On the other hand, the Economics Minister conceded that the growing influence of China, India, and other emerging economies "must be accounted for," and there was some consensus that these nations ought to be allowed to regularly join at least some sessions.[27]

The truth is that China and India are in a position to say "no thanks" to any lukewarm geopolitical embrace from the West. This is particularly the case with China, which every day seems to find a new arena in which to showcase its growing stature. For example, at the February 2007 meeting of the 65-nation Conference on Disarmament, China and Russia renewed their five-year-old initiative to establish an international accord against weapons deployment in outer space. In a not-so-subtle reference to the United States, the two nations distributed a working paper to delegates asserting that attempts to have global military dominance by the use of space "are counterproductive and jeopardize the security of all humanity." One country's bid to have "impregnable defenses," said the paper, is dangerous because it could "lead to new instruments of war and to an arms race."

In response to the Russo-Chinese proposal, U.S. Ambassador Christina Rocca said Washington was committed to peaceful uses of space but reiterated that it would pursue programs to ensure that its satellites and other spacecraft were protected.[28]

Interestingly, the conference took place a month after China launched a warhead from a ballistic missile to destroy an aging weather satellite—making China only the third nation, after the U.S. and Russia, to shoot down anything in space. Predictably, Washington criticized the incident as a provocative display of military capability, but it's not hard to imagine Beijing's response: "If you do it, we can do it. If you don't want us to do it, then come to the table."

China is also acting as a peacemaker in troubled Darfur, this time alongside rather than in opposition to the United States. Signaling an important shift in the Mainland's long-standing support for the oil-rich Sudanese regime, China's ambassador to the UN, Wang Guangya, played a crucial role in securing Sudan's agreement to replace the African Union contingent in Darfur with a larger hybrid AU-UN force. According to the *International Herald Tribune*, Wang's negotiating "earned the praise of the American special envoy for Sudan, Andrew Natsios, who recently affirmed that Washington and Beijing were largely working in concert on Darfur." The journal went on to say that in his push for a Darfur settlement, President Hu is showing his readiness to "position China as the protector of the repressed citizens of the region."

Similarly, during North Korea's missile and nuclear tests in 2006, China supported the imposition of UN-endorsed sanctions and stridently denounced its longtime ally—yet another indication of China's assumption of the role of global peacekeeper. More generally, China seems to have become a veritable pillar of strength on the UN Security Council. It is contributing an increasing number of troops to the UN force—now up to 1666—and has even taken the lead in the push for a deployment of peacekeepers to Somalia.

Chinese leaders have apparently become aware that "fence-sitting and providing unquestioned cover to allies" is ultimately more costly not only to global well-being but also to its own interests; thus diplomacy is suddenly becoming the centerpiece of China's foreign policy doctrine. According to the *Herald Tribune*, this shift in attitude represents "the next phase in China's efforts to demonstrate the unthreatening nature of its rise and allay fears that its political, economic and military footprint in the world will damage Western interests."[29]

As China rises in the East, Western influence in the hemisphere weakens—even in that surrogate-of-the-West—Australia. The new paradigm was evident in 2003, when visiting President Hu Jintao was allowed to address Australia's parliament, an honor previously granted only to visiting U.S. presidents. The following year, Australia's foreign minister defied Washington by insisting that Australia wouldn't necessarily join a U.S. intervention into a clash between China and Taiwan. Then, again in 2005, Australia refused to follow Washington's example and publicly press Europe to continue its weapons embargo of China. The Australians continue to make clear that they won't antagonize China at Washington's behest. Hugh White, a strategic studies scholar at the Australian National University in Canberra, summed it all up: "We do not expect the United States to retain the kind of unquestioned primacy that we all assumed at the end of the Cold War."[30]

On a broader canvas, Oded Shenkar delineates China's inevitable evolution from an economic to a geopolitical power. Within a decade [of 2005], he predicts, China not only will become the hub of a huge Asian market that will rival the economies of Europe and America, but it will also "be a broker and arbiter of global diplomatic affairs not only in Asia but the world over." China's growing military prominence will counterbalance the old dominance of the West, "redrawing the political and security map and turning what it sees as single player hegemony into a two- or three-player game." While maintaining its non-expansionist tradition, says Shenkar, China "will utilize its economic muscle in the service of a broader international and political agenda."[31]

China's reforms started in 1978, India's in 1991. The 13-year head-start explains to a considerable degree China's greater economic muscle today, as well as its greater geopolitical influence. But India's ascendance is assured, in no small part, thanks to the United States. As Edward Luce writes in *In Spite of the Gods*, "In March 2005 the Bush administration did something none of its predecessors had done. It announced it would play midwife to the birth of a new world power." The administration's declaration, notes Luce, followed upon a CIA report identifying India as the "key swing state" of the 21st century. What this meant was that the United States had—and has—every intention of strengthening India as a way of counterbalancing the influence of China in Asia and the rest of the world. This culminated in strategic alliance between the two nations encouraging is established nation's business to trade and invest with the other, especially with respect to the military market. India is one of the largest weapon buyer in the world, and it now has the currency reserves to pay for it.

For now, receiving a boost up onto the international stage from the United States suits India's purpose, as well as that of the United States. But soon enough India will outgrow its need for the midwife's solicitous care. It already seems clear that India does not relish the role of "strategic counterbalance to China" but rather, in Luce's words, "wants to remain equidistant from both China and the United States, while working for good relations with both." For example, Washington had fervently hoped that India would join "the coalition of the willing," but India was not willing. As senior advisor Brajesh Mishra told then-Prime Minister Vajpayee, "India does not have a dog in this fight."

Then there's India's relationship with Iran, a nation included in President Bush's "axis of evil." As we noted in an earlier chapter that India plans to seek oil and gas resources from Iran and is not reluctant to deal with the regime in power there—even if it courts U.S. displeasure in the process. In fact, the Helms-Burton Act, passed in the early 1990s, is supposed to trigger U.S. sanctions against any company that trades with Iran or Libya, but India's state-owned oil company, ONGC Videsh, appears willing to take the risk. As Luce writes, "it is hard to imagine that any U.S. sanctions on India would outweigh the economic benefits of securing a plentiful supply of cheap Iranian gas." Indeed, their critical quest for energy security will make the relationship between China and India, at least on that important issue, more compelling than that between India and the United States.

So we have what Luce calls "the triangular dance." Not that the interests and influence of other players like the EU, Russia, and Japan can be neglected entirely, but, as Luce writes, "in many respects the world appears to be on a trajectory where relations between the three big powers will outweigh all other ties as the 21st century unfolds."[32]

Cultural Fusion

"East is East and West is West," wrote Kipling at the end of the 19th century, "And never the twain shall meet." The second half of the 20th century proved him wrong, as young people around the world adopted the cultural product of the west—jeans and t-shirts, MTV, cell phones, coffee shops. History will no doubt describe the last decades of that century as the great era of Westernization. The 21st century will continue to prove Kipling wrong, but unlike its predecessor, the new century will usher in the era of Easternization. Following upon Chindia's burgeoning economic power and geopolitical influence, we can expect wide dissemination of Asian culture.

The new cultural flow will be different not only in direction but in content as well. Westernization exported technology, education, modernization and consumption, and the ever-new, fast-moving, media-centered culture of the West often seemed at odds with the traditional cultures of the developing world. While teenagers in the East might have embraced rock music and the lifestyle it symbolized, their parents likely lamented a "clash of cultures" in which theirs was overwhelmed.

Easternization, as I see it, will result not in a clash of cultures but in a fusion of cultures, as the West—always changing anyway—embraces Eastern food and clothing, arts and entertainment, and philosophical and spiritual values. For me, nothing epitomizes this cultural fusion better than the current craze of Christian yoga. From California to Georgia, Christian churches (and Jewish synagogues, too) are offering yoga classes as an additional way of "connecting to God." Devotees enjoy the physical and spiritual refreshment that yoga exercise offers but are less interested in its religious origins, so in some cases the yoga positions (like "the warrior" or "the cobra") are renamed to sound more Christian. Likewise, instead of having New Age or Eastern music playing in the background, Christian yoga is sometimes performed with the recitation of Bible verses. In any case, the fast-spreading phenomenon typifies what I see as the dominant cultural trend of the 21st century—the fusion of East and West.

Let's consider a few other examples—first in the basics of material culture (food, clothing, and living space), then in the arts and entertainment, then in the realm of religion and philosophy.

Material Culture

Indian curry has taken the West by storm, but nowhere is it more popular than in Britain. Depending on whom you ask, curry is anywhere from the

No. 1 favorite cuisine in Britain to the fourth-most favorite. One survey conducted in 2006 found that Indian was the second-favorite take-out food in Britain, which was not surprising. What was surprising was that the No. 1 spot did not belong to the standard fish and chips, but rather to Chinese take-out (more evidence of culture fusion). Specifically, the survey reported that 43 percent of respondents preferred Chinese take-out, 24 preferred Indian, while only 14 preferred fish and chips.[33]

There are currently 8,000 Indian restaurants in Great Britain, and leading supermarkets like Tesco do a brisk business in Indian ingredients and ready-made meals. According to one estimate, Britons consume some 23 million Chicken tikka masalas every year. All that ringing of the cash registers is sweet music to the ears of Kirit Pathak, son of L. G. Pathak, who in 1957 founded Patak Foods (dropping the "h" to make the name easier on the British tongue). The younger Pathak believes the company, which generates about £70 million annually in spices, sauces and ready-mades, is poised for booming growth. Which is why in 2006 he hired the N.M. Rothschild investment bank to undertake a review of strategic options to take the brand worldwide. Though its largest market is Great Britain (where it supplies ingredients to 75 percent of the Indian restaurants in addition to the supermarket business), Patak products are already available in 75 nations. The wild popularity of the cuisine may help Kirit Pathak realize his ambition of overseeing a dominant global Indian food brand with annual sales of £500 million.[34]

Of course, Chinese food has long been popular in the West, but here's a new twist. French restaurants are now encouraged to put out soy sauce and chili paste so Chinese tourists may spice up French dishes. So advises France's Tourism Ministry, which in late 2006 published a 65-page guide for tourism professionals titled, *Chinese Tourists: How Best to Welcome Them*. In addition to allowing Chinese visitors to infuse their French food with Asian flavors, the guide also recommends that tourism workers avoid sensitive political subjects, like the student riots on Tiananmen Square or the status of Taiwan or Tibet.

Some people, like Elisabeth Alles of France's League of Human and Citizens' Rights, object to such self-imposed censorship, but the tourism industry is unapologetic. The Chinese are traveling abroad like never before, bringing their culture (and their yuan) with them, and France is a major benefactor. Franck Paillard, Vice Director of the tourism promotion agency Maison de la France, notes that, in 2005, 650,000 Chinese visited France—up 12 percent from a year earlier—and he was all for doing whatever it took to making them feel at home.[35] After all, if the Chinese in Paris prefer "coq au soy sauce" to "coq au vin," what we have is culture fusion on the most basic level.

At the same time, Asian—especially Indian—clothing styles are making an impact on Western couture. Of course, India's textile industry has historically been one of the nation's most important, and today its clothing factories do a $5 billion export business. But only recently, as a feature in *BusinessWeek* points out, have Indian designers begun attracting a global following with their fusion of Indian motifs and Western styles. Suddenly, India is cool. According to Narendra Kumar, a leading designer known for his combination of Asian themes and Western looks, "Indian designers are able to use their Indian-ness to make their offerings globally appealing."

The world of high fashion is taking note. The work of designer Rina Dhaka now appears in international fashion magazines like *Marie Claire* and *Vanity Fair*, and her creations have graced the figures of mega-stars like Uma Thurman and Naomi Campbell. And in 2007, two other designers—Anamika Khanna and Manish Arora—became the first Indians to be invited to show their work at the Paris's annual Fashion Week extravaganza. The Fashion Design Council of India is hoping for a boost from Manmohan Singh's government—in the form of money to develop a seven-acre fashion hub, India's own Fifth Avenue, at Dwarka, on the outskirts of New Delhi. Regardless, India's growing influence on international high fashion, as *BusinessWeek* puts it, "will be one of the more interesting business stories to watch in the years ahead."[36]

Eastern culture is also exerting a growing influence on Western interior design—witness the widespread popularity of the ancient Chinese practice of feng shui. Feng shui, which translates into English as "wind and water," teaches that these two elements are the containers of "qi," the natural energy flow within and around all things. Thus, as untold numbers of Westerners have now learned, the goal of feng shui is to situate our dwellings and arrange our furnishings in such a way as to be attuned with the flow of qi. The energy-enhancing benefits of feng shui are said to have been enjoyed by such prominent Westerners as Donald Trump and Prince Charles, as well as by major corporations like Coca-Cola, Procter & Gamble, Hewlett-Packard and Ford.

Not to be outdone, India is now exporting *vastu shastra*, its ancient art of architecture and decoration. As Tatiana Boncompagni writes in the *Wall Street Journal*, "just when feng shui home accessories are hitting Bed, Bath & Beyond stores," here comes its "Indian cousin." Practitioners are advised to abandon feng shui's wind chimes, mirrors, and beaded curtains and replace them with natural fabrics, wood, pottery, flowers, and brass or copper—all in "sunrise or sunset colors."[37] Actually, both have in common the use of geometry to dissect living spaces into quadrants, and both have the same ultimate goal—to control energy in a way that promotes health, harmony, and happiness. Both also exemplify—like Eastern clothing and Eastern food—the extent to which Asian culture is infused into daily life in the West.

Arts and Entertainment

In March 2007, *The Namesake* opened to glowing reviews across the United States. Directed by Indian filmmaker Mira Nair, it tells the story of the Ganguli family's immigration to America, and of the inevitable problems that arise as the family adapts to American life while trying to hold on to their ethnic roots. Not the first film to deal with such a theme, certainly, but this one brought together two Indian artists with fast-growing reputations in the West.

Mira Nair, the Orissa-born director, won the Golden Camera Award at the Cannes Film Festival and received an Oscar nomination for her first feature-length film, *Salaam Bombay*! Her reputation has continued to grow with the release of *Mississippi Masala*, which profiled a family of Uganda-Indians living and working in Mississippi, and more recently, *Monsoon Wedding*, about a chaotic Punjabi wedding, which won the Golden Lion Award at the Venice Film Festival. She is now one of the world's most respected filmmakers.

To make *The Namesake*, Nair adapted the novel of the same name by celebrated American-Indian writer Jhumpa Lahiri. Before the publication of *The Namesake* in 2003, Lahiri blazed into the consciousness of Western readers with her debut collection of short stories, *The Interpreter of Maladies*, which won such prestigious prizes as the O. Henry Award, the PEN/Hemingway Award, and *New Yorker's* Best Debut of the Year.

The point is that Easternization will bring to the West more than an infusion of the East's material culture. It will also bring Asian ideas, attitudes, tastes, and lifestyles, as reflected in a veritable flood of books, movies, plays, TV shows, paintings, and music. That this should happen now is not surprising. Historically, the rise of economic power has resulted in the rise (and dissemination) of culture. Wealth fosters art, not the other way around. High culture grows up around wealthy cities, which almost always happen to be port cities, centers of international trade and commerce, from which cultural products are exported as surely as manufactured goods. So from Bombay and Beijing, from Bangalore and Shanghai, Asia's cultural influence will expand westward, fusing with and enriching the culture of the West.

The booming Indian art market provides a perfect example of how a country's rising economy can lift its cultural output, as well as an example of Eastern culture moving West. As the *Wall Street Journal* reported in 2006, the numbers are staggering. In 2004, works by four 20th-century Indian artists had sold for more than $100,000 at auction, smashing through that barrier for the first time. Just two years later, three Indian artists broke through the $1 million barrier. The *Journal* reports that the price of Indian art has been surging for five years, but that recently the acceleration has become downright dizzying. Together, Christie's and Sotheby's took in a whopping $31 million from Indian paintings in 2005. The figure for 2006: just under $70 million.

One of the most successful Indian painters is Anju Dodiya, whose work, like that of his contemporaries, has little in common with the depictions of Buddha or illustrations of the life of Krishna that have typically represented Indian art. Instead, Dodiya's work was influenced by his visits to museums in Paris, where he was struck by the work of Western modernists. "I started appropriating in a direct way from [David] Hockney and [Jasper] Johns and Picasso and [Philip] Guston," he told the *Journal*, "used them as a grammar of painting, juxtaposing my own images from India, creating a hybrid sort of thing." Having taken those Western influences home to India with him, Dodiya now finds his work gaining tremendous popularity in the West. An exhibit of his work opened the New York franchise of the Delhi-based Bodhi Art gallery, and his work was heavily promoted at Christie's and Sotheby's September 2006 auctions.[38] Dodiya shows how East may borrow from West, resulting in an interweaving of cultural creativity that both East and West then mutually embrace.

Granted, most of us are not art collectors, so the artistic fusion we're more likely to be aware of will be on the more accessible level of books and movies. Jhumpa Lahiri is far from the only Indian fiction writer making a name for herself in the West. Arundhati Roy's novel, *The God of Small Things*, won the Man Booker Prize, Britain's highest literary award. The prestigious Booker Prize has also been awarded to India's Salman Rushdie, for *Midnight's Children* in 1981. Of course, thanks to the notoriety arising from the publication of *The Satanic Verses*, which earned for the author the unique distinction of a *fatwa* issued by Ayatolla Khomeini, Rushdie has gone on to become India's best-known expatriate writer. He recently joined the faculty at Atlanta's Emory University. And while Indian writers generally have the advantage (for a Western audience) of an English-language education, we should also mention China's Ha Jin, who was studying at Brandeis University during the Tiananmen Square uprising in 1989 and who decided as a result to remain in America. His first novel, *Waiting*, won the National Book Award and the PEN/Faulkner Award, and his recent *War Trash* was a finalist for the Pulitzer Prize.

At the movies, Deepa Mehta joins Mira Nair at the top of the list of India's best known directors, but it's fair to say that, in terms of sheer renown, both are overshadowed by China's Ang Lee. The West's enthusiasm for Asian cinema became evident with the release in 2000 of Lee's *Crouching Tiger, Hidden Dragon*, which not only won five Academy Awards (including best foreign film), but also grossed $128 million in the United States alone—unheard-of earnings for a foreign-language film. Crossing the cultural divide, Ang Lee won the 2006 Academy Award for Best Director for the remarkable *Brokeback Mountain*. Talk about cultural fusion: a movie by a Chinese director, about a homosexual love affair between two cowboys, set in the mountains of Wyoming.

The trans-global appeal of Asian cinema, though, is best indicated by the success of India's "Bollywood," the largest film industry in the world in terms of movies made, and tickets sold. The global audience for Bollywood films is estimated at 3.8 billion, and Bollywood stars are better-known worldwide than their Hollywood counterparts. One gossip-column anecdote has it that Tom Cruise had to wait an hour at the Paris airport for Indian mega-star Shah Rukh Khan's entourage and fans to pass through. And when the beautiful Shilpa Shetty appeared to be the victim of racist bullying on the British reality show "Celebrity Big Brother," the entire Indian nation was outraged, and effigies were burned on the streets of Patna.

Bollywood produces a staggering 800 films a year, more and more of which are making headlines in the West. An industry first occurred in January 2007 when *Guru*, starring Aishwarya Rai and Abhishek Bachchan, had its world premier in Toronto. Across Canada, in fact, leading theater chains like AMC and Cineplex have been screening Bollywood films, often with more success than their Hollywood rivals. Filmgoers in Great Britain have also embraced the gorgeous Aishwarya Rai, whose *Bride and Prejudice*, a remake of the Jane Austen classic *Pride and Prejudice*, perfectly epitomizes culture fusion. But the aforementioned Shah Rukh

Khan may be the best proof of Bollywood's emergence in the West. "King Khan," as his fans call him, was not only named by *Time* magazine as arguably the most recognizable actor in the world, but in 2005 he was on the cover of *National Geographic*.

In February 2007, Lei Yixin, master sculptor from China, was chosen to create the statue of Martin Luther King that will be the centerpiece of the civil rights memorial now under construction on Washington's National Mall. Meanwhile, internationally known musician Kalyan Pathak has fused Indian raga with American jazz to produce a new synthesis he calls "ragazz." The examples continue to multiply. As I noted at the beginning of this chapter, it all comes down to numbers. By 2030, according to the World Bank, the number of middle-class consumers in China will exceed the entire U.S. population. The inevitable result, long-term, is that the West will be importers and not just exporters of culture. Uri Dadush, director of the World Bank's international trade department, puts it this way: "New fashions, new trends . . . are just as likely, indeed more likely, to start in China and India or Brazil as they are today to start in Europe or the United States."[39]

Spiritual Enrichment and Personal Values

Paradoxically, while Easternization makes itself felt in virtually every aspect of material culture, it will also offer a corrective to Western materialism, a philosophy the West now realizes it has pursued to an unhealthy extreme. Non-materialist values derived from Buddhism and Jainism will penetrate deeply into three dimensions of life that I characterize as (1) spirituality, (2) conduct, and (3) ecological balance.

Spirituality

In my view, the West will welcome an infusion of spirituality from Buddhism (common to both China and India) and also from Jainism, with its emphasis on the three principles of non-violence (ahimsa), relativism or pluralism (anekanta), and the rejection of possessions (anegraha).

That the Western culture is conditioned to violence is a truism. The violent content not only of movies but also of daily local television is a major shock to foreign visitors and anyone else not already immersed in the culture. Psychologists worry about the effects of violent imagery on children, and every thinking person has misgivings about commonplace depictions of mayhem and gore.

But few people actually know the extent to which violence has penetrated the fabric of our lives. Few people realize, for example, that each year there are at least 1.5 million reported incidents of violence in the workplace. The disgruntled employee who "goes postal" is perhaps the most familiar form of workplace violence, but there are many others, including hold ups at convenience stores. The annual cost of violent crime to business is a staggering $200 billion, and it would be much higher if you added in the cost to the community (for law enforcement, criminal justice, etc.) and the cost to victims in post trauma mental and medical care and disability. I emphasize that these figures are for the United States alone, and the costs are rising. In short, casualty of work place violence (and increasingly market place violence where customers take out their anger and frustrations on marketer's property, people and producers) is mindnumbing hundreds of thousands per year.

I believe that a nationwide anti-violence campaign will soon take root in the US probably by businesses and enterprises for their own business interests and that it may well enjoy the success of the nation's anti-smoking campaign. I also believe that Jainism's philosophy of non-violence will play a significant role in such a campaign. There is already an "Ahimsa Center" in California, and my guess is that more are on the way.

The second principle, anekanta (literally "non-one-endedness"), holds that there is no single right perspective. Let's recall the old fable about the five blind men touching the elephant: the one touching a leg believes he is touching a tree; the one feeling the trunk believes he is holding a snake; the one with the tail believes he has a rope, etc. Western rationalism insists that all five are wrong; Jainism holds that all five are right. The world offers a multitude of perspectives, each as valid as the next.

Such a view departs radically from the Western dualism of "either right, or wrong." And while dualism is the foundation of logic and mathematics, it also leads to dogmatism, bias, and absolutism—and, more perniciously, to ideological zeal, intolerance, and persecution of "the other". In Jainism, your god is as good as mine, and I fully support your right to believe in whatever doctrine you choose. In other words, Jainism is all about peaceful coexistence and mutual tolerance, and this too may be a principle the West is ready to embrace. It is already manifested via diversity and tolerance at workplace neighbors and other public places.

The third principle, anegraha, is most directly opposed to the West's culture of consumption. Anegraha teaches the downside of excessive consumption and material possessions; it reminds us that "too much stuff" is psychically and spiritually damaging. The pursuit of possessions is a perversion of the proper relationship of body and mind. It puts the desires of the body (which can never be completely satisfied anyway) in control. Jainism tells us to jettison the things we have accumulated—to divest, to share, and to keep for ourselves as little as possible. This is why Jains are involved in so many charitable endeavors, especially in education. Some 3,000 institutions of learning have been founded by Jains to date in India alone. In fairness, of course, we should note that such charitable work is not unique to Jainism. Christianity has an equally long and distinguished record, especially when it comes to bringing medicine and health care to areas of need. The Jains, though, have made their mark especially in education.

The anti-materialism at the heart of anegraha has always had its spokesmen in the West. In mid-19th century America, for example, Henry David Thoreau observed that "Most of the luxuries, and many of the so called comforts of life, are not only not indispensable, but positive hindrances to the elevation of mankind."[40] But those voices were hard to hear in the mid-20th century, as the rise of television—and the commercialization of mass markets—created an ever-increasing level of consumer desire. Now Easternization could help the pendulum swing back. "Simplicity" and freedom from desire are likely to become potent talismans in the new century—especially with the growing consciousness of what Western-style consumption has done to consumers, workers and citizens as well as the planet. Indeed, central to Jainism is the belief that all life is precious—human life, plant life, insect life. Consumption causes damage, and to leave a light footprint we must consume and possess as little as possible.

It is important to understand that the kind of enlightenment that follows from meditation, from the mind's control over the body's needs and desires, and from overriding the appetites of the flesh does not depend upon divine intervention. The Buddha taught that there is no supernatural intermediary between mankind and nirvana, and that he and the Buddhas who followed him were simply practitioners, teachers and guides. The Buddhist system of insight, thought and meditation was not revealed divinely, but by the understanding of the true nature of the mind, which could be discovered by anybody.

This idea, I believe, should appeal to the West today. It makes sense that affluent Western societies are now moving beyond the "primitive" need for a deity or external authority to fear and to worship, beyond the need to have religious wisdom packaged and distributed by the religious preachers (Europe may be somewhat ahead of the United States in this respect; Scandinavians are constantly amused by what they see as Americans' addiction to church-going.) The point, as I see it, is that Westerners have arrived at a place in their spiritual evolution where they see spirituality as something within themselves, rather than something imposed from without. They are approaching the Jainist principle of anekanta, with its openness to spiritual influences from any source, including the East. They may be coming to see that the beauty of the outdoors is a better reflection of the divinity of all life than inside of a cathedral, temple or synagogue.

To recapitulate: Westernization exported technology, materialism and modernization across the globe, but now we are moving back in the other direction—toward spirituality and a healthy de-emphasis of excessive consumption and possession of worldly goods. As Western philosophy moves in this direction, it will meet and fuse with Eastern philosophy and spirituality. Already Buddhism is the fastest-growing religion in the United States. It is estimated that the number of people practising Buddhism in America will triple—from 2 million to 6 million—by 2010. However, it will not be manifested in large edifices such as a cathedral.

A New Code of Conduct

Of course, eschewing institutionalized religion is the easy part, and it comes naturally to the affluent Westerner with his or her highly developed sense of individuality. Now the question is: has the supremacy of the individual in Western thought resulted in the erosion of respect not just for the church but for institutions generally—for school, for government, for family, for work. What does it say about a society where kids in the schoolroom take demeaning pictures of their teachers with their cell phones? We regard our Bill of Rights as sacrosanct, but have we gone too far in protecting individual liberty? Has the necessary authority of institutions been compromised? It's the old question of rights versus responsibilities. Absolute freedom, obviously, means anarchy.

For the East, the absence of a supreme being in the spiritual quest does not imply any lack of respect for social institutions. On the contrary, the institutions that bind society together are cherished in Eastern thought (perhaps all the more so *because* of the absence of the deity). The 1948 Universal Declaration of Human Rights (UDHR) was perhaps not so universal after all. At least Singapore's Lee Kuan Yew and Malaysia's Mahathir Mohamad didn't believe it was. These leaders argued that the declaration elevated the individual's rights over the collective—in clear opposition to "Asian values" that promote attachment to family, individual deference to societal interests, conservatism in social mores, and respect for authority.[41]

Lee Kuan Yew is a compelling figure here. John F. Kennedy's famous words—"Ask not what your country can do for you. Ask what you can do for your country"—became for Lee a principle of government. More interested in the duties of Singapore's citizens than their rights, the long-time Prime Minister was never going to win any accolades from the American Civil Liberties Union. He routinely asked his citizens to put the welfare of the whole society above their own, as when he instituted the draft in 1967, or, a couple of decades later, when he encouraged men to choose wives from the too-large pool of unmarried women with college degrees.

Singapore has become renowned worldwide for its strict enforcement of laws against anti-social behavior, and Prime Minister Lee has never apologized for his government's heavy hand. In 1994, when 18-year-old American Michael Fay was convicted in Singapore of spray-painting cars and other acts of vandalism, his sentence—which included six lashes across the back with a rattan cane—ignited an international furor. Lee was unmoved, explaining once again that U.S. condemnation of the caning stemmed from its worship of individual rights, as opposed to the Eastern emphasis upon the rights of society. America "dares not restrain or punish the individuals," he commented, "[but rather forgives] them for whatever they've done. That's why the whole country is in chaos." Even some Westerners were able to appreciate the efficacy of Singapore's system. As sociology professor and family violence expert Richard Gelles observed at the time, "It's not the severity that gives Singapore the lowest homicide rate in the world, it's the certainty of the punishment and the foreknowledge that you'd better not cross the line."[42]

Writing just after the incident, William F. Buckley juxtaposed Lee's tough policies against a Carnegie report that had just been released detailing the deterioration of America's social fabric between 1960 and 1990. Among the findings: the number of children born to unwed mothers increased from 5 percent to 28 percent; the number of children under age three living with one parent increased from 7 percent to 27 percent; children under 18 experiencing the divorce of their parents increased from 1 percent to 50 percent, and so on. Lee had no trouble explaining the figures. They amounted to "the breakdown of civil society."

Buckley cited a recent interview in which Lee turned to drug policy to illustrate the difference in the two societies. The United States concentrates on interdiction, flying around the world to help narcotic agencies wipe out the drug trade. That's an approach Singapore can't afford, says Lee. But what Singapore can do is pass a law allowing any customs officer or policeman who sees anybody in Singapore behaving as though he might be under the influence of drugs to haul the person in and have his urine tested. "In America, if you did that," says Lee, "it would be an invasion of the individual's rights and you would be sued." Buckley applauds Lee's assertion that "man needs a certain moral sense of right and wrong."[43]

Lee has also provoked the ire of Western rights groups with his attitude that the media should be subordinate to the state. For example, when international publications like *The Economist,* the *International Herald Tribune*, and the *Far Eastern Economic Review* accused him of nepotism (his son is the current Prime Minister), they have been threatened, sued or banned in Singapore. But Singapore was back in the spotlight in 2003, this time earning praise around the world for its prompt response to and containment of the SARS epidemic. What happened was that, without quibbling, the media carried out the government's plan: citizens who scrupulously followed health guidelines were featured in news reports; government officials were pictured in newspapers or on television submitting to the same procedures as anyone else; and, on the other hand, citizens who protested were publicly castigated for putting their own interests above those of society at large.

In Singapore, as international policy expert Tom Plate wrote in the *South China Morning Post*, "compliance with government policies— not just health measures—is viewed as a personal and community responsibility."[44]

The lesson Singapore teaches may not be entirely applicable to the West. But if the East errs in one direction, certainly the West errs in the other. We seem more anxious to stand up for the rights of the individual than for the rights of the group or institution that may be harmed by the individual's actions. Of course, institutions have a responsibility too, to add value to society, but in so far as they fulfill that responsibility, they are due respect from individuals.

Lee Kuan Yew's distinction between cost-causers (those after whom others have to clean up) and value-adders seems sensible. Perhaps it's time to think again about where the balance should be struck between rights and responsibilities. Perhaps this pendulum, too, is beginning to swing back, and the "Asian values" of family, community, and institution will find an increasingly warm welcome in advanced societies that now seem fragmented by individual rights, needs and desires. Maybe the "me generation" is ready to embrace the "we generation."

Culture fusion, I believe, will fashion a revised code of conduct, one in which strong institutions will foster in individuals the desire to be value-creators rather than cost causers. Under such a code, children won't bring weapons to school, not because of a zero-tolerance policy, but because taking a weapon to school should never occur to them in the first place.

Ironically, the West's individualism may well abet this trend, just as, more generally, the larger process of Easternization will meet with less resistance than did Westernization. Our very individualism—and weaker bonds to institutions and traditions—makes us open to change, even to a change in values.

Ecological Balance in Day-to-Day Living

I'm not talking about the "green revolution" here, although that's part of it. By "ecological balance" I mean living every day with the understanding that we are part of the vast web of life, and that everything we do affects the web—for good or for bad. Ecology means understanding that how we produce and consume our food, how we build and live in our houses, how we make and wear our clothing, and even how we compete with others—all these actions have consequences that ripple outward. Ecology, literally, is the branch of biology dealing with the interrelationships between organisms and their environment, and the term as I use it here stresses this interconnectedness.

Thus, the ecological view is holistic, the goal is harmony (as opposed to assertion of the self), and the route to the goal is through consciousness. These principles gained immense popularity in America's so-called counterculture during the 1960s and 1970s, thanks to the Indian ambassador of Transcendental Meditation, Maharishi Mahesh Yogi. The Maharishi was born in Madhya Pradesh in 1917 and, like so many other spiritual leaders, began his career as a scientist, earning the equivalent of a Master's degree in physics from Allahabad University in 1940. But then he spent a long apprenticeship under Swami Brahmananda Saraswati, and by 1955 was ready to assume the title "Maharishi" (or great sage). He began teaching his meditation techniques (to which he gave the name Transcendental Meditation) first in India, where he founded the Spiritual

Regeneration Movement, and then abroad. In America, his path toward ever higher levels of consciousness found an avid audience among young people disillusioned by the Vietnam War, and the list of his famous disciples ranged from musicians like the Beatles and Donovan to movie directors like Clint Eastwood and David Lynch.

The Maharishi's phenomenal popularity may have faded after the 1970s, but the holistic view that is ecology, continues to gain traction today as part of the growing global consciousness of manmade threats to environmental health. Also, the spiritual dimension of the movement continues to find leaders from India, and, in at least one case, another leader who began as a scientist. I'm thinking of Deepak Chopra, born in New Delhi and graduated from the prestigious All-India Institute of Medical Sciences in 1968. In fact, after emigrating to the United States in 1970, Dr. Chopra was for a short time a leader in the Transcendental Meditation movement, but he veered off to pursue a more specialized interest in the mind-body relationship. His belief in the interconnection between mind and body—and that self-awareness is the key to health—has led Dr. Chopra to become a leading practitioner of holistic medicine. In books like *Quantum Healing* (1989) and *Perfect Health* (1991), he introduced the West to Ayurveda, the traditional system of Indian medicine with its emphasis on maintaining health through the holistic balance of mind and body.

The holistic approach to healing is becoming increasingly mainstream in the West, thanks to practitioners like Dr. Andrew Weil, who, tweaking the name of the concept, founded the Program of Integrative Medicine at the University of Arizona in 1994. Weil's PIM combines alternative and traditional medical practices, with an emphasis on allowing the body to heal itself through nutrition, meditation and exercise. Integrative medicine has become so popular in just the dozen years since Weil's center was founded that there are now 31 such programs at medical schools across the United States, including at Harvard and the Mayo Clinic.

Holistic medicine, diets that recommend locally grown food, architecture that adapts to rather than displaces the natural landscape, clothing fashioned from indigenous material—all are expressions of the desire for ecological balance. The East, where the community as a whole has always been valued more highly than the individual, enjoys an inherent grasp of the ecological view. As the process of Easternization continues, the West's appreciation of ecology will strengthen.

In Conclusion

To recapitulate, cultural fusion is Christian yoga, as well as other forms of spiritual enrichment for the materialist West. It's the plethora of books and movies by Asian artists working out the conflicts of "East meets West." It's the Sudoku puzzle (which actually traveled East, where it became a huge hit in Japan in the 1980s, then returned West where it is now a phenomenon) sitting beside the crossword puzzle in American newspapers. It's the Western palate tingling to the spicy sensations of Indian curry and Chinese chili paste. It's *weiqi* (or GO), the ancient Chinese board game, being played in Western living rooms. It's the vibrant orange of Indian saris used as a theme color in trend-conscious Hallmark cards. It's the coming of Asia to Europe and America.

Cultural fusion, in short, represents the final step in Chindia's emergence onto the world stage. Economic power will confer geopolitical authority. Through those agencies Chindia's clout will be felt in banks and boardrooms, in bilateral and multilateral trade negotiations, and at the conference tables where global disputes are settled and peace treaties hammered out. But the cultural fusion that joins the East to the West will be something perhaps even more profound. It will be a meeting of peoples, a mutual embrace, a joining of hearts and minds, and, with luck, a step forward for the human race.

Notes

1. McGregor, Richard, "Starbucks Brews Up China Expansion," *Financial Times*, Oct 25, p. 26.
2. "Starbucks Gaining Ground in Tea-drinking China," *Financial Times Information / Global News Wire*, Nov 21, 2006.
3. Engardio, Pete (Ed.); *Chindia: How China and India Are Revolutionizing Global Business* (New York: McGraw-Hill, 2006), pp. 193-194.
4. "IBM India Clocks 37% Growth," *The Statesman* (New Delhi), Feb 2, 2007, p. 1.
5. Barboza, David and Michael Barbaro, "Wal-Mart Challenges for Top Spot in China," *Houston Chronicle*, Oct 17, 2006, p. 1 (Business).
6. Barboza, David, "Wal-Mart Expands in China As Its Own Growth Slows in U.S.," *New York Times*, Feb 28, 2007, p. C10.
7. Giridharadas, Anand and Saritha Rai, "Wal-Mart Set to Open Hundreds of India Stores," *International Herald Tribune*, Nov 28, 2006, p. 1.

8. Yee, Amy, "Nokia Leads the Way for Manufacturers," *Financial Times*, Jan 26, 2007, p. 6.

9. "Earnings at Nokia Climb 19%," *International Herald Tribune*, Jan 26, 2007, p. 16.

10. "China Business Could Double in Five Years," *Toronto Star*, May 30, 2006, p. D2.

11. Kranhold, Kathryn and Mei Fong, "Beijing Olympics 2008," *Wall Street Journal*, Oct 16, 2006, p. B1.

12. Christoffersen, John, "GE Expects Overseas Sales to Match Its Domestic Business," *Buffalo News*, Jan 16, 2007, p. B6.

13. Batson, Andrew, "China & the WTO: Five Years Later," *Wall Street Journal* (Asia), Dec 11, 2006, p. 32.

14. Halligan, Liam, "'The Process of Economic De-colonialization Is Not Yet Complete,'" *Sunday Telegraph*, Dec 3, 2006, p. 5.

15. Johnson, Tim, "Australia-China Ties Growing," *Sunday Gazette-Mail* (Charleston, WV), Jan 21, 2007, p. E5.

16. "Asia Free-trade Pacts Gain," *Wall Street Journal* (Asia), Jan 15, 2007, p. 2.

17. "India-China Trade Touches $24.9 Billion in 2006," *The Hindu*, Jan 31, 2007.

18. Wysocki Jr., Bernard and Michael M. Phillips, "U.S. Assets Entice Buyers," *Wall Street Journal* (Europe), Feb 23, 2006, p. 8.

19. Elliot, Larry, "America Is Living Beyond Its Means," *The Guardian*, Oct 2, 2006, p. 26.

20. Cordesman, Anthony, "Forging a New Asian Economic Bloc," *Financial Times Information / Gulf News*, Sep 28, 2006.

21. Nalapat, Madhav D., "Partnership for Peace, Prosperity, and Parity," *China Daily*, Feb 14, 2007, p. 11.

22. Pocha, Jehangir S., "Summit Forges Military Ties in Central Asia," *Boston Globe*, Jun 18, 2006, p. A18.

23. "EU/India Summit," *Europe Information Service*, Oct 13, 2006.

24. Jialu, Chen, "China, EU Start Talks on New Pact," *China Daily*, Jan 18, 2007, p. 1.

25. Bootle, Roger, "Lopsided and in a Time Warp," *Daily Telegraph*, Feb 12, 2007, p. 2.

26. McRae, Hamish, "We Fail to Work with China at Our Peril," *The Independent*, Feb 14, 2007, p. 33.

27. Williamson, Hugh, "Berlin Presses for Emerging Nations' Role at G8 Summits," *Financial Times*, Jan 25, 2007, p. 4.

28. Klapper, Bradley S., (AP), "An Arms Race in Space?" *Atlanta Journal-Constitution*, Feb 14, 2007, p. A7.

29. Kleine-Ahlbrandt, Stephanie and Andrew Small, "China Jumps In," *International Herald Tribune*, Feb 1, 2007.

30. Johnson, Tim, "Australia-China Ties Growing," *Sunday Gazette-Mail* (Charleston, WV), Jan 21, 2007, p. E5.

31. Shenkar, Oded, *The Chinese Century: The Rising Chinese Economy and Its Impact on the Global Economy, The Balance of Power, and Your Job* (Upper Saddle River, NJ: Wharton School Publishing, 2006), p. 162.

32. Luce, Edward, *In Spite of the Gods: The Strange Rise of Modern India* (New York: Doubleday, 2007), pp. 277-278; 287-288; 291; 294.

33. "Indian Food 2nd Favorite Takeaway in Britain," *Hindustan Times*, Oct 12, 2006.

34. Goodman, Matthew, "Curry Moguls Put Empire Up for Grabs," *Sunday Times*, Mar 11, 2007, p. 1.

35. Leicester, John, (for the Associated Press), "French Guide: Let's Not Offend Chinese," *Atlanta Journal-Constitution*, Jan 5, 2007, p. C3.

36. Bremner, Brian and Nandini Lakshman, "India Craves the Catwalk," *BusinessWeek Online*, Apr 5, 2007.

37. Boncompagni, Tatiana, "Goodbye, Feng Shui; Hello, Vastu Shastra," *Wall Street Journal*, Oct 10, 2003, p. 4.

38. Russell, Jacob Hale, "Collecting: India's Art Market Grows Up," *Wall Street Journal*, Dec 2, 2006, p. 3.

39. Lynch, David J., "Developing Nations Poised to Challenge USA as King of the Hill," *USA Today*, Feb 8, 2007, p. B1.

40. Thoreau, Henry David, *Walden; or Life in the Woods* (New York: Dover Thrift Editions, 1995), p. 8.

41. Wiwa, Ken, "Universal Human Rights, Whether You Like It or Not," *Globe and Mail*, Dec 14, 2002, p. A21.

42. Schorow, Stephanie, "Experts: Caning Works in Singapore, Not in U.S.," *Boston Herald*, Apr 14, 1994, p. 43.

43. Buckley, William F., "In Singapore, They Know How to Treat Crime," *Buffalo News*, Apr 15, 1994, p. B3.

44. Plate, Tom, "Singapore's Lesson for the World," *South China Morning Post*, Feb 1, 2007, p. 14.

5

Will the Rising Tide Lift All Boats?

It's tempting to describe the rise of Chindia as a tsunami that threatens to shake the foundations of the global economy, but I think such a metaphor is overly dramatic. In fact, the arrival of Chindia on the world stage should neither impede the continued growth of advanced economies nor overwhelm the efforts of less developed economies to follow in its footsteps. Quite the opposite. Today, the nations China and India are the growth engines of the global economy, without which economic growth everywhere else would likely stagnate. More generally, as my colleague Rajendra Sisodia and I argued in our 2006 book *Tectonic Shift*, the long journey toward economic prosperity we have been on since the 1800s, but which has been intermittently interrupted by wars (including the Cold War), appears to be back on track. We may well see the return of the Golden era—thanks primarily to the economic juggernaut of China and India.

The growth of the United States into a global economic power during the 70 years between the. Civil War and the end of World War I does indeed suggest that a rising tide lifts all boats. Lincoln's insistence that America move from an agricultural to an industrial economy meant, in effect, that Great Britain was forced to export the industrial revolution to these shores. But the establishment of factories and value-added manufacturing in America imposed no hardship upon Europe. America's rise helped fuel a growing world economy that was only shattered when the nations of Europe went to war with each other. Similarly, the rise of Chindia does not threaten the advanced nations from which it appears to be "stealing" low-wage manufacturing and service jobs. David Ricardo's theory of comparative advantage is as applicable today as it was when he formulated it in the 1820s. As long as the laborer is not exploited, production should go where costs are lowest, and the economies from which that labor migrates must redirect their resources to higher-value industries (where new, higher-wage jobs will be created).

As Ricardo believed, trade is the force that swells the tide and lifts the boats, not protectionist measures like tariffs and subsidies. Thanks to the reforms that opened the economies of China beginning in 1978 and India beginning in 1991, those two nations are now advancing toward undreamed-of prosperity, and lifting millions of their citizens out of poverty. But it is absolutely essential to recognize that as China and India mature, the low-wage work with which their journey began will be exported to less developed nations—in Africa, in South America, in Eastern Europe—so that those economies, in their turn, will begin to rise.

Thus it is that the rise of Chindia will benefit the whole world, developed nations and undeveloped nations alike, if "economic nature," so to speak, is allowed to run its course. Will the tide be allowed to rise? What can advanced nations do to enable the process? How will the other emerging economies be pulled up and into the mainstream? Let's consider both halves of the equation: First, the challenge that Chindia's rise presents to advanced nations; and second, the promise that Chindia offers to the less developed areas of the world.

The Challenge to the Developed World

The only threat to the advanced nations of the world lies in their own attitude toward the rise of Chindia. The West, in particular, must resist the impulse to respond out of fear or xenophobia, and all advanced nations, including those in Asia, must take an enlightened view of the emerging competition. The rise of Chindia is not a zero-sum game for the global economy as a whole. It is a win-win game. It is, in fact, an enormous opportunity for the advancement of global prosperity. But what, specifically, should the world's advanced nations do to help the dream become reality? Here are some recommendations.

Participate in Chindian Growth

In Chapter 4, we looked at several (mostly U.S.) companies whose growth strategies have focused on increasing their stakes in China's and India's consumer markets. This strategy is particularly important when sales in the domestic market are shrinking—as Coca-Cola vividly demonstrates. Cultivating international markets has been a part of Coke's strategy for decades, but it was Roberto Goizueta, Coke's leader during the glory days of the 1980s, who memorably articulated the vast promise of Asia. According to Goizueta's algebra, if Coke could increase consumption in China from three bottles a year per capita to 100 bottles a year, the company's growth in the 21st century would exceed its phenomenal success in the 20th. For those who doubted that such a goal could be realized in a poor country without infrastructure, Goizueta pointed to Mexico, now the nation with the world's highest per capita consumption of Coke, at 400 bottles a year.

Whether the Chinese ever achieve the 100-bottle-a-year mark remains to be seen, but the success of Coke's strategy in the developing world is beyond dispute. In the company's 2006 annual report, CEO Neville Isdell summed up the year by saying that flat growth (in case-volume) in the United States was more than balanced by healthy growth in emerging markets: 10 percent in Argentina, 15 percent in China, 26 percent in Russia, and 10 percent in Turkey. Sales in India grew at a more moderate 4 percent, but it was the first increase there in two years. Third-quarter 2006 figures were even more striking. Despite sales declines in both Japan and the United States, double-digit sales gains in China, Russia, and Brazil translated into global sales growth of 5 percent (the highest in six years), as well as a 14 percent increase in quarterly profit. Even Goizueta could not have foreseen that in 2006 international operations would account for 70 percent of the company's sales and 80 percent of its profit.

Coke's commitment to its global strategy was highlighted during the Asian financial collapse of the late 1990s. While other multinationals took flight, Coke remained steady. Douglas Daft, who was then head of the company's Middle and Far East Group, saw opportunity rather than danger: "This is the time to take advantage," he explained, "so you emerge stronger when the economy emerges." Analysts got the same message from CEO Douglas Ivester at a meeting in December 1997: "His point was that Coca-Cola will not recoil or pull back," reported one analyst. "Those that recoil have to start from scratch again." It was a lesson Coke had learned many times in many places—including Mexico just a few years earlier. In 1994, the year the peso collapsed, Coke's market share stood at about 55 percent. While investors fled, inflation soared, and job losses mounted to 1.5 million, Coke kept investing its dollars and pouring its soft drinks. Market share rose to almost 70 percent.[1]

(We might note as an aside that Coca-Cola's shares are going up too, part of a telling trend in corporate America right now. With the bottom falling out of the housing market, the first quarter of 2007 was supposed to usher in lean times on Wall Street. Instead, the Dow and the S&P 500 surged to all-time highs, due primarily to very robust earnings from American corporations. As Coke illustrates, these earnings to a very significant extent are being produced not at home, but in China, India, and other emerging markets.)

The United States is not the only advanced economy that must pursue this strategy of participation—as multinational corporations around the globe are coming to realize.

In late 2006, for example, France's Alcatel, through its Chinese subsidiary Alcatel Shanghai Bell, won a huge contract from China Mobile to create a full-scale, nationwide IP network. According to the deal, Alcatel will deploy its *7750 Service Router* and *5620 Service Aware Manager* (both for management of the internet) throughout 13 of China's most densely populated provinces and municipalities, including Beijing, Shanghai and Guangdong. The *China Economic Times* reported that with the completion of the deal, all the major Chinese operators—China Mobile, China Unicom, China Telecom, and China Netcom—have selected Alcatel's IP solution. Betting on China's future, Alcatel also signed a memorandum of understanding with Datang Telecom to help develop and support China's home-grown 3G standard, TD-SCDMA.[2]

Germany's Volkswagen illustrates the necessity of participating in Chindia's growth, as well as some of the difficulties. One of the first multinational carmakers to enter the Chinese market, via its joint ventures with Shanghai Automotive and First Auto Works, VW held the dominant position on the Mainland by the late 1990s, with more than 50 percent of total auto sales. The company even opened a $120 million R&D center in Shanghai in 1997 to develop a locally produced version of the Passat. But as demand soared in China over the next few years, the market fragmented; international players poured in and local manufacturers sprouted like weeds. By 2005, VW's market share had fallen to 30 percent. In 2006, it appeared to be leveling off at 18 percent. But as VW executives realized, 18 percent of a car market like China's was still a pretty good thing. As Winifried Vahland, President of Volkswagen China, explained, "There are 60 brands in China now. Fifty percent are global brands, 50 percent are local brands. Compared with the United States, which has altogether 37 brands in the market, China is more competitive."[3]

So, like Coke, VW is staying the course in China, with commendable results. While market share may not have increased, 2006 sales in China rose 24 percent over a year earlier. South America and Africa, incidentally, were VW's next-fastest growing markets for the year. Growth in India is coming. In November 2006, the company announced that it would spend $530 million to build a plant in the city of Pune, which is apparently envisioned as "the Detroit of India," although more recently the gravity is shifting to a southern port city of Chennai. Meanwhile, at home in Germany, sales grew at a modest 7 percent. First-quarter results from 2007 underscored the point. VW shipped a record 1.47 million vehicles during the period, up 7.9 percent from a year earlier. Sales in China led the surge, while on the domestic front, figures were down 4.9 percent.

Western financial institutions, like London-based HSBC, have a tremendous opportunity in Chindia. All those millions of consumers buying their first cars, homes, and appliances need loans, credit cards, and other services; new businesses need capital; and newly successful entrepreneurs need wealth management. That's why HSBC has invested close to $1 billion in the development of its retail network in India. The investment would no doubt be greater, but Reserve Bank of India regulations prohibit any foreign bank with an existing presence in the country from owning more than 5 percent of a domestic bank. In India, therefore, HSBC is focused entirely on "organic" growth.

Not so in China, where HSBC's investment totals more than $5 billion. There, its network of 30-plus outlets constitutes just one prong of its two-prong strategy: i.e., to grow its own organic business while continuing to work with domestic partners like the Bank of Communications and insurance giant Ping An. In fact, HSBC's stake in those companies was expected to produce some $630 million profit in 2006, compared to $52 million from its branch network operations—giving impetus to its ambitious plan to have the organic business producing half of its China profits within five years. In any case, 2006 was a banner year for the company's business in Chindia. Midyear earnings were up 30 percent from a year earlier, driven by strong growth in both China and India.

We might add that what is true of advanced economies in the West is true of all advanced economies, including those in the East. In Japan, for example, Toyota knows that its ambition to become the world's No. 1 carmaker is entirely dependent upon its success in China, the world's fastest-growing car market. Toyota has announced a goal of garnering 10 percent of the China market by 2010 and is working feverishly with its Chinese partners to ramp up production and sales. In 2006, Toyota's venture with Guangzhou Automobile produced the first Chinese-built Camry, already an import favorite, and the locally-made version is priced to move fast. Then there's Sony, which already in 2005 had invested $1.1 billion in the Mainland. Of course, some of this investment is on the manufacturing end, with the video products, games, and mobile equipment bound for export. But China is also Sony's third-largest market, behind only the United States and Japan, and it's predicted to surpass its domestic market in just a few years. These numbers say it all: In 1997, Sony's first year of operation in China, it generated about $20 million in revenue. Since then, sales of consumer electronics have risen 100-fold, surpassing $2 billion. Total Sony sales in China are expected to produce some $8 billion in 2008.

As for South Korea, its trade figures with China tell the story. When diplomatic ties were established in 1992, trade between the two nations totaled $5 billion. Fifteen years later—an anniversary marked by Wen Jiabao's first visit to South Korea in his office as China's Premier—the figure stood at $130 billion. In the process, China became South Korea's largest trade partner, largest importer, and largest overseas investment target. Equally remarkable, South Korea is now China's third-largest trade partner, behind only Japan and the United States. It's no wonder that Premier Wen described his visit as "substantial and fruitful" and noted that future cooperation between the two nations looked promising.[4]

Even tiny Singapore is looking for growth in Chindia. In 2007, Singapore Airlines substantially increased its schedule of flights to most major Indian cities, including Chennai, Delhi, Bangalore and Calcutta. At the same time, it was working out a deal with Wipro to consolidate its reservations operations in Australia, New Zealand, the United States and Canada and move them to a call center in Mumbai. More significantly, the airline has long been rumored to have an interest in investing in China. As of late 2006, the company was trying to acquire 25 percent (the maximum allowable under Chinese regulations) of China Eastern, one of the three major carriers on the Mainland.

Wake Up and Smell the Coffee

Yes, the competition from China and India is going to be even more fierce than the competition we faced from Japan and Korea, but that may not be such a bad thing. It might just create a healthy sense of urgency inside the walnut-paneled offices of old-line corporations. It may shake some business leaders out of their lethargy and complacency; it may prove a needed corrective to the arrogance and denial that have weakened the competitive fiber of many once-great Western companies.

In my most recent book, *The Self Destructive Habits of Good Companies and How to Break Them*, I have documented why good companies fail. Most of them acquire seven bad habits on their way to greatness including denial, arrogance, complacency and internal turf wars.

The point is: corporations in advanced economies don't need to fear competition from Chindia. They need to face it. And they can.

Looking at America in particular, it should be noted that productivity of the American worker matches or exceeds that of any worker in the world. This is what Indian IT services companies are now discovering as wages at home begin to rise. Yes, wages in America are still higher, but productivity is excellent, discipline is good, turnover is minimal. The wage trade-off is worth it, and Indian companies are now looking to expand their talent pool in America.

Or consider foreign carmakers like Honda, Toyota and Hyundai. Honda opened its first U.S. manufacturing plant in Marysville, Ohio 25 years ago, and now employs 16,000 workers in Ohio alone. The people who fume that buying "imported" cars takes jobs from U.S. workers probably don't realize that 80 percent of the automobiles Honda sells in America are built here. The assembly plant Hyundai opened in Montgomery, Alabama in 2002 now employs 3,100, and the nearby engine plant, set to open in 2008, is expected to employ another 600. Kia, Hyundai's affiliate, plans to open an assembly plant in West Point, Georgia in 2009 that will generate, directly and indirectly, approximately 4,500 jobs.

However, none of these foreigners is building plants in America as fast as Toyota. Americans' love for Toyota autos appears matched by Toyota's devotion to American workers. The company's biggest U.S. plant, in Georgetown, Kentucky employs 7,000 workers and since opening in 1988 has produced nearly 5 million Camrys. Toyota announced in 2007 that it had chosen Tupelo, Mississippi as the site of its eighth North American assembly plant. But as Toyota North America's the then president Jim Press puts it, "There will probably be a ninth and a twelfth plant. I wouldn't mind 15 plants."[5] The company is now building about 2 million cars in America every year and is perfectly willing to draw attention to its commitment to the American workforce. Commuters getting off the escalator at one Capital Hill Metro stop are greeted by a big red banner reading: "386,000. Bird watchers in Nebraska. Kilometers to the Moon. Jobs created by Toyota in the U.S."[6]

What's going on in the U.S. auto industry proves that there's nothing wrong with the American worker, but there may be some problems up the chain of command. The *Wall Street Journal* offered some interesting observations on the November 2006 meeting between executives of the Big Three and President Bush. Predictably, the executives from Detroit came to complain about the "unfair competition" from abroad and its harmful effects on the "American auto industry." But the *Journal* wanted clearer definitions: "What does it mean to be a domestic U.S. auto manufacturer today?" It noted that, according to 2004 figures, some 29 percent of all the cars and light trucks made in America were produced in foreign-owned manufacturing plants. It also reported that every one of the 10 top-selling cars of 2006—including the Toyota Camry, the Honda Accord, and the Nissan Altima—was produced in U.S. facilities. The *Journal* concluded that, in fact, the U.S. auto industry as a whole was quite healthy, and that the problems faced by the Big Three were the result of "self-inflicted wounds" like weak product lines and bad management decisions. Detroit came to Washington looking for a bail-out, but the *Journal* counseled against it: "Consumers have more choices in what to drive and better quality than ever. And prices are competitive. Government intervention in a market this healthy can only increase the chances that it won't stay that way."[7]

American corporations shouldn't need government bail-outs or subsidies, nor should they presume that they are the best just because they are American. American companies need to wake up, reassert themselves, and then become the best all over again. Many like IBM, HP, and GE have already committed to this philosophy with stunning results.

Some, like Harley-Davidson, have successfully completed it. The venerable Milwaukee-based manufacturer (and for many years America's only motorcycle maker) went public in 1965, and in 1969 was bought by American Machine and Foundry (AMF)—which has gone on to fame as America's leading operator of bowling centers. But by the late 1970s, with sales and quality slipping, and a deluge of Japanese bikes flooding the American marketplace, AMF put Harley up for sale. When no buyers stepped forward, 13 AMF executives pooled their resources and bought the company in 1981. As one of those investors, Jeffrey Bleustein—who would eventually rise to CEO in 1997—recalled, "[We] didn't want to go into the history books as the company that let Harley-Davidson perish."

Still, it was a roll of the dice that might not have come up a winner. A step-child that AMF had badly neglected, Harley was in poor health. AMF had a new strategy that Harley didn't fit into, explained Bleustein, "and if we grew, that created a bigger problem for AMF." When the team of investors took over, they had to pretty much start from scratch, looking at everything from product redesign, to manufacturing processes, to marketing strategy. "We really had to reinvent the company," Bleustein admitted, but the new owners' had one thing to build on: Harley's strong brand, and a loyal following of dealers and customers. The engineering team set to work with a new "materials as needed" (or MAN) manufacturing application, which improved quality and efficiency by having parts and materials purchased only as needed. At the same time, the marketing division dreamed up the Harley Owners Group (or HOG), devoted to expanding the irresistible aura of the Harley cult. Organized in 1983, by the time of the company's 100th birthday in 2003, it had grown from 90,000 members to 700,000.

Admittedly, Harley did get help from the government—a Reagan-era tariff against the Japanese imports, which increased from 4.4 percent to 49 percent in its first year and was to be annually lowered until it returned to 4.4 percent after the fifth year. To its credit, Harley didn't need five years. After the fourth year, AMF/Harley petitioned for an early termination of the tariff. (Of course, the U.S. car industry also got help from Reagan, who pressed Japan for "voluntary export quotas." The difference is, Detroit now wants more help.)

By the time Bleustein and his fellow owners took the company public again in 1986, one of the greatest turn-arounds in U.S. automotive history was complete. By 1987, Harley had regained 25 percent of the U.S. heavyweight-motorcycle market, up from 16 percent just two years earlier. That centenary year, 2003, marked 17 straight years of growth, and along the way (in 1999) Harley had bested Honda in the U.S. market for the first time in 30 years. A new milestone was reached in 2006, when the company made its first move into China with the opening of a Harley-Davidson dealership in Beijing.

Current CEO (and 36-year company veteran) James Ziemer summed up what the Harley comeback was all about: "Jeff and his team did a lot of great things with really no cash. It was a lot of brain, a lot of effort, a lot of confidence in the company during some rough times."[8]

In short, American—and Western—corporations must answer the call. In industries where we once led and would like to lead again, we need to follow the example set by Harley-Davidson. Leaders must inspire their companies with vision and passion, and a commitment to return to the top. I should add that in many critical sectors, like education and health care, we continue to lead the world. In those industries we must be dedicated to holding that position and to avoiding the pitfalls of arrogance and complacency.

Again, the message here is positive. Competition from Chindia, like the fabled poison of Mithridates, should not kill us. It should make us stronger. At the same time, we need to face the fact that sometimes the right move is to get out.

Exit Smart

At the same time, we need to face the fact that sometimes the right move is to get out. In the famous words of Kenny Rogers, "You've got to know when to fold 'em." New companies are born and old ones die every day; whole industries come and go. As technological advances render old processes obsolete, and as the fulcrum of the global economy shifts toward Chindia, old money will increasingly need to find new opportunity. The point here is: when it's your time to go, exit in an anticipatory mode and get highest valuation for your assets. That is, exit smart.

Actually, Americans have shown a certain knack for this. In 1998, Bob Eaton sold Chrysler to Daimler-Benz for $37 billion. In 2007, Daimler divested Chrysler by selling it to Cerberus Capital Management for roughly *one-sixth* of that 1998 sale price. Similarly, when Coca-Cola decided it wanted to get out of the motion picture business in 1989, it sold Columbia Pictures to Sony for $1 billion more than it had paid just seven years earlier.

Exiting, though, is just the first step. The second step is putting your resources (your money, your people, your expertise, your patents, etc.) to work somewhere else. Your exit shouldn't be a disappearance; it should be a transforming migration. Good examples abound.

Monsanto Chemical Works was founded in 1901 to manufacture saccharin. The chemical sweetener was linked to cancer in laboratory rats in 1977, but by that time Monsanto had already transitioned into textile chemicals and synthetic fibers. As the textile industry fled to Asia, Monsanto made its move from textile to agricultural chemicals, developing blockbusters like Lasso and Roundup. It didn't stop there. The company's interest in developing seeds that tolerate Roundup while resisting insects led to a new focus—on bioengineering crops like soybean, corn, cotton and canola. Monsanto is still in the chemistry business, but it continues to stay ahead of the competition by finding new applications for its capabilities.

Or take Arm & Hammer brand baking soda. The product was created in 1846 to be used in bread baking, and making bread rise remained its purpose for 100 years. But when homemakers stopped baking their own bread, the maker (Church & Dwight Co.) had to find new applications—a task at which it succeeded brilliantly. The product's cleansing and foaming properties brought Arm & Hammer toothpaste into American households after World War II. Then, when newer products like Colgate and Crest pushed it out of that market, it found a new application as a laundry detergent (a "natural," non-phosphate product, good for the environment and beneficial for people who were allergic to other detergents.) Baking soda's effectiveness as an odor killer also began to be exploited, opening up a huge market (not just inside refrigerators, but also in cat litter boxes and on carpets.) Most recently, the product's health benefits are coming to light. The company manufactures a medical-grade sodium bicarbonate for use in kidney dialysis, and sports medicine research reports that a spoonful of baking soda dissolved in water or juice provides an energy boost.

Yet another example comes from DuPont, which invented nylon when the communist revolution in China disrupted the supply of silk. The company produced its first pair of nylon stockings in 1940 and a few years later was manufacturing nylon parachutes for the war effort. After the war, when other synthetics took over the hosiery market, nylon found new life as an upholstery fabric. It was a short leap from there to wall-to-wall carpeting, and from there to artificial turf. Now nylon is replacing metal in the human-parts industry—finding use in heart valves and hip prosthetics.

Woolworth offers a great example from the retail sector. The classic five and dime seemed to be staring at its own demise when—unlike the visionary Sears—it failed to foresee the suburban mall phenomenon. But instead of going belly-up, Woolworth migrated into specialty retailing. It milked the Woolworth brand and invested the returns in the shoe business, first by buying up Kinney and then, spectacularly, by creating Foot Locker. Now Woolworth/Foot Locker has the last laugh at the expense of Sears, which finds itself still locked into the department-store model. One of its departments is the family shoe center, selling shoe lines of various types to men, women and children. But for the most popular lines—sports shoes for walking, running, playing and loafing—the family isn't shopping at Sears. It's shopping at Foot Locker, Lady Foot Locker and Kids Foot Locker.

These examples illustrate our knack for exiting smartly in the face of domestic competition. Now we must apply those lessons to foreign competition. Japan created the paradigm with its strategy of "vacating markets," or giving up industries in which it was no longer competitive and migrating up the value chain. It began its post-war journey by specializing first in textiles, steel and shipbuilding, and in each case developed an improved technology that would accelerate its push for dominance. It was synthetic fabrics in the textile industry, blast furnace technology in steel, and riveting to replace nuts and bolts in shipbuilding. Once it had brought these industries to maturity, and with less developed nations prepared to copy the technology and reduce costs, Japan moved onward and upward—to consumer electronics, automobiles and machine tools.

Right now Americans are drinking orange juice from Brazil. In fact, America has now become a net importer of agricultural products. To what endeavor will Florida's and California's citrus growers migrate? And how about Western makers of clothing, shoes, toys, carpets, furniture and auto parts? There's going to be a whole lot of exiting going on. But business leaders who see the future clearly will also find many destinations to which to migrate.

Let Investment Flow In

In my defense of the American worker, I noted the eagerness of Japanese and Korean carmakers to build factories in this country. At the same time, it's widely assumed that all we get from China and India is cheap goods and services. But just as happened in the case of Japan and Korea, Chindia's export model is giving way to the investment model. Today, Indian and Chinese corporations are going global, no less than their Japanese and Korean counterparts, expanding into advanced nations either by building plants and facilities for their own companies or else by buying up entire foreign companies.

In Chapter 1 we looked at a couple of examples—Lenovo's purchase of IBM's PC unit, for example, or, even more spectacularly, Mittal Steel's purchase in 2006 of Arcelor, Europe's largest steel manufacturer, for $34 billion. Other examples continue to stream across the headlines. In February 2007, India's largest aluminum maker, Hindalco Industries, paid $5.7 billion for Atlanta-based aluminum company Novelis. A month earlier, Tata Steel bought the Anglo-Dutch steelmaker Corus Group for $12.9 billion. In April 2007, New Delhi-based Essar Global agreed to buy Minnesota Steel Industries and, as part of the deal, to invest $1.65 billion to build a 2.5 million ton-a-year steel plant in northern Minnesota.

Meanwhile, during April and May of 2007, China sent a business delegation led by a ranking member of the Ministry of Commerce on a $15 billion spending spree across the United States. Its immediate fruits were $4.3 billion worth of technology contracts in California, and, on the other side of the continent, a $30 million electrical parts factory to be built in Barnesville, Georgia, promising to employ 350 people. This was just one of five separate "buying missions" headed westward out of China during 2007, as Beijing continued to encourage its corporations to invest overseas. According to Ma Xiuhong, the Ministry official, representatives from 208 Chinese companies will be scouring 23 U.S. states, looking to do big business with machinery, electronics and household companies.[9]

Such investment is a boon for the advanced nations into which it flows. The building and operation of plants creates jobs. The buy-out of companies often generates huge sums of cash that can be used to create whole new businesses. The competitive environment all-around gets a healthy jolt. The presence of Toyota, Honda, Sony and Samsung in the West has had a bracing effect on the auto and electronics industries and has been of incalculable benefit to consumers. The industries haven't dried up; the markets haven't shrunk. Investment in-flow from Chindia will be similarly positive.

Moreover, in industries where advanced countries continue to lead the developing world, China and India will be buying on a scale commensurate to their size and needs. Perhaps the most critical of those industries is defense, as illustrated by India's commitment to buy some 126 multi-role fighter aircraft ($10 billion worth) over the next decade. The United States, needless to say, dearly hopes to be the seller. China, with only 7 percent of its land considered arable, is expected to be a net importer of agriculture by 2035, which is why that the Ministry of Commerce official, on her swing through America, suggested that America's soybean and cotton farmers would also be getting some of China's business. Health care and health management constitute another area where advanced nations hold a sizeable lead, and where Chindia's imports will be substantial.

It's interesting to note the historical shift: in the old model, the North (the advanced nations of Europe and North America) did business with the South (the developing world) mostly to its own advantage. Now the tables have turned: the South (epitomized by China's $1 trillion in foreign currency) has become the rainmaker. But that's okay. The advanced nations need the rain.

Ride the Crest of Innovation

I suggested in an earlier chapter that affordability, scarcity and environmental issues will spur a wave of Chindian innovation, but surely the problems of world poverty, diminishing natural resources and environmental deterioration will push innovation in advanced nations as well. Whether East or West, what an exciting time it must be to be a scientist, engineer, researcher or inventor! The challenges the world faces today are sure to stimulate ideas, innovations and technologies heretofore undreamed of. There is no reason to suppose that the West will forfeit its position as world leader in knowledge creation.

Let's look briefly at two areas—energy and nanotechnology—where research is meeting the world's most critical needs and where researchers in developed nations are continuing to lead the way.

Today the world runs on oil. It is a diminishing resource, and until a better source of energy becomes viable, innovation must focus on environmentally sustainable ways to extract the oil we do have. Canada's "oil sands" provide one example among many that might be cited. These oil fields in Alberta constitute one of the largest crude oil deposits in the world, but extraction is problematical. The water that gets mixed with the fine clay from the oil sands cannot be reclaimed, so the clay forms thick tailings (material left over after ore processing) with high water content, consuming two to three barrels of water for every barrel of oil and requiring enormous ponds for containment. Now a new partnership between Imperial Oil and Alberta Ingenuity (the Imperial Oil-Alberta Ingenuity Centre for Oil Sands Innovation) will invest $15 million in research over the next five years to solve the problem of how to extract the oil without using water and creating the tailings. The center's scientists have no doubt that the goal—clean bitumen with minimal water consumption—will be achieved; more important, the new technologies developed by the partnership will be applicable around the world.[10]

Tomorrow, if we're lucky, the world will not run on oil. It will run on hydrogen—which will become the energy of choice first in automobiles. General Motors' Rick Wagoner says GM will have a hydrogen fuel-cell powered car for sale by 2010, but it looks like Honda will beat GM to the punch and put its first fuel-cell autos on the market in 2008. A prototype, the FCX Concept car was on display at California's Laguna Seca racetrack in late 2006. Journalists were invited to test drive the vehicle and, generally, they were amazed. The car is sleek and luxurious; it's plenty fast for accelerating onto the expressway; it's wonderfully quiet; and it covers about 300 miles on a "tank full" of fuel, giving it an average energy-equivalent economy of 106 mpg. Most promising of all, it emits nothing but water. According to Andrew English, one of the journalists lucky enough to go for a spin, despite the many obstacles still to be overcome, "the FCX Concept is a superb-looking, entirely practical vision of the future. It is also eminently desirable, and I want one."

About those obstacles: Though the engine emits only water, it emits enough (eight gallons per tank full of fuel) to cause ice or fog problems during winter. A much bigger problem is cost. Honda's concept car cost $5 million, and the models Honda plans to sell in 2008 will definitely not be for mass consumption. A conservative estimate is that it'll be another 10 years before any real mass market rollout, and even then the FCX, with a probable cost of roughly $65,000, will obviously be for the affluent. And then there's fuel storage, probably the biggest obstacle holding back hydrogen's development. Right now there are very few hydrogen fueling stations in the United States and no great incentive to build them either—since the cars aren't on the road yet. "It's a chicken and egg problem," says Yozo Kami, Honda's revered "father of the fuel cell." The solution is one of those public-private partnerships I recommended in Chapter 3—in this case one where automakers, energy companies, and the government all place their money on the hydrogen bet in such a way that the cars and the fuelling stations appear at the same time. To its credit, the Bush administration has made a small step in this direction, committing $1.2 billion to develop the necessary infrastructure.

In the meantime, Honda and the other fuel cell developers are working on their own solutions, like solar-powered hydrogen generators that, ultimately, produce heat and electricity for the home while generating hydrogen to run the car. Now we're talking about the hydrogen economy.[11]

While we await the hydrogen energy revolution, other doors to the future are being opened by nanotechnology. Investment statistics reveal the global frenzy now going on in nanotech: Worldwide, $9.5 billion was spent on R&D in 2005, and by 2008, global demand for nanotech materials, devices and tools will exceed $28 billion. The U.S. market will expand from $3.3 billion in 2008 to $20 billion by 2013, while the global market for textiles using nanotechnology will reach $13 billion by 2007 and $115 billion by 2012.

The numbers also show that developed nations clearly outpace emerging nations in nanotech investment. The United States is the largest spender, at 27 percent of global investment. The Japanese are second with 24 percent, and roughly that same amount is being invested by Western Europe (Germany, the UK, and France). The remaining quarter of the investment pie is divided among China, Russia, South Korea, Canada, and Australia.

But what is nanotechnology? It is the ability to manipulate microscopic material at the atomic level. Its applications are so vast that they impinge upon virtually all other areas of technological advancement, including energy. Enthusiasts say nanotechnology has the potential to put us in affordable solar-powered homes and hydrogen-fueled cars while turning our nastiest wastewater into clean, pure drinking water. Its economic impact is beyond measure. Lux Research, which specializes in the nanotech sector, predicts that 15 percent of the world's manufacturing output could be made with nanotechnology by 2014. An estimated 2 million workers would be needed worldwide to create the forthcoming $2.6 trillion worth of products.

The technology is already increasing the storage capacity of computer discs, and it's being used to make stain-resistant clothing, sunscreens, eyeglass coatings that reduce glare and longer-lasting tennis balls, among other applications. But it's the future that boggles the mind. Researchers expect nanotechnology to do everything from reducing pollution to enabling doctors to kill cancer cells without damaging healthy ones. At Cornell, nanotech scientists are developing sensors to detect disease-causing organisms in water—a huge step forward in protecting people from life-threatening illnesses.[12]

Global business is not merely paying attention, it is pushing the frontier. In April 2007, researchers at IBM's Almaden Research Center in California announced the latest milestone: a way to not simply look at clusters of atoms but—for the first time—to look inside them. The ability to see the structure of individual atoms in three dimensions, say IBM's researchers, could open new realms of nanotechnology that might let semiconductor engineers create even smaller and more powerful computer microprocessors, or help biotech researchers develop new types of drugs. According to Dan Rugar, Manager of Nanoscale Studies at IBM, the discovery "represents a huge breakthrough in structural molecular biology."[13]

In these and other critical areas at the forefront of knowledge creation, the United States and other developed nations are sure to remain on the crest of innovation. Chindia will narrow the gap—as it should—but its gradual ascent into the knowledge economy should not be construed as a threat to the developed world. On the contrary, it can only help promote the global prosperity desired by the East as well as the West.

Create "Blue Ocean" Opportunities

While on the subject of innovation, let's consider what W. Chan Kim and Renee Maubourgne call "value innovation." This concept—figuring out new ways to create value for customers—is at the heart of their much-praised book *Blue Ocean Strategy*. The book advises companies that there is a way out of the "bloody red oceans" of intense competition, i.e., by creating your own new market space where competition is nonexistent or irrelevant. The "strategy canvases" of companies competing in red oceans tend to converge—competitors selling similar products to similar consumers and seeking incrementally to build market share, as with Coke v. Pepsi. But by "redefining the problem," companies can create a *divergent* strategy that leads them toward their own blue ocean. The book offers innumerable examples of the blue ocean strategy. Let's look very briefly at two.

Cirque du Soleil, the authors point out, has achieved in just 20 years the level of revenues that took Ringling Bros. and Barnum & Bailey—global leaders in the circus industry—more than a hundred years to attain. How? Not by competing against traditional circus, but rather by appealing to a whole new group of customers and thus creating "uncontested new market space." Competing against traditional circus would have no doubt meant more (or more exotic) animals, performers with more star power, maybe even four rings instead of three. Such measures, of course, would have raised Cirque's cost structure without substantially driving new value to the consumer. Instead, rather than trying to offer a better solution to the same old problem—adding more fun and thrills to traditional circus—Cirque redefined the problem: it combined the fun and thrill of circus with the intellectual sophistication and artistic richness of the theater. Moreover, Cirque got rid of some of the traditional circus's most burdensome costs, like animal acts and star performers, and thus was able to achieve both differentiation and low cost. Since it was giving its customers a new theater-like entertainment experience (value innovation), it priced its tickets against those of the theater rather than the circus and thereby created a leap in value for itself also. Twenty years later, there are still no competitors in Cirque's blue ocean.

Two years after its introduction, Yellow Tail wine, a product of Australia's Casella Wines, had become the fastest-growing brand in the history of either the Australian or the U.S. wine industry, and the No. 1 wine import into the United States, surpassing every brand from France or Italy. By August 2003, it was the No. 1 red wine (in a 750-ml bottle) sold in the United States, even beating out the California labels. Like Cirque du Soleil, Yellow Tail decided not to compete within the traditional industry. Instead, it saw what the wine industry failed to see: that there was a huge market out there (beer drinkers, cocktail drinkers, and other drinkers of non-wine alcoholic beverages) that needed to be tapped. Its truly profound insight was that all the points on which traditional wines competed (fancy enological terminology, vineyard prestige, flavor complexity, aging quality, upscale labeling) were a complete turn-off to this vast untapped market of drinkers. These people saw the wine industry as pretentious and saw choosing wine as too much trouble (and possibly embarrassing). What Yellow Tail did, then, was redefine wine. It built a strategy on selling points alien to the traditional industry: easy to drink, easy to select, and a source of fun and adventure. It offered only two choices, a white (Chardonnay) and a red (Shiraz); it took everything remotely technical and jargon-ridden off the bottle, and in its place put its striking, vibrant kangaroo (orange and yellow on a black background). Thus, like Cirque, it differentiated itself, drove down its own costs, drove up value for consumers, and created a vast blue ocean.[14]

It's not difficult to think of other examples. After World War II, thanks to the rapid rise of the soft drink industry, people were preparing funeral rites for the poor old coffee. Then Starbucks came along and redefined the coffee-drinking experience, opening up a vast market (the student population and young professionals) that no one could have foreseen. Wal-Mart pulled off a similar feat in retailing. Here was a moribund industry (the stand-alone discount store) that Sam Walton breathed new life into by doing the unthinkable—taking it into small towns. He was scoffed at: *How do you expect to succeed in small towns like Bentonville?* Walton's famous answer encapsulates the blue ocean strategy: "Hit 'em where they ain't." Today, Wal-Mart is the world's largest corporation, in revenues surpassing General Motors, Exxon Mobil and General Electric.

Enterprise Rent-A-Car provides a particularly vivid example. While Hertz, Avis, and then Budget fought over the "suits and shorts" market of business and vacation travelers pouring through the nation's airports, Enterprise set its sights on an entirely new market—the at-home family in need of a spare car for unforeseen circumstances. If your car has broken down, or if you've been in an accident and your car has to spend a few days in the body shop, or if your car is back at the dealership for routine maintenance, you are in Enterprise's hands. Instead of vying for that expensive close-to-airport real estate, Enterprise opened cheap storefronts in strip malls across the country—so many of them, in fact, that the company claims to have an office with 15 minutes of 90 percent of the nation's population. What a blue ocean Enterprise swam into! As of 2005, the company's total fleet numbered 600,000 vehicles, roughly twice that of Hertz, and it continues to open 400 new locations a year.

As Kim and Maubourgne point out and as these examples illustrate, value innovation is not necessarily a matter of creating new technology. Often it is a matter of new thinking about an old problem. On the other hand, sometimes blue oceans are indeed created by new technologies. Sometimes a new technology will push out an older one and send an industry soaring into the stratosphere. Think of Henry Ford's Model T, the mass production of which transformed the automobile from an expensive toy for the wealthy into a necessity for the common man. The dimensions of Ford's blue ocean are measured by the fact that, thanks to the Model T, the company's market share of the auto industry surged from 9 percent in 1908 to 61 percent in 1921. We are seeing a similar transformation in the print media, where information is increasingly being delivered via the Internet. The phenomenal success of Google suggests the depth of the blue oceans that beckon to technology pioneers like Larry Page and Sergey Brin. While I'm online, I might note also that the Internet is transforming higher education, opening up a vast market of non-traditional students for whom getting a college degree is now a real possibility.

Even more dramatic, new technologies can sometimes trigger whole new industries. Innovators that bring new products to the marketplace, creating desires (and eventually needs) that consumers never realized they had before, chart the widest blue oceans of all. It would be hard to think of a better example than television, a product that didn't exist when many of us were born, but without which life today would be unimaginable. Or take cell phones—a product that just a few years ago seemed a symbol of conspicuous consumption, but is now a necessity for every member of the household. Of course there's also the personal computer, not only massive in itself but also the progenitor of huge sub-industries like computer gaming.

Indeed at the intersection of the Internet (or the IT industry more generally) and consumer electronics, new industries are being created all the time. Let's take a look at telematics, the industry that's combining computers with wireless communications inside of automobiles. *USA Today* spotted the new trend in 2005: "Pimp my ride" was out; "geek my ride" was in. The fully "geeked" ride would put "a PC in your car with a touch-screen panel in the dashboard, Wi-Fi antenna, iTunes pumping music through speakers, Global Positioning System (GPS) tracking, video games, e-mail and technology that can both keep your attention on the road and help you sue anyone who rear-ends you." One aficionado with a Wi-Fi enabled PC in his car described being able to stop outside of any Starbucks with Wi-Fi, connect and download his e-mail, then touch a button on his screen to have a voice synthesizer read his messages aloud to him as he drove down the road.[15]

Is there a blue ocean of opportunity here? Apparently so. In a 2006 study conducted by Accenture, eight of 10 U.S. car owners reported that they were looking for some form of in-vehicle technology in their new cars. And they're getting what they're looking for. Today electronics comprise 18 percent of all the raw material purchased by auto makers, and the manufacturers are paying more for microprocessors than for steel. Carmakers have their electronics engineers working overtime to meet consumer demands, as Toyota's Scion FUSE demonstrates. This avatar of the new has a media station running the length of the dashboard that can accommodate MP3 or iPod players, laptops, and any other electronic information storage and display devices. Passengers can watch movies or play video games on dual-display, 10.5-inch video screens, or use the Wi-Fi connection for e-mail or instant messaging.[16] Volkswagen, meanwhile, is working on a high-tech bumper sticker—a wafer-thin, highly flexible foil that can display text and images like a computer monitor and thereby allow drivers to communicate with those behind them. And a global trends manager at Ford foresees the day when your car's steering wheel will be used to monitor heart rate and other vital signs and send the information to your physician's computer.

Here we see telematics as one facet of a broader technological phenomenon—machine to machine communications, or M2M. The technology that for several years has allowed for remote reading of gas and electric meters is suddenly exploding in its range of applications. Vending machines can now send information to a central computer to indicate that they need to be restocked. Lottery machine terminals in grocery and convenience stores communicate with the central system. Sensors attached to machine parts like electric motors and compressors use a cellular network to let a central server know when they are overheating or being stressed by too much vibration. Young companies like DataRemote, SensorLogic and nPhase are getting more orders than they can fill, in an industry that researchers say is now moving "from the introductory to the growth stage." How fast it will grow depends on whom you talk to. Juniper Research, which tracks the telecom industry, predicts the world market for M2M business will increase from $20 billion in 2006 to $76 billion in 2011. French research firm IDATE is not so conservative; it predicts a $264 billion M2M industry by 2010.[17]

With machines getting smart enough to talk to each other, and with the car evolving into a mobile platform for the Internet, why not let the car take over the job of personal assistant? I see it working something like this: my smart refrigerator, Internet enabled to keep track of everything inside, detects that I'm running low on orange juice or that my baking soda is beginning to lose its odor-absorbing ability. It will send a signal (wireless, of course) to my car's on-board computer, and my computer— by text or by voice—will remind me to pick up the necessary items on my way home from work. Road assistance, like GM's On-Star, is just the starting point.

Here's another way to look at the whole new-industry phenomenon: Originally, product manufacturing led to services—purchase a car, then have it serviced as needed. But now the opposite is true: providing services is creating products, creating manufacturing sectors, creating new industries. The new paradigm is most evident in health care, where research into new treatments for chronic disease is constantly splintering and subdividing the medical products industry. Take Medtronic, for example, which developed the first cardiac pacemaker in 1957 (and the implantable version in 1960) and in the process gave birth to a new industry.

Combine service, medical products and M2M technology, and you've got Japan's burgeoning "smart toilet" industry, now valued at about $625 million. It makes sense that Japan, with its love of gadgetry and obsession with cleanliness, would develop toilets that, as *BusinessWeek* reports, "deodorize the room, play music to drown out unwanted noise, spray your buttocks, cleanse the bowl, and close the lid after you're done." But Japan also has an aging population and a tradition of in-home care for the elderly, so the smart toilet also has sensors and microprocessors that transform it into an in-house doctor. It tests sugar-levels in urine and detects blood in fecal matter. It diagnoses liver complaints or kidney ailments and can even confirm pregnancy. There's also a monitor (next to the toilet-paper roll) to measure blood pressure. In development now is wireless technology that will enable the medical data to be sent to the doctor's office across town. Japan's Toto Ltd. is the industry leader, but frankly, Toto's blue ocean is starting to get crowded. Nihon Safety and Matsushita Electric are but two of the dozens of companies moving into the sector.[18]

More generally, as the West's baby-boom generation moves into retirement age, services across the board will become growth industries. Millions of retirees will need not only to be kept healthy, but to be kept safe (advanced home alarm systems), solvent (wider range of financial instruments), and entertained (recreation-oriented communities). The companies who bring new approaches to meeting these needs will prosper.

And finally, a vast source of blue ocean opportunity exists in what might be called the "knowledge storehouse" of the advanced nations—its decades of investment in proprietary knowledge creation, its patents, its inventions, the great body of work that has earned the lion's share of Nobel Prizes and other top awards. Some of this knowledge rests with governments, some with corporations. In either case, its commercialization affords a huge, long-term opportunity. When the government declassified cell phone technology, for example, a trillion-dollar industry was launched. On the corporate level, IBM released the technology that allowed the creation of SAP, illustrating the benefits that often follow when scientists (or managers) become entrepreneurs. In the years to come, as more of this proprietary knowledge is put to commercial advantage, who knows what industries might blossom?

The Promise for Emerging Nations

If the rise of Chindia should reinvigorate the economies of advanced nations, where markets are mature and growth has slowed, think what it promises to the less developed nations of the world, where markets are yet untapped and the engines of growth have yet to be ignited. Let's now consider how Chindia's rising tide will not only float the ocean liners of the developed world but will also lift the frailer craft of emerging economies.

Investments in Infrastructure

In an earlier chapter I mentioned the historic summit in Beijing in November 2006, attended by leaders from 48 African nations. The fruits of that meeting are summarized as follows: $1.9 billion worth of deals, including a rural telephone system in Ghana, an aluminum factory in Egypt and a highway in Nigeria. This followed the $8.3 billion deal signed by China Civil Engineering Construction Corp. to build an 815-mile railway between the Nigerian cities of Lagos and Kano, the most expensive international construction project ever undertaken by a Chinese business. India's considerable investment in Africa also includes projects in Nigeria; its state-run oil exploration company, Oil & Natural Gas Corp., is investing $6 billion in a power plant and railroads there in return for stakes in the nation's rich oil fields.

This is the old British colonial model without the colonialism: that is, invest where the natural resources are. My point in Chapter 2 was that China and India have a vast thirst for the oil, gas and other natural resources to be found in abundance in Africa and other developing nations, and that their infrastructure investments are a matter of enlightened self-interest. But the developing nations in Africa, Latin America and elsewhere need Chindia's investment every bit as much as Chindia needs the natural resources. Indeed, a World Bank study published at the end of 2006 revives an iconic phrase to describe Africa's new economic ties to China and India; the study's author, Harry Broadman, declares that "this new Silk Road represents a significant, and to date, rare opportunity to accelerate Africa's growth, expand intra-African trade and hasten the continent's integration into the global economy."[19]

The developing nations of Latin America are another favorite target of Chindian infrastructure investment. As I noted earlier, many of these projects are in energy, iron ore and steelmaking—like Shanghai Baosteel Group's joint venture with Companhia Vale do Rio Doce (CVRD) to build a $1.4 billion steel mill in Brazil, or ONGC-Videsh's exploration of the vast heavy oil reserves in Venezuela's Orinoco River belt region. China's commitment to invest $10 billion a year for 10 years (starting in 2004) continues to outpace India's Latin American spending spree, but India's investments in the region are moving beyond the energy and steel sectors into pharmaceuticals, agriculture and IT services. To cite just a few examples, Dr. Reddy's Laboratories spent $60 million on a pharmaceuticals plant in Mexico in 2006, and, in 2007, Bilcare began construction of a plant in Brazil for the manufacture of pharma packaging material. United Phosphorous has built a plant to manufacture agricultural chemicals in Argentina, while the Birla Group is building a carbon black plant in Mexico. As for IT, Tata Consultancy Services has set up software development centers in Montevideo and Brazil. Writing in *Financial Express*, Ministry of External Affairs official R. Viswanathan calls the deluge of investment activity "another kind of Amazonian downpour."[20]

The fact is that Chindia's growing wealth is allowing it to seek investment opportunities all over the developing world—in Eastern Europe, in the Middle East and in other Asian nations. The impact cannot help but be positive—just as it was when Great Britain invested in America's infrastructure, or later, when advanced nations began investing in China and India.

A New Wave of Export Economies

Why will Chindia's infrastructure investments be a boon for emerging economies? Because they will boost trade; specifically, they will create a surge in export activity out of those developing nations, exports destined for the huge markets of China and India. There is no measuring the need of China and India for the raw material to be found in Africa, Latin America, Eastern Europe, and Central and South Asia; Chindia's infrastructure investments will help those emerging nations reach their export potential. First Japan and Korea, then China and India depended on the export model to jump-start their economic growth. Now it's the turn of the less developed nations—and China and India are helping make it happen.

Again, these exports will be massive in the energy sector—in oil, coal and natural gas—but they will also cover the entire range of natural resources, from food, to forest products, to precious metals. For example, Brazil's $137 billion total export business derives not only from iron ore, but also from soybean, coffee, and other agricultural products; China is now Brazil's third-largest export partner. Similarly, Chile, where China has moved into second place as an export partner, ships out $58 billion worth of copper, fruit, fish and paper products. China has also become the second-largest importer of goods from Zimbabwe, goods that include cotton, tobacco, gold and ferro-alloys. And the export economies of South Africa and the Congo are built around diamonds, gold, platinum, copper, cobalt and other minerals. At the same time, the steady movement of additional millions of Chinese and Indians into the consumer class will help drive export activity in developing nations around the globe. Like China and India just a couple of decades ago, these emerging economies lack their own substantial consumer markets, but Chindia gives them one, just as Chindia is helping them develop the infrastructure required to extract, produce and deliver their exports to that market.

Chindian Outsourcing

At the second Expo Central China in Henan Province in April 2007, Singapore Senior Minister Goh Chok Tong suggested to Chinese Vice Premier Wu Yi that China begin moving its manufacturing offshore.

Singapore wouldn't mind having some of China's manufacturing work, said Goh, but China really needed to consider outsourcing to countries like Vietnam, Indonesia, Malaysia and Thailand. Why? Goh explained that the move would ease China's troublesome trade surpluses with the United States and Europe, and substantially diffuse the issue of revaluing the yuan.[21]

Sound advice, and prescient. China, and India too, will certainly begin the process of offshoring in the coming years, but not necessarily for the reasons Goh suggests. The real reason is global economic inevitability. China and India will conform to the pattern established by the advanced nations of the West, and then followed by Japan, Taiwan, and Korea. Moreover, since the rise of China and India is happening so rapidly, we'll witness this next step in their economic evolution sooner than we might expect. China will soon begin thinking about redirecting its own labor force into industries more valuable than low-end manufacturing— chip manufacturing, for example, rather than the current shoe and toy manufacturing. China will recognize its own advantage in letting those jobs go to Africa, Vietnam, Bangladesh and other emerging nations. The phenomenon has already begun in India's IT services sector, where wage pressures are pushing salaries up and gnawing away at the cost advantage. IT giant Wipro, in fact, has already opened centers in Brazil and Romania. Of course, outsourcing from Chindia will further fuel the export boom that will lift the economies of undeveloped nations.

Chindian Export of Education and Health Services

With its billion-dollar deals and sky-high visibility, that China-Africa summit in Beijing in November 2006 got all the headlines. But by the time the historic event took place, China had already offered 18,000 scholarships for African students to study in China, dispatched 15,000 medical personnel to Africa and treated some 170 million African patients. For its part, India aspires to be a global education powerhouse. It has already exported education institutions to Singapore and Dubai, and its Manipal Group has established a medical school in Malaysia.

Great Britain's experience in India demonstrated that infrastructure means more than manufacturing plants; it encompasses education, health and civil systems too. This powerful lesson has obviously not been lost on either India or China, who no doubt recognize its salient point: such "value-added infrastructure" will not only help lift developing nations out of poverty and illness; it will also guarantee returns on Chindia's investment. The factories, mines, ports, railroads and communications systems China and India build in developing nations will need educated people to operate and manage them. Both China and India have excellent institutions of higher education and, especially given both nations' commitment to distance learning, education becomes a highly valuable and exportable asset. Over the coming decades, we can expect Chindia's investment in the developing world to evolve from brick-and-mortar infrastructure to knowledge, medical, and other "higher" industries.

In Conclusion

To reiterate then, the ascent of Chindia in no way threatens the advanced nations of the world, nor should it cast an intimidating shadow over the less developed nations. On the contrary, Chindia should offer a healthy and invigorating challenge to the advanced economies, and at the same time serve as a beacon of hope to the rest of the world. In particular, its vast consumer market will offer advanced nations a much-needed arena for growth, and provide poorer nations an opportunity to develop their export-driven economies.

So yes, Chindia's emergence may indeed prove that a rising tide can lift all boats. Today, without question, Chindia is the growth engine of the global economy, without which boats all over the world would be floating listlessly, or sinking even. If China and India manage to rise peacefully, as they promise to do, their arrival as key players on the world's stage should be universally welcomed.

But we should recognize also that Chindia does not represent the final act in the drama. Today, for good reason, the world's eyes are riveted upon these two nations. But tomorrow, as the storyline dictates, their mighty engines will begin to sputter, and they will take their turn as aging, affluent nations whose economies have matured. Which is as it should be, since, at that point, the fast-emerging nations in Africa, South America, Eastern Europe and Southeast Asia will be eager to take their turn. Count on it: before the 21st century is half gone, doomsayers in China will bemoan the loss of manufacturing jobs to Africa, and IT engineers in Bangladesh will be offering their services for one-third the going rate in Bangalore.

The journey continues.

Notes

1. Gramig, Mickey H., "Coca-Cola: Full Speed Ahead in Asia Strategy," *Atlanta Journal and Constitution*, Jan 18, 1008, p. 1.
2. "Alcatel Signs New Deals in China," *Comtex News Network*, Nov 28, 2006.
3. Wong, Kandy, "VW Close to China Sales Target," *South China Morning Post*, Nov 13, 2006, p. 2.
4. Ying, Ding, "Connecting with East Asia," *BeijingReview.com*, Apr 19, 2007.
5. Wilson, Paul, "Can Toyota Have a Future in Ohio," *Columbus Dispatch*, Feb 11, 2007, p. G1.
6. Thomas, Ken, "Wrapped Up in Red, White and Blue with an 8th U.S. Plant," *South Florida Sun-Sentinel*, Mar 7, 2007, p. D1.
7. "Detroit and Bush," *Wall Street Journal* (Asia), Nov 21, 2006, p. 13.
8. Maria Cecil and Andra Maria "Brashness, Brains Revived Company, *York Daily Record* (York, Pa.), Jul 17, 2005, p. 10.
9. Chapman, Dan, "Georgia Lands Chinese Factory," *Atlanta Journal-Constitution*, May 12, 2007, p. C1.
10. "New Research Centre Will Seek Ways to Reduce Water Use in Oil Sands," *Canada NewsWire*, Feb 27, 2007, p. 1.
11. English, Andrew, "Here Comes the Future," *Daily Telegraph*, Nov 25, 2006, p. 1 (Motoring). Also, Steve Maich, "Reinventing Your Wheels," *Maclean's*, Mar 5, 2007, p. 40.
12. Kelly, Erin, "Nanotechnology: Environmental Boon or Bane?" *Gannett News Service*, Apr 19, 2006, p. 1.
13. Keefe, Bob, "IBM Researchers Peek into Atoms," *Atlanta Journal-Constitution*, Apr 23, 2007, p. A5.
14. W. Chan Kim and Renee Maubourgne, *Blue Ocean Strategy: How to Create Uncontested Market Space and Make the Competition Irrelevant* (Boston: Harvard Business School Press, 2005), pp. 3-4; 13-16; 24-35.
15. Maney, Kevin, "PCs Could Make In-Dash Splash," *USA Today*, Sep 7, 2005, p. B.5.
16. Brown, Warren, "With 'Telematics,' the Futuristic Is Now," *Washington Post*, Apr 16, 2006, p. G2.
17. Bruce, Allison, "M2M Data Communication Businesses Thriving," *Ventura County Star*, Mar 20, 2007; also Burt Helm, "Giving Machines the Gift of Gab," *BusinessWeek Online*, July 11, 2005.
18. Hall, Kenji and Hiroko Tashiro, "Potty Talk from Japan," *BusinessWeek Online*, Jan 3, 2007.
19. "World Bank Study Finds China, India Boost Africa's growth," *BBC Monitoring Asia Pacific*, Nov 14, 2006, p. 1.
20. Viswanathan, R., "Another Kind of Amazonian Downpour," *Financial Express*, Jan 4, 2007.
21. "SM Goh Suggests China Move Manufacturing, Investments Outside," *channelnewsasia.com,* Apr 27, 2007.

6

The End of the Journey:
Economic and Political Reform

I perhaps appear to have taken it for granted that the rise of India and China into economic superpowers is a foregone conclusion, a matter of economic necessity. But there is a caveat. After all, the free market depends upon the existence of two great institutions, capitalism and democracy, and neither of these institutions is in perfect health in either India or China. Both institutions will need to become stronger in both nations, and that may not be easy. I have discussed the "new innovation imperative"—the need for Chindia to invest in R&D in order to move up the value chain to knowledge creation. I see evidence that this is happening. But here is another imperative, equally urgent. For the dream of prosperity to be fulfilled, China and India must strike the balance between capitalism and democracy that will suit the unique needs of these to ancient but newly vibrant nations.

Though the United States' rise to dominance was hobbled for almost a century of slavery, once that "peculiar institution" was abolished, America's free-market economy and transparent democracy propelled it quickly forward. I should note, however, that America was a new nation, unencumbered by older institutions like monarchy, theocracy, or feudalism, unburdened by long history and vested interests. The nations of Europe that now enjoy Western-style democracy and capitalist economies have traveled difficult roads to arrive there—deposing kings, for example, or rejecting the authority of the Church of Rome. Similarly, the nations of Eastern Europe are presently in turmoil as they attempt to work through the transition from communism to capitalism, and from authoritarianism to some form of democracy.

We might expect then, that China and India—ancient civilizations with rich cultures and entrenched ideologies—will encounter serious obstacles in their journey toward capitalism and democracy. Nor should we assume that India, to which Gandhi and Nehru brought a sort of democracy after independence, will have the easier journey. Both nations face real difficulties.

At the same time, there's no escaping the imperative—for a very simple reason. Utterly unlike the rise of America, as well as Great Britain before it, China and India are arriving on the world stage at the same moment as the global dissemination of mass media. Thanks to the Internet, information—real information in "real time"—is available to everyone everywhere. This is the true significance of mobile telephony, especially with the 3G technology that turns mobile phones into miniature Internet-connected TV sets. As I noted in Chapter 3, thanks to their mobile phones, struggling farmers in India now know the real price of grain and don't have to take the middle man's offer. But they also know which politicians in New Delhi are exploiting the poor for political gain.

I participated in a conference in 1990, where Ted Koppel, anchor of ABC Television's *Nightline*, was one of the featured speakers. He made the point that Poland's Solidarity movement began to gain force once contraband news videocassettes were smuggled into the nation. Such is the power of democratization of information. The number of television and radio channels in India is now exploding. In China, social unrest is the *bête noire* the Party fears the most. And it should. Information is the genie that can never be stuffed back into the bottle. An informed population is hard to subdue or deceive, and the people in China and India will increasingly demand both a government and an economic system that responds to their needs.

On the other hand, the embrace of capitalism and the reform of government in both nations must be a careful and deliberate process. Neither India nor China need the unbridled capitalism that characterized America's so-called Gilded Age, and that now seems at least partly responsible for post-Communist Russia's economic and political tumult. Also, just what shape a "Chinese democracy" ought to take, and exactly how India should address the confusion that now besets its politics are complex questions, and their answers will no doubt lead to the kind of change that makes those in power very uncomfortable. But again, change must come. Two and a half billion people will demand it.

Let's look first at India, then at China, examining the obstacles each will face in adopting and steering these institutions, and also suggesting some directions in which the journey might profitably lead.

Indian Capitalism

We must first acknowledge that India harbors a fundamental mistrust of capitalism. The origins of this sentiment are as old as the caste system, which conferred ultimate respect upon the Brahmin class. Indeed, amassing wealth was anathema to the Brahmins, for whom the purpose of life was to accumulate wisdom, not riches. Thus gurus and fakirs were the idealized members of Indian society, and after them came the warriors, the defenders of the realm. The traders (today's business people and entrepreneurs) occupied the third rung in the hierarchy, above only the laboring class.

This deeply entrenched prejudice against money-making was by no means weakened when Nehru came to power. On the contrary, Nehru was much more socialist than capitalist, and the state-controlled economy he put in place hindered India's growth for decades. Even today, though the "License Raj" has been largely dismantled through the reforms of 1991, India's bureaucrats cling to whatever power they can still exercise over the business community. Edward Luce reminds us of Gurcharan Das's witty assessment at the end of his long career as Head of Procter & Gamble's India operations: "In my thirty years in active business in India, I did not meet a single bureaucrat who really understood my business, yet he had the power to ruin it."[1]

In India today there is also a huge (and growing) chasm between the rich and the poor—which makes for an intriguingly complex problem. On the one hand, it contributes to the antipathy toward capitalism on the part of the government, since it enables the government to point at the wealthy industrialists as the cause for the gap. The government, of course, wants to be viewed as the solution to, not the cause of, India's massive poverty. And it's true that capitalism in its raw state does not have much of a social conscience; it can certainly make a few wealthy at the expense of the many. But it's also true that only capitalism—an enlightened capitalism—can alleviate the problem of India's poverty. The government's efforts have failed abjectly. Moreover, the poor know it. They have seen small-scale entrepreneurism at work in their villages and have seen standards of living rise as a direct result.

Another problem for capitalism in India is that, for many in this traditional society, capitalism is the face of Westernization, the force that threatens to alter and even erode India's values and culture. Capitalist-driven Westernization, with its implicit celebration of materialism, is deeply at odds with the renunciation of the world and liberation from the karmic cycle that lie at the heart of Hinduism—the religion practiced by 80 percent of Indians. It's not hard to understand that many Indians might take offense at the kind of capitalism that paves the way toward Western-style consumption, Western values and Western material culture. We in the West don't always get it, but India's devotion to its own traditional values was much in evidence at an AIDS awareness benefit in New Delhi in April 2007. When Hollywood actor Richard Gere hugged and kissed Bollywood actress Shilpa Shetty (not even on the lips, mind you), demonstrators in the streets of Mumbai burned effigies of the American movie idol, while others shouted out, "Death to Shilpa Shetty."

With these impediments in mind, let's look at how capitalism—or what kind of capitalism—might work effectively and productively in India.

In our recent book *Tectonic Shift*, my coauthor and I drew an analogy between a free-market economy and Freud's analysis of the human personality. As we try to imagine what Indian capitalism might look like, the analogy seems again useful. It goes like this:

The free market is a wild force, representing the rawest form of economic energy. Unrestrained, it is capable of good (as an agent of production), but since it fulfills its own needs without regard to the consequences for society as a whole, it is also capable of harm. We compare this to the human ID, the childlike and impulsive part of the personality that seeks its own pleasure and demands instant gratification.

Raw market forces are harnessed and directed by entrepreneurship, which meets its own needs by meeting the needs of others. It creates goods and services, for example, and enters them into the marketplace where they become available to consumers. Yet without some regulation from outside or above itself, entrepreneurship itself can "get out of control" and violate its implicit agreement with stakeholders. Or, most commonly, it tries so aggressively to satisfy one stakeholder—investors—that it neglects its commitment to one or all of the others—customers, employees, suppliers, and the community. Entrepreneurship, then, is analogous to the ego, the rational mind that satisfies the pleasure demands of the ID while remaining conscious of—though not always acceding to—long-term consequences.

But like entrepreneurship, the ego demands governance, which it finds in what Freud called the superego. Freud saw this as the last part of the personality to develop—the final evolution beyond selfishness and toward acknowledgment of the greater social good. Herein lies our higher nature, our moral sense, our desire to "do the right thing." In our economic system, it typically corresponds to the government, which formulates policies that channel the energy of entrepreneurs in ways that serve the interests of both business and the society at large. Rightly construed, both the superego and the government are forces for balance; they allow the ego, or the entrepreneur, to reach its fulfillment while at the same time creating value for the world at large. On the other hand, in some people and in some economic systems, the superego and the government have too much power. The person in this case is paralyzed by fear and guilt and may be unable act productively. The entrepreneur is regulated out of business.

The lesson here for India is one that has been learned, sometimes painfully, by most capitalist economies. The entrepreneurial impulse needs restraint; it needs to be channeled in a positive direction. It may need a Sherman Antitrust Act to curb its natural instinct toward monopoly. It may need a Food and Drug Administration to slow its haste to rush untested products into the marketplace. It may need federal regulation of a variety of sorts. But, to reiterate, the object to be sought is not power of government over business, or vice versa, but a balance that weighs the importance of a healthy business environment against the well-being of society. Consider, for example, how the pro-labor Wagner Act of 1935 was amended 12 years later by the pro-business Taft-Hartley Act. Or think of the U.S. industries (like the airlines) that, having been regulated for a number of years, were subsequently deregulated. Neither business nor the force regulating it is always "right," but out of their opposition comes a healthy equilibrium.

In India, the reforms of 1991 unleashed the pent-up spirit of entrepreneurism, and as yet, the government's attempts to keep this spirit under control have produced not equilibrium but disorder. In the nation's old-line industries, the industrialist depends for his success on exploiting regulatory loopholes and offering bribes. The situation was perfectly illustrated when Rupert Murdoch, in the late 1990s, paid a visit to Dhirubhai Ambani, who until his death in 2002 was the head of Reliance Industries. The media tycoon was looking for opportunities to expand his empire in India and had already met the top government officials in New Delhi before arriving in Mumbai for his meeting with the titan of Indian business. Ambani asked Murdoch whom he had met in the capital, and Murdoch listed the Prime Minister, the Finance Minister, and others. "Ah, you've met all the right people," replied Ambani. "But if you want to get anywhere in India you must meet all the wrong people"— by which he presumably meant all the corrupt government officials and bureaucrats.[2]

India is rife with corruption, as the whole world knows. But, as I like to say, "It takes two to bribe." India's capitalists need to take the high road. By offering bribes, they perpetuate the system and continue to empower the bribe-taker. By resisting the temptation, they would initiate change and at the same time improve the image of the business community. And yet the system is deeply entrenched. I recently attended a conference in India at which one of the speakers was the brilliant Union Minister in charge of the *Panchayat Raj* (governance at the village level), Mani Shankar Aiyar. Given that the theme of the conference was the further opening of India's economy, it was surprising to hear this minister speak out against market reforms. But his logic was arresting. He noted that politicians are caught in the middle. They must court the vote of the masses—85 percent of the population—but, once elected, they are expected to carry out the agenda of the 15 percent who have the money to get what they want.

Capitalism in India must elevate its reputation, and indeed, some of the nation's successful entrepreneurs are trying to lead the way. Azim Premji, for example, whose majority stake in Wipro Ltd. has made him one of the India's richest man, understands the importance of wearing his wealth lightly. He dresses plainly, flies economy class, and recently upgraded to a Toyota Corolla. He manages his company professionally, rather than paternalistically, and has avowed that nepotism will have no part in its future leadership. He has a reputation for uncompromising integrity and a commitment to serving all of his company's stakeholders, particularly his employees and his customers. And he is trying to make India a stronger nation. His eponymous Foundation is engaged in a massive program to improve primary education throughout the country, and its efforts have already had an impact on millions of schoolchildren in the interior regions of 16 states. It may have been an advantage for Wipro, and for the IT industry as a whole, that IT is one of the new sectors that grew up outside the umbrella of state control. But in any case, Premji and Wipro offer an example of what capitalism in India can aspire to.

Of course, capitalism in India is still unnecessarily hampered by the government and by government regulation. The most egregious example is that, as a legacy of the License Raj, the nation's greatest economic assets continue to be owned by the government. These are the state-controlled enterprises like the oil companies, the telecommunications companies, and even the nation's biggest carmaker, Maruti. They are the nation's economic crown jewels, and should have the autonomy and governance of large private enterprises such as Tatas and Birlas. Why?

Because they have the scale to be globally competitive. India needs to implement the Chinese model, where the government is playing the role of investor rather than owner and allowing its enterprises to adopt a capital market structure and be listed on global stock exchanges. As a result, companies like Lenovo, Huawei, Haier and China Mobile have become global powerhouses, returning to the government not only investment earnings but also tax dollars.

Indian CEOs of Public Sector Units (PSUs) are often frustrated by the whims of the government representatives who sit on their boards, and by the rules and regulations that render their companies uncompetitive. The CEO of ONGC, Subir Raha, took early retirement. Insiders say he got embroiled in a power struggle with the union minister and *lost*. What's known for sure is that eight months later (February 2007) the government had still not been able to find a successor. As reported in *Financial Times Information*, "The episode raises the larger question of corporate governance in Public Sector Units and the role of the government as the dominant shareholder." The incident also proves, says the newspaper, that "PSUs are treated as handmaidens by the government" and it "certainly does no good to the latter's reformist credentials."[3] Perhaps more than anything, this story illustrates the uphill battle capitalism must fight to gain acceptance in India's circles of power.

Still, at the root of the problem is capitalism's unsavory image. The harm that capitalism does (in perpetuating a corrupt system, for example) is magnified, while the good that it does is obscured by fears—perpetuated by bureaucratic elites—of Westernization, culture erosion, and threats to the hallowed concept of Swadeshi. It can help itself by placing social interests at the top of its agenda, by actively working with the government as well as with NGOs to tackle the huge problems of poverty, substandard rural education, and environmental degradation. It can espouse a bottom-up platform, looking for opportunities to bring not just products but entrepreneurism itself to the bottom of the pyramid (opportunities which, as I noted in an earlier chapter, are numerous and inviting). But capitalism needs help, not hindrance, from the government. The state was ingenious enough to create a vast bureaucracy, the License Raj, in order to stifle the free market. Let it now use that ingenuity not merely to enable capitalism but to channel its boundless energy to the benefit of the nation as a whole. A post-Nehruvian anti-capitalism still forms the ethos of the bureaucratic elite, but in the meantime the masses have fallen in love with capitalism. The government needs to catch that spirit.

Indian Democracy

Unfortunately, before India's government can help capitalism, it will have to reform itself. Like Indian capitalism, Indian democracy faces serious challenges that must be overcome if the nation is to continue its upward journey.

In the first place, democracy came too suddenly to India, enfranchising a largely illiterate nation. Improving education is the first step to improving India's democracy, because uneducated people with the vote are easily exploited. Of course, people without voting rights can also be exploited, but it may be better not to vote for people who intend to deceive you. Indian politics has been hijacked by people who know how to play the game of the poor. But for 60 years, this has proved to be a negative game with losers on all sides.

A good example of how the game turns out was supplied by the crisis of 1975, when Indira Gandhi shut down the government for 19 months. Predictably, the protests that forced her hand were sparked by her failure to "remove poverty," which had been her campaign promise. Thus the cycle is illustrated. The uneducated poor are manipulated by the promises of the politicians, the promises are broken, crisis looms, yet the poor remain poor and stand ready to be exploited again. As I noted above, India's government cannot solve the problem of poverty—at least not until the bureaucracy seeks the help of capitalism. But it always promises to do so. This truth was proved again with the Rural Employment Guarantee Act of 2005, the flagship legislation of the Congress Party-led coalition that returned to power in 2004—largely on its promise to "remove poverty."

The centerpiece of the program is the guarantee of 100 days of minimum-wage manual labor in the countryside to anyone who wants it. The labor is that which has traditionally been consigned to India's poor: filling in potholes, mending river embankments, and clearing irrigation channels. Which is to say, the work itself accomplishes nothing. It will all have to be done again after the next rainfall or monsoon. That's bad enough. What's worse is that, despite the program's huge expense—up to 10 percent of India's annual budget by 2009—it doesn't do anything to upgrade the skills of the people it is designed to help. As Edward Luce points out, it doesn't even invest "in genuine rural infrastructure, such as all-weather roads, proper electricity supply, or new agricultural technologies. Such investments would stimulate greater economic activity, which would be much likelier to create lasting employment for the rural poor."[4]

What is it that continues to make India's democracy so ineffectual? One way to put the problem is that India's democracy has evolved from one party trying to do too much to too many parties capable of doing too little. Back in power after the 2004 elections, the Congress Party (the party of the Nehru-Gandhi dynasty) is now a coalition of six parties, which don't necessarily have a great deal in common. For example, one of those six parties—in fact, the second largest after the Congress Party—is the Muslim-Yadav Party, the alliance between the Muslims and the Yadav caste (mostly cowherders) that holds power in the impoverished and until recently, virtually lawless Bihar state in India's north. This is the party that since 1990 has been led by the notorious Lalu Prasad Yadav, and subsequently, after he was briefly imprisoned in the late 1990s, by his wife, Rabri Devi. (Lalu's indictment on corruption charges, by the way, did not prevent him from being named to the powerful post of Minister for Railways in 2004 when the coalition came to power.) It's hard to imagine what coherent political platform could bind together these two extremes—the flagrantly renegade MYs and the Brahmin idealists of Nehruvian legacy.

This fragmentation is both a cause and an effect of a further problem with India's democracy: decentralization of power. Parties are formed at the local level, and general elections send the leaders of these parties (and their cronies) to serve in the Lok Sabha, or House of People. (Members of the less powerful upper house, the Rajya Sabha, or Council of States, are elected by state legislatures in proportion to the state's population.) Since there are virtually no criteria for standing for office, sometimes the general election will send popular movie stars to the Lok Sabha; sometimes it will send criminals. Whatever party or coalition of parties can round up the greatest number of seats in this 545-member legislative body picks the Prime Minister. But after all the giving and taking, the coalescing and breaking apart, how much power can the prime minister have? The current Prime Minister, Manmohan Singh, came to power with the reform of the bureaucracy as his top priority, but there has been slow reform because the Prime Minister has no power. Many here in the United States believe that the office of the President has arrogated way too much power to the executive branch, but, clearly, India has too little power at the top.

No less an authority than former President A. P. J. Abdul Kalam, nearing the end of his term in office, called for an end to coalition politics and the "rapid evolution to a two-party system" in India.[5] But short of a constitutional amendment, how do you limit the number of political parties? A place to start might be with U.S.-style transparency in the matter of campaign contributions. Let India admit openly that political campaigns are costly and that politicians need money; let India at least attempt to institute a system where that money changes hands over rather than under the table. Let it be a matter of public record as it is in the United States: here are the people and institutions who support this candidate, and here is the amount of their contribution. The influence of Political Action Committees (PACs) and lobbyists in the U.S. in publicly known and in the age of the Internet, it is permanently digitized for everyone to see. The recent fund raising compaigns by both Democratic and Republican candidates for party nominations for presidential elections in 2008 is a good example of this transparency. Since nobody wants to be on record as giving money to a scoundrel, such transparency might very well have the effect of reducing the number of politicians, the number of parties, and the complexity of coalitions.

In fact, there are two dominant parties in India—the Congress Party and the Bharatiya Janata Party (the India People's Party). But while the Congress Party has been vitiated by lingering socialist ideals and an entrenched bureaucracy, the BJP has been co-opted by the ultra-conservative Hindu nationalist movement. Nevertheless, we see here a pale image of the American system: a party of the left (Congress) and a party of the right (BJP). If both were to move to the center and purge their unwholesome elements patronage in the Congress Party, religious extremism and violence in the BJP), India might have the beginnings of a viable two-party system.

Whatever the exact number, fewer parties would have the huge additional benefit of creating political alignment between state and federal government, where now there is none. Too much power now devolves to the states, a problem made much worse by the uneven distribution of wealth among them. States in the south are booming, led by bustling cities like Hyderabad, Bangalore and Chennai, while those in the north are impoverished, densely populated, and poorly educated. The lack of centralized power is one of the reasons that India's federal government is unable to solve the nation's endemic problems.

It's not so much that India needs a change in leadership; rather, its leadership needs a change in mindset. What India needs is "servant leadership"—i.e., "I am in politics to serve the nation, not to exploit it for personal or party gain." It's not difficult to see India's problems, but to fix them will require leaders with strength, determination and will. As R. A. Mashelkar, the retired Director General of India's Council of Scientific and Industrial Research, explains it, India has "three Ds"—democracy, demographics, and diversity. But for these to fulfill their potential, India must embrace the fourth "D"—discipline.

Chinese Capitalism

In March 2007, on the last day of the National People's Congress, China's government passed a law providing sweeping new protections for private businesses and property. A concession to the growing economic importance of the private sector, the new law offers all the same protections for private as for public property. With economic reports showing that the private sector, including foreign investment, was now accounting for 65 percent of gross national product and 70 percent of tax revenues, the vote of Party delegates was lopsided: 2,799 in favor of the new law, and 52 opposed. The handful of opponents consisted largely of scholars and retired officials who lamented the state's diminishing role as the guiding hand of economic progress; they feared the law would be a vehicle for the kind of unrestrained privatization that would widen the income gap between rich and poor. Their arguments had forestalled passage of the law for the 14 years it had been under consideration, but the government ultimately bowed to reality: private property was increasing every day and its protection "is the urgent will of the people."

China's leaders also had to face the truth that the state-owned segments of the economy weren't in the best of health. As the law was coming up for a vote, China's Labor Minister reported that jobs would have to be found this year for another 5 million laid-off state enterprise workers. So China took another step toward a free-market economy, bolstering in particular the rights of house buyers, who have pushed urban home ownership to 80 percent. According to news reports, the new law gives people the right to own "their lawful incomes, houses, articles for daily use, means of production and raw material. Deposits, investments and returns on such assets are also protected."[6]

What a remarkable turn of events! Indeed, despite the fact that one nation is the world's largest democracy and the other the world's largest communist state, China's economy over the past half-century has followed a path oddly similar to India's. When Nehru ascended to power in 1947, he handed control of the economy to the state. Similarly, China's 1949 revolution transferred to the state the ownership of all property and brought to an end the people's rights of ownership. Neither nation prospered. In 1966 and 1967, India was saved from mass starvation by shipments of more than 14 million metric tons of grain from the United States. In China, during the three years of the Great Leap Forward (1959-1961), 14 million Chinese died from famine (by official records; the actual total may be three times higher). In both nations, pro-market reforms (China's beginning in 1978, India's in 1991) have increased prosperity.

Yet, despite its booming growth, and despite the legislative progress cited above, China's move toward capitalism is just as halting and fraught with problems as India's. China, too, has an ancient antipathy to capitalism; its Mandarin class, like India's Brahmins, consisted of bureaucratic elites whose attainments were intellectual rather than material. And in China, like in India, capitalism is associated with Western hegemony and the encroachment of Western (mostly American) values. Working against these prejudices, as well as against Party doctrine, capitalism in China still has a "long march" ahead of it.

It's instructive to note, for example, where the new property rights law comes up short. It conspicuously rejects any change to the system of "collective" ownership of rural land, meaning that farmers will still have only "usage rights" to their property, rather than any legal title that can be bought and sold. Lacking such title, the farmers are still subject to seizure of their land whenever local officials deem a better use for it (not too different from the case of the SEZs in Bengal, discussed above). Worse, when local officials are permitted to seize farm lands and rezone them for commercial use, the door swings open wide for bribery and corruption—an impediment to the workings of the free market in China no less than in India.[7]

An even greater issue, as China attempts to enter the global marketplace, is its failure to protect intellectual property—its own and that of other nations. For multinational corporations attempting to do business in China, the losses to piracy and counterfeiting are staggering. Depending on what figures you look at, China's share of the global counterfeit trade ranges from between $19 billion and $80 billion annually, and the losses suffered by foreign firms operating in China are estimated to be $20 billion a year. Procter & Gamble loses as much as $150 million a year, and Nintendo reported that intellectual property rights (IPR) violations cost it $650 million in 2002 alone. Yamaha estimates that five out of six motorcycles sold under its name in China are bogus.

For emerging nations, the temptation is strong. As Oded Shenkar points out, "In a world where developing a new car routinely exceeds a billion dollars, piracy and counterfeiting remove a steep barrier to new entrants and allow those falling behind to catch up on the cheap." In

China, moreover, all the ingredients are in place to make the temptation overpowering: a weak legal system with little enforcement power; no open and independent media; a lack of transparency in government operations; and worst of all, local officials with plenty of authority and little oversight. As the ancient Chinese axiom has it, "The sky is high and the emperor is far away." Consequently, local officials not only turn a blind eye to IPR violations, they depend on the revenue those violations produce. Shenkar notes that most of China's 100-plus car manufacturers would be out of business if they had to pay for development costs.[8]

Is China even trying to reform this system? Some commentators don't think so. In *China Inc.*, Ted Fishman writes that "Convincing the Chinese to enforce intellectual-property protections means convincing them to give up one of the primary practices that have nourished their economic miracle. It is a hard sale."[9] But China insists that it is trying to clean up its act. In March 2007, the China Council for the Promotion of International Trade (CCPIT) and the U.S. Chamber of Commerce co-sponsored the grandly titled "Global Forum on Intellectual Property Rights Protection and Innovation" in Beijing—an event attended by more than 500 high-level government officials and senior corporate experts from China, the United States, the European Union, Japan, Korea, India, and other nations.

China's Vice Premier Wu Yi was there, assuring the audience (and the world) that China was fully committed to the protection of IPR and that enforcement and international cooperation would be strengthened. A new "national strategy" was forthcoming later in 2007, promised Wu, covering a full range of IPR topics. Moreover, statistics already showed enforcement on the upswing: 3,634 prosecutions of IPR cases in 2006, 12.6 percent more than in 2005. At least one foreigner, U.S. Chamber of Commerce president Thomas Donohue, came to China's defense. "The Chinese government works hard to deal with IPR protection issues," he told a press briefing, and "is making serious progress" in its fight against infringement.[10]

State councilor Chen Zhili made the key point that "IPR protection is in the long-term interests of China" since China is quickly evolving into "a major country in terms of intellectual property rights." To illustrate, she noted that in 2006 the State Intellectual Property Office received 573,000 patent applications and more than 7,000 trademark applications—20 percent more than in 2005 and higher than the number received by the U.S. Patent Office. Chen averred that protecting IPR "is vital for fostering a good environment for foreign investment," but she also begged the international community for patience. Britain has had 300 years, the United States 200 years, and Japan 100 years to formulate sound IPR policy, Chen noted, and the issue begs for "cooperation, understanding, and effort from all sides."[11]

The Bush administration apparently was not impressed. Two weeks after the global forum, the United States announced that it would file two formal complaints against China at the WTO in Geneva. The first accuses China of setting "excessively high thresholds for launching criminal prosecutions" against makers and distributors of pirated products like DVDs and CDs. The second targets China's rule that some of the most popularly counterfeited goods—books, movies, music, and computer software—be handled solely by state-owned importers, a policy that can delay distribution of legitimate goods and give counterfeiters a window of opportunity. U.S. trade representative Susan Schwab characterized the problem as "more than a handbag here or a logo item there; it is often theft on a grand scale." China questioned the wisdom and validity of the action and particularly its timing. The threshold for criminal prosecution has already come down, noted Song Hong, Head of International Trade Research at the Chinese Academy of Social Sciences. And Tian Lipu, commissioner of China's Intellectual Property Office, responded that it was "not sensible" to file a WTO complaint "right when China is forging ahead with its IPR protection efforts."[12]

In early October 2007, the unthinkable happened! A Chinese court penalized Shwab, the French group in industrial circuit breakers, a record $55 million for violating Patent Rights of a Chinese company and insisted on cease and desist from copying the Chinese Patent Protectoral law and consumer market. This incident makes it difficult to say who imitates whom.

Whether China is still dragging its feet or making reasonable progress on the IPR issue, the certain fact is that it still has a long way to go. And perhaps no issue is more important to China's continued development of an open economy. As Shenkar observes, "IPR protection is a key element in all free market economies, underpinning the incentive to innovate, develop, invest, and produce."[13]

China also has further to go in the development of its financial institutions—its banks and financial markets—but again, it appears to be moving in the right direction. Six years after the nation's entry into the WTO in 2001, it has to a considerable degree fulfilled its promise to open up its financial sector. As proof, it boasts that three of its "big four" state banks are now favorite targets for investors both domestically and abroad.

Over the same period, nonperforming loans have been cut in half, down to 7.5 percent. Moreover, at the Third National Financial Work Conference in early 2007, the government pledged continued reforms, with the goal of eventually matching "international best practices." In particular, new regulations will need to enhance supervision of financial markets—to improve transparency on transactions, on financial performance, on mergers and acquisitions, and the like. A report from the Central Bank in May 2007 put the case plainly: "Institutional improvement is a priority as China's financial market is far from mature."[14]

While it makes the necessary structural reforms, China, no less than India, must make certain that it moves toward a sustainable capitalism. China's capitalists must proactively embrace the dual-interest model, making sure to serve society at large as well as the interests of the corporation. Let's call it "enlightened capitalism"—where wealth creation and wealth distribution occur at the same time. In capitalism of advanced nations, the distribution (back to society) is largely a function of taxes, collected by the government and then distributed according to the needs of society. Enlightened capitalism distributes wealth as soon as it is created to all stakeholders—investors, employees, customers, suppliers, and the community. It does not exploit the community's human and natural resources (a zero-sum game) but rather enhances both, the true path to sustainability. The Internet will prove to be a great enabler of enlightened capitalism. In China especially, with its lack of independent media, bloggers are everywhere, sharing information and enforcing a grassroots transparency whether the Party likes it or not.

The good news is that many business leaders in China appear ready to embrace the kind of capitalism that will redound to the credit of the nation as a whole. At the 27th China Daily CEO Roundtable Luncheon in October 2006, the topic under discussion was "Corporate Social Responsibility," and the conference's overriding message was that China's dream of a "harmonious society" will only be realized in the context of CSR. "Just two years ago, no one was talking about CSR," said William Valentino, a Bayer (China) executive who chaired the CEO Roundtable, but the idea has now permeated China's business environment: "The concept of a harmonious society," he explained, "is really China's rephrasing of the concept of CSR, sustainable development and human rights in China." He went on to explain that the burden of China's social and environmental problems is so great that "economic development will stop somewhere if we do not try to do something about it." And by "we," Valentino pointedly referred to business leaders: "The social contract has been moved from the industrial to the private sector because great wealth, power and influence are now in this sector. We should be leaders in the CSR movement."

CSR, as these business leaders see it, is not charity. It is "dual-interest" capitalism. It is the enlightened capitalism that creates and distributes wealth simultaneously. It is good for business and good for society. For example, Shanghai Pudong Development Bank (SPDB) began its initiatives to conserve natural resources in 1997 by introducing advanced technologies to create an online, paperless office. It also set up a designated website through which it collects donations for HIV patients, money from which has already helped hundreds of orphans with HIV in Henan Province. "We have invested a lot of money," said Ma Li, the bank's executive vice president, "but we have also reduced our costs and risks and improved management efficiency. We also enhanced our image and branding, which would have a long-term effect." Valentino adds that CSR can also confer benefits on corporate identity and integrity: "We live in a very interconnected world. It should not be a give-and-lose situation but a win-win one."[15]

A similar and relatively successful dual interest capitalism is the popularity of microlending which began in Bangladesh (Grameen Bank) and now implemented in India by ICICI Bank. It has resulted in generating many successful entrepreneurs especially among illiterate poor women. At the same time, the leading institution has practically zero default and one of the highest return on loans. In other words, it is not zero sum game but creating a win-win positive sum game between the bottom of the pyramid masses and traditional financial institutions.

It should also be noted that China, like India, has a widening gap between rich and poor, and a vast majority of the population at the bottom of the pyramid (BOP), both of which are potential triggers for social unrest. Here again is an opportunity for capitalism to show its human face. Chinese capitalists are now taking full advantage of the business boom in the nation's eastern provinces, especially in east-coast cities like Nanjing, Shanghai and Guangzhou, while China's vast interior remains impoverished. Forward-looking entrepreneurs will partner with the government to take that wealth and that business activity westward. Military installations, health centers, infrastructure projects—such enterprises would create employment, which is the bedrock of economic progress. The point is that, if it is to be sustained, China's capitalism must make sure to address the needs of the BOP.

Finally, individual entrepreneurs can do a great deal to "rebrand" capitalism as a force for social good. In fact, they need to, or else their vast wealth could become a source of dangerous resentment. The philanthropy of Americans like Bill Gates and Ted Turner have set a high standard here, but it's one that can be met and, in fact, is being met by people like Hong Kong-based billionaire Li Ka-shing, said to be the world's richest man of Chinese descent.

Like India's Azim Premji, Li is a fabulously successful businessman whose tastes and lifestyle have remained simple. Chairman of the global conglomerate Hutchison Whampoa, Li favors simple black dress shoes and a cheap Seiko wristwatch. More to the point, Li, like Premji, is distributing his wealth with a generous hand. His philanthropic foundation has already disbursed more than $1 billion, most of which has been dedicated to education and health care, including many projects in China's western provinces. As he received the 2006 Malcolm S. Forbes Lifetime Achievement Award, he encouraged other Asian entrepreneurs to "adopt a culture of philanthropy," which he describes as an investment in the future. Recently Li ascended to the upper echelon of enlightened capitalists when he pledged to bequeath to his philanthropic foundation (which he refers to as his "third son") one-third of his wealth, a fortune estimated at $19 billion.

Wealth confers power, and power used constructively can solve many problems. By working to alleviate China's massive poverty, by addressing health and environmental issues, and by nudging the government on human rights issues, China's capitalists can be instrumental in bringing about the "peaceful rise" that the nation's leaders claim to be dedicated to.

Chinese Democracy

A free market pushes naturally toward an open government. Capitalism democratizes wealth and democratizes information. It welcomes the rule of law, under which it operates healthily. It is abused and perverted by corruption and stifled by authoritarianism. As China opens its economy, can it keep its government closed? We are finding out right now, but I have to believe that the answer, ultimately, will be no.

In the spring of 2007, nearing the end of their five-year terms, China's Party leaders could be heard talking about democratic reform of government. Party journals and state-run media were publishing commentaries by retired officials and academics on "political system reform" and the need for "socialist democracy." Top leaders even authorized the publication in April 2007 of the pro-democratic political reflections of Lu Dingyi, a veteran of the Long March who advocated political change before his death a decade ago.

But is the push for reform real or illusory? At a minimum, the flurry of articles suggests that the terms "democracy" and "freedom" have lost their old taboo. "What we're seeing is a repudiation of Deng Xiaoping's edict that the Party should focus exclusively on economic development," said Lu De, an influential economist who has pushed for greater political pluralism. Lu is the son of Lu Dingyi, Propaganda Chief and Deputy Prime Minister under Mao. After he fell out of political favor during the Cultural Revolution (1966-1976), Lu Dingyi spent 13 years in custody. It was his "reflections," as recorded by son Lu, that have just been published.

Lu De gives Hu Jintao and Wen Jiabao credit for realizing that political change and economic change have to proceed hand in hand. "Of course, they must move step by step. It will not be one big leap and we're there," says Lu, now an advisor to China's State Council on economic policy. Moreover, some top officials are actively pushing for reform and hope that Hu will devote his second term to broadening the use of elections rather than relying almost exclusively on top-down appointments within the Party structure. One of those is none other than Vice President Zeng Qinghong, Hu's most influential colleague within the Party. Zeng, in fact, advocates increasing the number of senior officials who participate in the selection of Hu's eventual successor (in 2012).

On the other hand, it's quite possible that Hu and Wen are simply posturing. As Hu's first term as Communist Party chief comes to an end, he may find it expedient to project the image of a progressive who wants to improve governance and reduce corruption. After all, as the old truism has it, those with power are generally reluctant to relinquish it. And China's top leaders like to obfuscate the issue by arguing that their one-party system has long practiced democracy, in the sense of governing on behalf of "the people." After all, it is the "People's Republic." As Joseph Kahn astutely observes for the *International Herald Tribune*: "Even some top Chinese intellectuals who favor more political pluralism tend to define democracy in instrumental terms, as a force that can help Party leaders stay in touch with the people and provide a popular check on corruption rather than as the core of a new political system in which people choose their leaders in free elections."

Even more ominously, many China watchers have noted that while Hu struck a progressive pose when he became Party chief in 2002, he has since hardened his position. Based on his repeated crackdowns on journalists, lawyers and rights advocates, it may be that divergent political views are less tolerated in China today than they were five years ago.[16]

Right now the labor rights movement in China is the best illustration of why China must eventually move in the direction of democracy—and also of the government's ambivalence about such movement. The pressure is building in China. The gap between rich and poor is widening at the same time that Internet- and cell phone-enabled information is breathing a spirit of restlessness into the nation's workers. According to China Labour Bulletin, a Hong Kong-based rights group, in 2004 alone 3 million workers joined a total of 57,000 protests nationwide.

What's happening now is that workers are beginning to flex their muscles because there is no longer an infinite supply of them. Labor shortages are beginning to affect productivity in the manufacturing strongholds of Guangdong, Fujian and Zhejiang Provinces. Incomes are rising, if slowly, in the countryside, tempting more and more young people to stay at home rather than migrate to the cities. "Workers have more choices than before," says Huang Huiping, Deputy Chief of the Labor Bureau in the Pearl River Delta city of Dongguan. When employers have to compete to lure workers and retain them, and when workers begin to realize what's going on, conditions improve and wages rise.

So what role is the Party playing in the "emancipation" of the worker? Well, Hu's government has ordered local Labor Bureaus to ensure that work sites are safe and that migrants get paid fairly and on time. Also, the government banned migrant worker detention centers in 2003. But when it comes to workers' organizations, the government's tolerance extends only as far as the "official" union: the All-China Federation of Trade Unions (ACFTU). Anybody trying to set up an independent union is in trouble. In 2002, for example, two workers who organized protests against unpaid wages and pensions at a ferro-alloy plant in the northeast city of Liaoyang were sentenced to seven- and four-year sentences, respectively, on charges of "subversion."

As Lee Cheuk Yan, general secretary of the Hong Kong Confederation of Trade Unions, explained to *BusinessWeek's* Beijing Bureau Chief Dexter Roberts, the government supports the ACFTU because it acts as a safety valve, allowing workers to let off steam so "grievances don't build up." The government "wants to show the workers that there is an organization to represent them. But it still represents predominately the interest of the Communist Party." Lee, who has been blacklisted from the Mainland ever since his participation in the Tiananmen Square protests, can refer to his own experience when he speaks of the current regime's obsession with political control and stability—"politically more controlling than even the Jiang Zemin regime," he says—but his most interesting observation concerns the futility of government repression.

"In a way [government officials] are helpless," he says. "That's because the only way to fight corruption is if you have transparency and democracy. They always try to do it from the top down. But actually they need to allow bottom-up supervision."[17]

Actually, China needs more bottom-up government. In contrast to India, where there are too many parties, too much decentralization, and too little power at the top, China's single party rules in a state of insularity—which cannot be sustainable forever. Even more than its workers, China's fast-growing middle class will increasingly demand representation in government, just as the Party will also feel mounting pressure to allow an independent judiciary and an independent media.

Is the creation of an opposition party the key to the way forward in China? Not necessarily. In my home state, Georgia, the Democrats ruled for 130 years. More relevant, no doubt, is the example of Singapore, where the single-party government created by Lee Kwan Yew has brought peace and prosperity for decades. In Europe too, dominant single parties—like Helmut Kohl's in Germany, for example—have achieved great economic success.

Yet openness to dissent is a characteristic of great governments, and China's Party leaders may decide that it is in their interest to allow the emergence of a second party. An opposition party would bring the big picture into clearer focus and allow Party officials to be exposed to valid, if challenging, streams of thought. Like the ACFTU, an opposition party would allow alternative points of view to be aired and thus serve to dissipate dissension. As I like to say, "A dissatisfied customer with no choice is a terrorist." Disenfranchised people have no choice but to take the law into their own hands. And again, the democratization of information will inflame any resentment that smolders below the surface.

So, an increasingly democratizing China might mean what, then: Wider participation in the selection of Party officials? The creation of one or more opposition parties? A judicial branch of government outside of Party control? An independent media? An unconstrained labor movement? But these are—if we may borrow the term—revolutionary changes. Why would the Chinese government sanction any of them? Especially a regime that, as Lee Cheuk Yan believes, values political stability and control above all things?

The reason is that in the long term the system as it exists today will not be able to maintain stability and control. Lu De is correct in that with economic progress must come political progress. Those first market reforms in 1978 initiated a process that continues to build momentum—witness the astounding growth of the nation's economy. The new private property laws constitute another significant step forward. To resist or retard the force that has been set in motion might very well incite the instability and unrest that the Party leadership dreads. Once granted, rights and freedoms are difficult to rescind. Likewise, too rapid a change (as we've seen in the former Soviet Union) can prove chaotic.

Thus it seems likely that China's "peaceful rise"—if it does indeed happen—will entail a gradual move away from authoritarianism. We needn't expect the sudden emergence of universal suffrage and a Western-style democracy, but we can expect, I believe, a program of "disciplined democratization" that will move hand-in-hand with continued economic reform.

In Conclusion

As we have said before, in today's globally interconnected world, economics tends to trump politics. The Chindian boom has been built on foreign investment, and foreign investment favors an environment that promises long-term stability. Moreover, thanks to that economic juggernaut, both China and India now find themselves as emerging global powers—nations with which even the United States must deal judiciously, and on even terms. In other words, pro-market reforms have brought these two nations a long way over the last couple of decades. It seems most unlikely that their leaders would choose to kill the goose that lays the golden egg.

Notes

1. Luce, Edward, *In Spite of the Gods: The Strange Rise of Modern India* (New York: Doubleday, 2007), p. 51.
2. Luce, p. 7.
3. "Uncertainty at the Top in ONGC," *Financial Times Information*, Feb 11, 2007.
4. Luce, 200.
5. "Kalam for Two-Party Polity," *Financial Times Information*, May 11, 2007.
6. Bodeen, Christopher (AP), "New Law Puts Capitalists on Par with State-Owned Companies," *Atlanta Journal-Constitution*, Mar 17, 2007, p. A3.

7. McGregor, Richard, "Farmers Are the Last to Benefit," *Financial Times*, Mar 9, 2007, p. 7.

8. Shenkar, Oded, *The Chinese Century: The Rising Chinese Economy and Its Impact on the Global Economy, the Balance of Power, and Your Job* (Upper Saddle River, NJ: Wharton School Publishing/Pearson Education, 2006), pp. 82–88.

9. Fishman, Ted, *China Inc.: How the Rise of the Next Superpower Challenges America and the World* (New York: Scribner, 2006), Afterword, p. 313.

10. "Vice Premier Says China to Protect Copyright More Effectively," *BBC Monitoring Asia Pacific*, Mar 27, 2007, p. 1.

11. Miller, Tom, "China a Source of Global Innovation," *South China Morning Post*, Mar 28, 2007, p. 7.

12. Montgomery, Lori and Ariana Eunjung Cha, "Taking a Harder Line on Piracy," *Washington Post*, Apr 10, 2007, p. D1; also see John McCary, "U.S. Takes Trade Dispute to the WTO," *Wall Street Journal*, Apr. 11, 2007, p. 9.

13. Shenkar, p. 82.

14. "China's Central Bank Urges Stricter Legal Supervision on Financial Market," *BBC Monitoring Asia Pacific*, May 30, 2007, p. 1; also see "Financial Reform," *China Daily*, Jan 22, 2007, p. 4.

15. "CSR Begins to Take Solid Shape," *Financial Times Information – Asia Intelligence Wire*, Oct 27, 2006.

16. Kahn, Joseph, "Among China's Elite, Talk of 'Democracy,'" *International Herald Tribune*, Apr 19, 2007.

17. Engardio, Pete (Ed.), *Chindia: How China and India Are Revolutionizing Global Business* (New York: McGraw-Hill, 2007). See "Waking Up to Their Rights," pp. 266–272); also "A Blacklisted Labor Leader Speaks Out," pp. 275–278.

Final Thoughts

The message of this book is hopeful. The future is uncertain, but the present day makes clear that China and India are rising, and much evidence suggests that this trajectory will continue. Moreover, I'm convinced that Chindia will help lift the nations rising behind them, and at the same time help maintain the vigor of the world's mature economies. I believe that the rise of Chindia will be a force for global prosperity—and even a force for peace—as the two nations pursue the kind of economic and political reform that will enable the journey to continue.

But readers may ask: What about the so-called "race to the bottom," the ugly underside of globalization? It's interesting: Karl Marx clearly foresaw the global economy—that is, a world in which national and religious identities had been swept away by the irresistible tide of global capitalism. Actually, Marx relished that vision, because he figured that in such a world, without the illusory comforts of "God and country," workers would be forced to recognize their plight. Trapped by their capitalist masters in the race to the bottom, the workers would at last rise up and throw off their chains.

That Marx, more than 150 years ago, could have so clearly predicted a globalized economy is pretty amazing, but even he would have to concede that the worker revolution has yet to materialize. Why? Because, thanks to free markets, standards of living are rising, not sinking. And as standards of living rise, more and better jobs are continually being created. That's why, despite all the fear-mongering about off-shoring, America's unemployment rate has held steady at a healthy 5 percent.

I don't wish to minimize the very real issues that surround globalization, but the drift of history since the end of World War II is discernible, and it is in this momentum of history that I place my confidence. As my coauthor and I put it in *Tectonic Shift*, during the last quarter of the 20th century governments everywhere were withdrawing from what Lenin called the "commanding heights" of the economy and allowing more freedom to the workings of the free market; I am not alone in believing that economic growth and rising standards of living have resulted. Francis Fukuyama writes that over those 25 years, "liberal principles in economics—the 'free market'—have spread, and have succeeded in producing unprecedented levels of material prosperity, both in industrially developed countries and in countries that had been, at the close of World War II, part of the impoverished Third World." More germane to our discussion here, Fukuyama also sees a connection between capitalism and democracy: "A liberal revolution in economic thinking has sometimes preceded, sometimes followed, the move toward political freedom around the globe."[1]

My confidence also rests on the tendency of strong economic relationships to promote strong geopolitical relationships. Fukuyama makes the point that democratic nations seldom, if ever, make war on one another, but free-market economics takes that logic one step further: nations with strong economic ties—or, in Thomas Friedman's words, nations that are both part of the same major global supply chain—are extremely unlikely to go to war with each other. Friedman calls it the "Dell Theory of Conflict Prevention," and Michael Dell, who does much business in China and India, helps define it: "These countries understand the risk premium that they have," and they're "pretty careful to protect the equity they've built up." Dell's visits to China have convinced him that the changes there are good for China and for the world. As he tells Friedman, "Once people get a taste for whatever you want to call it—economic independence, a better lifestyle, and a better life for their child or children—they grab on to that and don't want to give it up."[2]

Envisioning India's future, Gurcharan Das sounds a similar note. He foresees "the irresistible spread of competitive markets and social democracy. The preoccupation of the people will be with a rising standard of living, with social mobility, with the peaceful pursuit of middle-class values and culture, influenced increasingly by the homogeneous global culture." This is a trend, says Das, "which promotes peace, stability, integration, flexibility, and rationality."[3]

Following this trend toward liberal, capitalist democracy, China and India will become part of what Fukuyama calls the "post-historical" world, in which the "chief axis of interaction between states would be economic, and the old rules of power politics would have decreasing relevance."

There would still be discrete nations, as Fukuyama envisions this world, but economic interdependence would have rendered military conflict counterproductive, and therefore unlikely. He concedes that China is still far from having achieved democracy, but the movement in that direction is irrevocable. "The current leadership of China seems to understand that it cannot turn the clock back on economic reform, and that China will have to remain open to the international economy." This, in turn, rules out any return to a confrontational Maoist foreign policy.[4]

But perhaps Fukuyama is being optimistic, and perhaps I am too. It's possible that the scenarios I've sketched here could take a darker turn:

- Rather than pushing Western corporations to become more competitive and more visionary, maybe the fast-rising Chindian multinationals will simply overwhelm them, drive them out of business, and double or triple Western unemployment rolls.

- It's possible that China's and India's quest for natural resources will turn nasty and the competition between the two thirsty nations will turn bellicose.

- Maybe Chindian innovation will prove unequal to the monumental tasks that lie ahead—the ascent into a "knowledge" economy, the alleviation of widespread poverty and the restoration of environmental health.

- Chindian hegemony could prove to be ruthless rather than benign, with a return to colonial-style exploitation vis-à-vis its relations with less developed nations.

- And of course it's possible that markets worldwide will crash, that the Chindian boom will collapse, and that hardliners in both nations (Hindu extremists in India, Cold-War communists in China) will seize the moment to reverse the momentum of progress and reform.

Any and all of these are possible and, as always, there's good money to be made in predicting worst-case scenarios. I can only say that to me they seem unlikely, even far-fetched.

I believe in the reality of what I see happening in China and India: millions of people finding new jobs, improving their lot in life, enhancing their hopes for their children; two nations rising to positions of economic and political parity with the developed world and pulling up the poorer nations behind them; two nations whose spectacular ascent has been the result of economic reform rather than military conquest, and who appear committed to the peaceful journey.

I also believe that economic pragmatism and enlightened self-interest are powerful (and related) philosophies and that, perhaps more than in any previous era, the world of the 21st century is ready to embrace them.

The rise of Chindia brings with it opportunity on a scale never before contemplated. Why not believe that the door will be opened?

Notes

1. Fukuyama, Francis, *The End of History and the Last Man* (New York: Bard, 1992), pp. xiii–xiv.
2. Friedman, Thomas, *The World Is Flat: A Brief History of the Twenty-First Century* (New York: Farrar, Straus and Giroux, 2005), p. 421.
3. Das, Gurcharan, *India Unbound: From Independence to the Global Information Age* (New Delhi: Penguin Books India, 2000; revised 2002), p. 307.
4. Fukuyama, pp. 276–277.

Index

Author's Profile

 Dr. Jagdish (Jag) N. Sheth, the Charles H. Kellstadt Professor of Marketing at Emory University's Goizueta Business School , has been teaching and writing on global business for 35 years. An internationally renowned speaker, writer, and thinker, he has given more than a thousand keynote addresses, seminars, and presentations in more than 20 countries. His vast experience in Asia includes his role as advisor to the government of Singapore on how to position that nation in the region's emerging economy. He is also the founder of the India , China and America (ICA) Institute, a nonprofit organization created to provide a sustainable, non-governmental platform to identify and drive economic synergies among those three nations. The Institute works with research fellows and policy advisors to supply the latest information and opinion to policy makers, business executives, and thought leaders worldwide.

Dr. Sheth's widely-read and much-translated books have secured his reputation for innovative thinking and groundbreaking concepts across the spectrum of global business. His best-selling *Clients for Life* (coauthored with Andrew Sobel) was the first book to illuminate the transition from the role of "expert for hire" to "trusted advisor"—a message of critical importance to all professional service companies. His *The Rule of Three* (with Dr. Rajendra Sisodia) propounded a radical new way of viewing the competition in a given industry. It was developed into a seven-part documentary that aired on CNBC (India) and has been translated into five languages. In *Tectonic Shift: The Geoeconomic Realignment of Globalizing Markets* (with Dr. Rejendra Sisodia), Dr. Sheth was the first argue that advanced economies will find it necessary for their own survival to do business with the developing world. And in his just-released *The Self-Destructive Habits of Good Companies* he formulated the arresting proposition that it is often not the competition that brings ruin to otherwise good companies, but rather their own self-destructive behavior.

Dr. Sheth's close working relationship with business and professional leaders around the world, his contacts with the media, and his immense popularity as a speaker ensure his fresh and provocative ideas of a wide and enthusiastic audience.